OpenGL Graphics Through Applications

Robert Whitrow

OpenGL Graphics
Through Applications

 Springer

Robert Whitrow BSc, PhD
London Metropolitan University, UK

ISBN: 978-1-84800-022-3   e-ISBN: 978-1-84800-023-0

British Library Cataloguing in Publication Data
A catalogue record for this book is available from the British Library

Library of Congress Control Number: 2007938325

Printed on acid-free paper

9 8 7 6 5 4 3 2 1

Springer Science+Business Media
springer.com

Preface

This book is the result of teaching computer graphics for one and two semester, year two/three undergraduate and postgraduate lecture courses in Computer Graphics. Throughout the book, theory is followed by implementation using C/C++ and complete programs are provided with suggestions for change to enhance student understanding. During 30 years of university teaching the author has become aware of the frustration that many students suffer, of code fragments that 'never quite work' and programs that on a different system require system dependent additions! With this in mind all the programs given have been tested using MS C++ v6 and most have been tested using Solaris 4.2 and Borland C++ v5.

There are a number of texts which give a more in depth approach to the OpenGL pipeline and repetition has therefore been avoided by referencing such texts for the interested reader. The objective is to get students immersed in graphics applications as rapidly as possible, to develop confidence, which in turn leads to experimentation, which is so vital to the enthusiastic programmer. Theory and practice have been developed in parallel so that in many cases the reader begins to understand the strengths and weaknesses of a particular algorithm.

After a rapid 'getting started' introduction we look at the structure of bit map (.bmp) files as a precursor to understanding audiovisual files (.avi). This work forms a foundation for later sections on image processing and texturing. These are very simple file structures that can be converted from other image file formats using commercially available software packages. The chapter introducing image processing covers edge detection, enhancement and data capture from CAT scans. Theory and practice can be quite different and some processing appears more of an art than a science due to the variability in the image quality and the nature of the image itself. The example of edge finding on CAT scans where different slices may have well defined edges and other more fuzzy edges due to gray hair is not always apparent to the eye. We address these problems with alternative solutions with varying degrees of success to enable readers to comprehend that algorithmic development is still an inexact science for such applications.

In Chapter 4 we move to the first chapter, which might be considered to be computer graphics with all the mathematics that is required. I do not encourage students to skip over these areas of understanding for the 'black box' approach will only get you so far and gaps in knowledge at an early stage will come to haunt one later on. The toil of getting to grips with material will be amply repaid as students grow in knowledge – although I am aware that many avoid the joys of mathematical rigor!

Early on in computer graphics students are often heard to say; "why is there no error message and nothing on the screen?". Knowing where one is in 3D space has been another difficult area to communicate. Conceptually compressing a 3D model onto a 2D screen does not come easily to many students' minds and here we introduce viewing. In OpenGL the viewing process is concerned with two operations; the mapping an object into a viewing volume for screen display and called the PROJECTION process, while the orientation and size operations on the object is referred to as the MODELVIEW process. Being in the wrong place, whether viewer or object can leave nothing on a screen and much confusion as how to proceed. The author maintains that there is little alternative to debugging than printing out a few well-chosen coordinates to see if they lie in the field of view! With practice one becomes aware of location, but in the early stages 3D space seems like learning to fly in cloud – few reference points and a degree of panic if you don't trust your instruments (coordinate values in our case).

Lighting begins to bring realism to displays and in this section we cover the different forms of lighting available and see the effects as we move objects in relation to a light source. We also link the early work on the transformations as we see how illumination varies across a surface and adjust the surface properties to produce highlights.

In Chapter 7 we return to bit map images and use them to cover surfaces with pictures, initially on simple flat planes and then develop linear mapping methods for more complex surfaces. We introduce the concept of mapping onto terrain with a given height profile to simulate the idea of mountains and valleys. Multiple textures are used to simulate scenery as seen through windows and the changes apparent from movement in a room are implemented. An introduction to 3D texturing is included and finally reconstruction of 3D volumes from 2D CAT scan slices.

Object orientation has played a lesser part in the text up to this section and we now use the concept to build artifacts based on work in the previous chapters. Objects such as cylinders and 'stretched cubes' are textured with an appropriate image and result in building blocks for furniture. The tables built are then placed within the context of say a room to introduce students to applications of furniture and room decoration. The writing rather than only using objects has proved fruitful in student projects, where an understanding of mass manufacture has led students to consider in some depth the flexibility required in design for object use to be economic.

The final chapter considers the development of curves and surfaces using Splines and Bezier interpolation and fractals. A section on fractals explores the role they can play in adding objects to scenery and outlining complex shapes.

Approach

This book sets out to solve problems by complete example rather than discursively hint of how it may be done. We live in an era of mass education where as ever, the very able thrive without much need of teaching but where the large mass of students have less access to staff due to funding constraints. Some believe technology will overcome these obstacles and the author believes that one contribution to the solution of the problem is doing by example. However, a black box recipe approach leaves students vulnerable when circumstances change and thus I have included theory followed by worked examples. The initial implementation sometimes produces inefficient code and I have left this deliberately in order that students can follow where algorithms originate from theory. Good program design and efficient code comes from an in depth understanding that is the result of a long process of assimilation.

Supporting Material

Support materials may be found may be found on the accompanying Springer web site http://www.springer.com/978-1-84800-022-3
   They include:

   Program code
   Data files
   OpenGL include files
   OpenGL link libraries from the Mesa site.

Robert Whitrow
Department of Computing
Communications Technology and Mathematics
London Metropolitan University, UK

Acknowledgements

The enthusiasm of my students has made a major contribution to making this text possible. I would particularly thank George Fordham, A Saadat, Paul Kunka, Abid Khan, Michelle Stafford, Cecille Boulanger, Paul Armstrong and many others whose names escape me now who I learnt from and who inspired me with their enquiring minds and never ending questions. Their work and efforts are part of this book and without out meeting first hand the problems of learning, I would have never been driven to write this text.

As with any course, material develops over time and occasionally the original source can be easily forgotten. In this text I have referenced sources that have been particularly helpful in my teaching, developing this text and will be valuable to readers who wish to explore further as supporting material.

I would also thank Dr Ronnie Burton who first welcomed me to his OpenGL course in the autumn of 2001 and with his encouragement suggested I take a teaching role in the presentation at London Metropolitan University. Ronnie unstintingly gave of his time and knowledge, which made this work possible. I cannot let pass the support of Professor Jim Yip and Professor Ian Haines who appointed me and provided the time and space to complete the text. Their enthusiasm, encouragement and leadership was an example to all – thank you.

As with many tasks there is often a frequently hidden unseen support in the background – my wife Despoulla who has cajouled and pressed for completion when I could find reasons for vaccilation! I recognise and thank her for the persistent determination that was a major contribution to the success of the work.

The primary purpose of education is to make one's mind a pleasant place in which to spend one's leisure – S.J. Harris

Contents

1 Getting Started 1
   1.1 Introduction 1
   1.2 Access to Libraries 2
   1.3 Data Types 2
   1.4 Terminology 3
   1.5 The OpenGL Utility Toolkit–GLUT 3
   1.6 Our First Program 4
       1.6.1 Drawing Primitives 7
       1.6.2 Gaps, Lines and Blobs 10
       1.6.3 Other Line Types 11
       1.6.4 Surface Patterns and Polygon Stippling 12
       1.6.5 Character Generation 15
   1.7 Parametric Representation of Curves 17
       1.7.1 The Growth or Logarithmic Spiral 19
   1.8 Approximation and Processing Efficiency 21
       1.8.1 Line Drawing 22
       1.8.2 The Digital Difference Analyser 23
       1.8.3 Bresenham's Algorithm 25
       1.8.4 Bresenham's Algorithm for a Circle 27
   1.9 Problem Solving Through Graphics 31
   1.10 The Application Programming Interface (API) 34
       1.10.1 The OpenGL Utility Toolkit (GLUT) Library 34
       1.10.2 Mouse Interaction 35
       1.10.3 Keyboard Interaction 36
   1.11 Exercises 37
   1.12 Conclusion 37

2 Image File Formats 39
   2.1 Introduction 39
   2.2 The Bitmap File 39
       2.2.1 Bitmap-file Structure 40
       2.2.2 A Typical File Layout 41

2.2.3   Reading and Drawing a Bitmap File 42
2.2.4   Creating a Display Window 45
2.2.5   Creating the Image for Display 46
2.2.6   Monochrome Bitmaps.............................. 46
2.2.7   A General Class for Input of Bit
        Map Files 47
2.2.8   Manipulating Bit Maps – Embossing 49
2.3 Audio/Video Interleaved (AVI) File Format 51
2.3.1   Chunk Hierarchy 53
2.3.2   An Example of Web Cam Display 55
2.3.3   Compression 58
2.4 Exercises 59
2.5 Conclusion 59

3   Image Processing.. 61
3.1 Introduction... 61
3.2 Finding Objects 61
3.2.1   Edge Detection................................ 62
3.2.2   Numerical Implementation 63
3.2.3   Sobel Operator 63
3.2.4   Convolution 64
3.2.5   Laplacian Operator 66
3.2.6   Smoothing and Edge Finding 69
3.3 Histogram Equalisation 71
3.4 Component (object) Labelling 73
3.4.1   Exploring Connectivity (1)......................... 74
3.4.2   Exploring Connectivity (2)......................... 76
3.4.3   Multiple Regions 77
3.5 Drawing on the Screen and Data Capture 77
3.5.1   Outlining of Areas of Interest on Images 80
3.5.2   An Approach to Automating Edge Detection 82
3.6 Exercises 85
3.7 Conclusion 85

4   Transformations 87
4.1 Introduction... 87
4.2 Representing Points and Vectors........................... 87
4.2.1   Vector Dot Products 89
4.2.2   The Vector Cross Product 89
4.2.3   Using the Cross Product to Provide Colour Variation
        to a Cylinder................................... 91
4.3 Coordinate Systems 94
4.4 Transformations 95
4.4.1   Rotation 96
4.4.2   A Simple Example of Rotation 98

| | | 4.4.3 | General Rotations About Any Point | 99 |

4.4.3   General Rotations About Any Point 99
4.5   The Model View Matrix 103
4.6   Adding Some Movement 103
      4.6.1   Movement of Composite Objects....................... 104
      4.6.2   The Orrery 104
      4.6.3   The Internal Combustion Engine 107
      4.6.4   Arms, Robots, Actuators and Movement 113
      4.6.5   Data Capture of Limb Movement 114
      4.6.6   Animation – A Walking Robot......................... 116
4.7   Collision Detection 120
4.8   Exercises 124
4.9   Conclusion 124

5   Viewing and Projection 125
    5.1   Introduction... 125
    5.2   Vertex Pipeline 125
    5.3   The Viewing Process 126
          5.3.1   Engineering Drawings............................. 128
    5.4   Orthographic or Parallel Projection 132
          5.4.1   From Real World to Screen Window 132
          5.4.2   Inside the Matrix 134
          5.4.3   Getting to Grips with Where Things Are 137
          5.4.4   Perspective Projection 139
          5.4.5   Understanding the View 143
    5.5   Exercises 145
    5.6   Conclusion 146

6   Lighting and Colour 147
    6.1   Introduction... 147
    6.2   The Electromagnetic Spectrum............................... 147
          6.2.1   Colour 148
          6.2.2   Mixing Colours 149
          6.2.3   The Shading Model 150
    6.3   Lighting and Illumination 151
          6.3.1   Setting up the Lighting 152
          6.3.2   Addition of Specular Light 157
    6.4   A Synthetic Face 162
          6.4.1   Getting the Vertex Coordinates 162
          6.4.2   Moving the Eye and Light Source Together 163
    6.5   Shadows – A Projection..................................... 164
          6.5.1   Derivation of the Shadow Outline Using Equation
                  of a Line 164
          6.5.2   A Polygon Moving Shadow 166
    6.6   Exercises 168
    6.7   Conclusion 169

7   Texture Mapping 171
  7.1   Introduction 171
  7.2   The Mapping Process 171
  7.3   Setting up Textures 172
     7.3.1   Drawing the Texture 174
  7.4   Mapping onto Curved Surfaces 176
     7.4.1   Mercator Lines of Projection 176
     7.4.2   Quadric Surfaces 177
     7.4.3   Mapping onto a Spherical Surface 178
     7.4.4   Mapping one Image to Sphere 182
     7.4.5   Cylinder Texturing Mapping 184
     7.4.6   Mapping to a Circle 185
     7.4.7   Mapping to a Cone 186
     7.4.8   Mapping onto a General Surface 189
     7.4.9   Mapping onto a Contour Surface 191
  7.5   Adding Some Movement – A Rotating Hemisphere 193
     7.5.1   Movement via the Mouse 196
  7.6   Using Bit Maps to Provide Context 200
     7.6.1   Blending 202
     7.6.2   Manipulating Pixels 206
  7.7   Three-Dimensional Texturing 212
     7.7.1   Simulation of a Spherical Object 213
     7.7.2   Building a Solid Model of a Head 219
  7.8   Exercises 226
  7.9   Conclusion 226

8   Objects to Artefacts 227
  8.1   Introduction 227
  8.2   Artefact Hierarchy 227
     8.2.1   Construction Double Sided Squares 228
     8.2.2   A Box as a Basic Building Block 232
     8.2.3   Building a Table 233
  8.3   Integrating to a System 235
  8.4   Changing the Furniture Style 243
  8.5   Exercises 247
  8.6   Conclusion 247

9   Curves, Surfaces and Patterns 249
  9.1   Introduction 249
  9.2   Fitting a Line or a Curve 250
     9.2.1   Straight Line Fitting to Data Points 250
     9.2.2   Lagrange Polynomials and Curve Fitting 251
     9.2.3   A Practical Approach to Curve Fitting 251
     9.2.4   Curve Fitting Using Cubic Splines 252
     9.2.5   Surface Construction from Contour Maps 256

9.2.6   A Spline Surface Construction 258
9.2.7   Bezier Curves 260
9.2.8   General Curve Representation 263
9.2.9   The Beginning's of a Bezier Surface 267
9.2.10   Using Rotation to Sweep Out a Ring................. 271
9.2.11   Patching a Surface 271
9.3   Complex Shapes and Fractal Geometry 274
9.3.1   Introductory Concepts............................. 275
9.3.2   Reduction Copying 276
9.3.3   Implementation of a Sierpinski Gasket 278
9.3.4   Pascal's Triangle 280
9.3.5   The Sierpinski Gasket in 3 Dimensions 280
9.3.6   Order Out of Chaos – A Non-deterministic Gasket? 284
9.3.7   An Alternative Idea for a Tree or Plant 290
9.4   Koch Curves 292
9.4.1   Further Thoughts on the Koch Snowflake 295
9.4.2   Self-Similarity 296
9.4.3   Random Koch Fractals 298
9.4.4   Back to Trees and Bushes 300
9.5   Brownian Motion 304
9.5.1   Fractalised Lines 305
9.5.2   Fractal Surfaces 307
9.6   Exercises 310
9.7   Conclusion 311

Appendix A 313
A.1 Starting up VC++ 6.0 313

Appendix B 317
B.1 Bresenham's Line Algorithm – General Conditions 317

Appendix C 319
C.1 Matrix and Vector Algebra 319
C.2 Matrix Addition or Subtraction........................... 319
C.3 Matrix Multiplication.................................. 319
C.4 Matrix Vector Multiplication............................. 320
C.5 Example of Matrix Multiplication 321
C.6 Shearing Matrices.................................... 321

Appendix D 323
D.1 Equation of a Plane 323

References 325

Index of Functions....................................... 327

Index 329

Chapter 1
Getting Started

1.1 Introduction

Most software is about getting some output from input data after processing – OpenGL graphics is no different! Rather than describe the intricacies of the OpenGL system, which have already been covered in other texts (Hill, 2001; Angel, 2006), we shall enter practically and begin using the system in order to develop our understanding. A lot of ground will be covered in this chapter although the author hopes you won't notice this, nor worry too much, if there are parts you do not initially understand! We shall use a range of examples that illustrate how to achieve simple outcomes that can be incorporated into other applications later on. Understanding comes from the confidence of getting things working and a lot of detail does not help in the early stages. Keeping the detail to a minimum in the early stages of this text has required compromises, so do not worry if at the start you appear to be using functions that appear as 'black boxes', you will grasp the reason and purpose later on as concepts are explained and assimilated.

OpenGL is designed to be device independent to allow portability between various computer platforms. It is referred to as an API (application programming interface), that insulates the programmer from device differences and how they vary from one system to another. Windows programming is an *event* driven system operating on a first come, first served basis and managed by an *event queue* of *callback* functions – what we might call interrupt service routines. The callback functions govern what happens when we say press a key or move the mouse and later in this chapter we shall describe some of the actions required to make use of these events. We use C/C++ in this text due to its' widespread use in the OpenGL community and predominance over the past ten years. The software infrastructure history is such that while we can call the OpenGL libraries from other languages, it offers little advantage at this time and in commercial terms is expensive. I leave the language arguments to others in the profession although transfer to different environments has proved relatively painless to my students.

R. Whitrow, *OpenGL Graphics Through Applications,*
© Springer-Verlag London Limited 2008

1.2 Access to Libraries

Although the OpenGL interface provides platform independence, the set-up of libraries and header files varies across systems and compilers and we cannot hope to cover all such variations. However many university students will be using this text with a PC in their room and will require some knowledge of how to set up their system. For reasons of cost the set up is designed to be economical and based around commonly available (free) software. A useful stripped down MS C++ compiler comes with the widely available book by Deitel (2003) and further explanation is provided in the appendix to this chapter at the end of the book on installation and where to put the OpenGL libraries. There are also a number of sites from where OpenGL software may be freely down loaded as will be noted in our first program. Depending on which release of OpenGL you use, the number of header files included may need to be different. In the rest of this book we shall be using the Mesa libraries 1.5 obtained from http://mesa3d.sourceforge.net/. The mesa releases that I compiled are available for Windows (on the accompanying Springer web site) and Linux versions can also be obtained from the sourceforge website. The required location of direct link libraries and header information is given in Appendix A.

Typically the initial header inclusions for a Windows system will include

```
#include <windows.h>
#include <GL/glut.h>
```

plus any other library access (maths.h etc) that you may require. This will be slightly different on Linux where if you are using X windows then a likely include will be

```
#include <X11/Xlib.h>
#include <GL/glut.h>
```

and Mac OS X systems and readers should consult with sites such as http://developer. apple.com/graphicsimaging/opengl/ or http://www.linuxjournal.com/article/5534 for header and directory information relating to their particular system. If you are including any of the latest extensions these will probably be downloaded from www.opengl.org and stored locally in the same directory as your source files.

1.3 Data Types

As various versions of compilers are released along with different platforms the size of data types often vary. OpenGl provides a prefix (GL) to many data types to ease portability and a list of these are given in Table 1.1

Most of the types are self-explanatory. When a **u** occurs, it is to indicate all bits are used for storing numerical values of say a colour level.

Table 1.1

C/C++ type	Data Type	OpenGL name & Suffix	
signed char	8 bit integer	GLbyte	b
short	16 bit integer	GLshort	s
int or long	32 bit integer	GLint, Glsizei	i
float	32 bit floating point	GLfloat, GLclampf	f
double	64 bit floating point	GLdouble, Glclampd	d
unsigned char	8 bit unsigned number	GLubyte, GLboolean	ub
unsigned short	16 bit unsigned number	GLushort	us
unsigned int or long	32 bit unsigned number	GLuint, GLenum, GLbitfield ui	

1.4 Terminology

Before we start there is some basic terminology that you will see in most graphics textbooks and should understand. The following are used in this text.

Rendering: The process whereby computer software creates or draws an image from a model.

Model: An object constructed using points, lines and polygons delineated by vertices.

Vertices: Locations in the space representing the object. This may be Cartesian space or a space representing other entities.

The final rendered image is made up on a screen as pixels (screen locations with a given colour). The pixel colour values are stored in memory as bit planes and when combined are referred to as a frame buffer. The depth of the frame buffer determines the colour resolution to which images can be displayed (8 bits would provide 256 intensities for a single colour).

1.5 The OpenGL Utility Toolkit–GLUT

The OpenGL library only contains rendering commands that are independent of operating system. It is not capable of opening windows or responding to interrupts from a mouse or keyboard. The GLUT libraries (Kilgard, 1996) provide such a facility and are available from the Mesa site already mentioned and on the accompanying web site described in Appendix A. The commands to set up a window in which we may render an object are as follows.

```
glutInit          (&argc, argv );                    //initialise GLUT
                                                     //library
glutInitDisplayMode ( GLUT_SINGLE | GLUT_RGB );  //Single buffer with
                                                     //RGB colour model
glutInitWindowSize  ( width, height );           //window size in pixels
glutInitWindowPosition( x-position, y-position ); // & position on
                                                     //screen
```

```
glutCreateWindow  ( "Window Title" );    // create an OpenGL window
glutDisplayFunc ( Rendering Function );  // Display image from
                                         //Rendering Function
glutMainLoop ( );                     // get GLUT functions above executing
```

These are usually found in the main function of most OpenGL programs. The GLUT library is particularly important in that it provides a window creation that is independent of both Microsoft and Unix and thus platform independent. Throughout this text we shall use the GLUT library rather that facilities that depend on one operating system or another. The author is aware of efficiency arguments used for and against this approach but over the years has experienced system changes that have been at least irritating when using system dependent functions and at worst catastrophic when commercial upgrades are introduced.

The toolkit used above can be broadly divided into two components: the Window creation and initialisation and the registering and processing of the callback functions associated with different devices on the computer. glutInit() initialises the GLUT library and should be the first function call. glutInitDisplayMode() defines the display modes such as the type of pixel storage and whether single buffered usually used for static displays or double buffered when using animation. glutInitWindowSize(width, height) specifies the window size and glutInitWindowPosition () specifies the position of the GLUT window in (x, y) pixels on the screen. It is a good idea to position this away from the console window if input/output takes place via the latter. glutCreateWindow () creates a window of the size defined with a title bar and name.

After window initialisation there are a number of functions associated with calling functions used to draw, update and interact with the display. glutDisplayFunc() is used to specify the function used to render or draw the window contents or redraw them after some interaction with an existing display. Other functions we shall use later in the text that permit user interaction include glutKeyboardFunc (), glutMouseFunc () and glutPostRedisplay (). Finally GLUT programs enter an event (interrupt) processing loop, which never ceases using glutMainLoop (). The callback functions registered with the program for different tasks by the GLUT kit will be called when events such as mouse movement, pressing a key or rendering require them. This is akin to real time programming where we wait for an event or interrupt to occur and then execute the appropriate action or function. Program termination occurs if we close the glut window or use a 'break' as a result of a key input or a mouse click.

1.6 Our First Program

This is a 'get you started' program with all that is required to get a dot on the screen in a window. In this first chapter we shall give complete programs that are very short and may be read at leisure. In later chapters only relevant code fragments are given, while complete programs are also provided on the accompanying web site.

The height and width in pixels of our window for displaying results in this example is 250×250 and the top left hand corner of the window is positioned at (x, y) location (180,90) on the screen of the computer. The window title is written in the top bar as 'Display a Dot'. Comments indicate the role of the OpenGL functions in the program.

```cpp
#include <iostream>          //dot.cpp
#include <windows.h>
#include <GL/glut.h>
using std::cout;

GLsizei wh = 250 ;   // initial height of window
GLsizei ww  = 250 ;   // initial width of window

void Displaydot ( void );
void MyInit   ( );

void Displaydot ( void ) {
  glClear ( GL_COLOR_BUFFER_BIT ); //clear pixel buffer
  glBegin(GL_POINTS);    // render with points
    glVertex2i(40,210); //display a point
  glEnd();
  glFlush();
}

void MyInit ( void ) {
  cout << glGetString(GL_VERSION) <<"\n";
  cout << glGetString(GL_VENDOR) <<"\n";
  glClearColor ( 1.0, 1.0, 1.0, 0.0 ); //white background
  glColor3f(0.0f, 1.0f,0.0f);            // green drawing colour
  glPointSize(10.0);                     // 10 pixel dot!
  glMatrixMode ( GL_PROJECTION );
  glLoadIdentity ( );
  gluOrtho2D ( 0.0, (GLdouble)ww, 0.0, (GLdouble)wh ); //Display area
}

void main(int argc, char **argv) {
  glutInit               ( &argc, argv );
  glutInitDisplayMode    ( GLUT_SINGLE | GLUT_RGB );
  glutInitWindowSize     ( ww, wh );  // window size
  glutInitWindowPosition ( 180, 90 ); // & position on screen
  glutCreateWindow       ( "Display a Dot" );
  MyInit ( );
  glutDisplayFunc ( Displaydot );
  glutMainLoop ( );
}
```

The function MyInit () is used for setting up the rendering environment which in this case has a white background in the GLUT window using glClearColor (1.0, 1.0, 1.0, 0.0); to set the colour; the object to be drawn is green glColor3f (0.0f, 1.0f, 0.0f); and setting the size of the dot to be drawn as 10 pixels glPointSize (10.0). The colours red, green and blue (RGB) are set to be 1.0 when fully on or 0 when off using glClearColor () and glColor3f (). The glMatrixMode (GL_PROJECTION) and glLoadIdentity ( ) functions set up the projection identity matrix used by the routine gluOrtho2D (0.0, (GLdouble) width, 0.0, (GLdouble) height) to project the object coordinates onto the screen from (left, bottom) position to the (right, top) position of the screen. The centre of the window is by convention (0, 0) with the top right defined as (1, 1) and the bottom left as (−1, −1) with all points on an object being scaled to these limits. In this example we have a window of 250 × 250 pixels superimposed in the main computer screen window of whatever operating system we are using. For the first example this means that the largest object we can completely display has vertices that must lie between values of (−125, −125) and (125, 125). The size of the glut window measured in centimetres is whatever fraction 250 is of the screen display being used (800 × 600 in the authors case). We shall describe the projection viewing process in more detail in Section 5.4.2 but for now just use it in order to get started and leave the detail for later.

There are two lines of code using the glGetString ('name') function which are not strictly required but used for illustrative purposes so that students can find out about the version and supplier of the OpenGL they are using and possibly keep up to date with later versions as they become available.

The callback function Displaydot (void) is where the rendering of objects takes place. The GLUT executes this function whenever is needs to; for example when we first draw the window or make alteration to the image when animating objects. The callback function is referenced by the glutDisplayFunc() from the GLUT library.

The Displaydot (void) rendering function clears the pixel buffer of colour values where the image is to be stored. Rendering is a process of drawing between Cartesian points or vertices in the window and we use the command glVertex2i (x-position, y-position); to perform this operation. In this example we are using two parameters for a two dimensional space and each parameter is an integer. To draw an object delineated by vertices we use the functions glBegin(mode); and glEnd(); where mode defines the type of drawing (points, lines, polygons etc.). The final function glFlush() tells the program to execute these commands rather than wait for any further graphics commands later. Without this OpenGL will often wait for a number commands to queue up before executing and students can be left wondering why nothing occurs on the screen.

The resulting output is given in Fig. 1.1.

The version and author of the Mesa library is shown in the black console window and the green dot appears in the GLUT window next to it with the title bar. The bottom left hand corner of the window is 0,0.

Fig. 1.1 Console and graphics windows

1.6.1 Drawing Primitives

We have used a limited set of drawing primitives and we will now begin to generalise capabilities. Drawing is accomplished using points, lines, polylines and polygons all of which are defined by vertices. OpenGL provides beyond the primitives of points (GL_POINTS) to include a segmented lines (GL_LINES) facility, to have joined lines (GL_LINE_STRIP) and closed loops (GL_LINE_LOOP). Further surfaces may be patched using polygons, triangles and quadrilaterals. A set of primitives required to render the image occur between the lines glBegin() to glEnd(). glBegin() takes an argument Glvalue that governs how the vertex list is to be processed.

```
glBegin(Glvalue);  start of vertex list where argument
      |            Glvalue specifies the geometric
      ↓
                   primitive to be constructed at vertices
      Value                        Meaning
GL_POINTS            individual points at vertices
GL_LINES             individual line segments
GL_LINE_STRIP        connected line segments
GL_LINE_LOOP         connected line segments including
                     first and last
GL_TRIANGLES         vertex triples interpreted as triangles
GL_TRIANGLES_STRIP linked strip of triangles
GL_TRIANGLES_FAN   linked fan of triangles
GL_QUADS             vertex quadruples interpreted as 4 sided
                     polygons
GL_QUADS_STRIP       linked strip of quadrilaterals
GL_POLYGON           boundary of simple, convex polygon
glEnd();
```

The vertex rendering us accomplished using glVertex2i(...) and the flexibility is illustrated in the following:

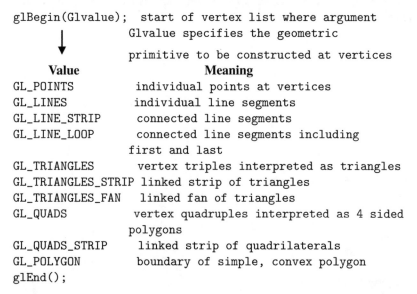

The order in which points are connected should be consistent (all clockwise or all anticlockwise). The presentation of vertices where GL_LINE_STRIP, GL_TRIANGLES_STRIP etc are used requires such consistency for drawing purposes.

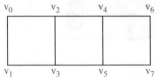

GL_TRIANGLE_STRIP v_0-v_1-v_2 **then** v_2-v_1-v_3 **then** v_2-v_3-v_4 etc.

GL_QUAD_STRIP v_0-v_1-v_3-v_2 **then** v_2-v_3-v_5–v_4 **then** v_4-v_5-v_7–v_6 etc.

Joined up line segments end to end are called polylines and OpenGL calls uses STRIP or LOOP in the parameter name to render in this manner. We can use this facility by storing vertices in an array to render an object.

In the following example the coordinates of the letter 'R' are read from disc and drawn. The disc file R.txt can be created in any text processing facility such as Notepad in Windows or vi in Linux after drawing the letter R on graph paper and reading off the x, y coordinates of the vertices.

```
10   10
10  100
30  100
45   80
30   70
10   70
45   10
```

```cpp
#include <iostream> //line_poly_file.cpp
#include <fstream.h>
#include <windows.h>
#include <GL/glut.h>

GLsizei wh = 250;
GLsizei ww = 250;

void DisplayLines  ( void ) ;
void MyInit ( ) ;

void DisplayLines ( void ) {
GLint xj, yj, j;
  glClear ( GL_COLOR_BUFFER_BIT ) ;
  fstream inStream;
  inStream.open("R.txt", ios ::in);
  if(!inStream) {cout << "File would not open\n";
```

```
        return;
   }
      glBegin(GL_LINE_STRIP);          //render a series of vertices
         for (j=1; j<=7; j++) {
         inStream >> xj >> yj;         //read from disc file
         cout << xj << " " << yj <<"\n";
         glVertex2i(xj,yj);
   }
      glEnd();
glFlush();
}


void MyInit ( void ) {
  glClearColor ( 1.0, 1.0, 0.0, 0.0 );//set window buffer as yellow
  glColor3f(0.0f, 0.0f,1.0f);          //draw R in blue
  //glLineWidth(5.0);                  //try different line thicknesses
  glMatrixMode ( GL{\_}PROJECTION );
  glLoadIdentity ( ) ;
  gluOrtho2D ( 0.0, (GLdouble)ww, 0.0,(GLdouble)wh );
  //draw R in this space
}
void main(int argc, char **argv) {
  glutInit ( &argc, argv );
  glutInitDisplayMode ( GLUT_SINGLE | GLUT_RGB );
  glutInitWindowSize ( ww, wh );
  glutInitWindowPosition ( 150, 90 );
  glutCreateWindow ( "Display R" );
  MyInit ( );

  glutDisplayFunc ( DisplayLines );
  glutMainLoop ( );
}
```

Fig. 1.2 A simple line
drawing display

Just as with the dot drawing program we could define the size of the dot, so with we can with line width by use of the function glLineWidth () with a real argument specifying the line thickness. The default is 1.0.

1.6.2 Gaps, Lines and Blobs

In Fig. 1.2 we drew a simple connected line that was able to describe the complete object in terms of (x, y) coordinates that was in this case, a letter R. Most drawings are made up from more complex combinations of lines that may be continuous, isolated from other parts of the drawing and areas (blobs) of colour that may be filled in. To illustrate these functions we have supplied a data file (snoopy3.txt), which is a digitised version of one of my hand drawn 'snoopys' (apologies to the artists amongst the readers!). While the previous example could be represented with Cartesian coordinates alone, we now need to add extra data to indicate the new facilities of line disconnection and blob filling for our dog Snoopy.

As one sketched the Snoopy it soon became apparent which lines were continuous because it was easy to draw without any hand movement other than wrist bending, while discontinuities required a pencil lift from paper. Similarly blobs of colour required over writing to fill in an area. To provide such *data driven* facilities we have introduced two variables beyond the Cartesian point representation of the vertices. Lines are separated by an indicator for the number of points in any given line stroke and a further variable which specifies whether we only wish to draw lines or fill in a region surrounded by the points using the drawing mode GL_POLYGON. Typical data for a line will look something like the following:

$$4\,1$$
$$12.5\,0$$
$$11\,2$$
$$10.5\,5$$
$$10.1\,7$$

where the line is specified by four coordinates and an 'l' to indicate a line rather than a filled blob indicated by 'f'. We read each line of data from file together with the indicator as to the type of drawing required for it. The display function follows with a typical output in Fig. 1.3.

```
void DisplaySnoopy (void) {
char line_fill;
GLfloat xj, yj;
int j, no_of_pts;
fstream inStream;
inStream.open("c:\\rob\\Graphics\\cppgr\\snoopy3.txt", ios ::in);
if(!inStream) { cout << "File would not open\n";
                          return;
                        }
glClear (GL_COLOR_BUFFER_BIT);
glScalef(5.0, 5.0, 1.0);
```

```
do {
  inStream>>no_of_pts>>line_fill;                    //next line
  if(line_fill == '1') glBegin(GL_LINE_STRIP);       //lines
           else glBegin(GL_POLYGON);                  // or blobs
    for (j=1; j<=no_of_pts; j++) {
                    inStream >> xj >> yj;             //cartesian coordinates
                    glVertex2f(xj,yj);
    }
  glEnd();
} while((no_of_pts = inStream.get()) != EOF); //end of file terminator
glFlush();
}
```

Fig. 1.3 Snoopy from blobs and discontinuous lines

In Fig. 1.3 we see that the points representing the nose of snoopy were preceded by an 'f' to facilitate the graphical filling using GL_POLYGON. The function glScalef() has been used since the digitised coordinates made the image rather small. A similar result could also be obtained by changing the window image range to gluOrtho2D(0.0, (GLdouble)ww/4, 0.0, (GLdouble)wh/4). Data input for lines in a normal text file is terminated with end of file. Besides GL_POLYGON the graphics primitives, GL_TRIANGLES, GL_TRIANGLE_STRIP, GL_TRIANGLE_FAN, GL_QUADS and GL_QUAD_STRIP also permit the colour filling of objects.

1.6.3 Other Line Types

In Fig. 1.3 we drew Snoopy with a continuous line and filled in the nose with the colour blue. OpenGL also permits drawing of discontinuous or stippled lines with a pattern governed by a bit pattern that we can define by an unsigned integer parameter using the function glLineStipple (GLint sfactor, GLushort pattern). The function has two parameters defined as follows:

pattern - a bit pattern where a 1 means draw and 0 means no drawing
sfactor - is a scale factor where we multiply the number of 1's or 0's by this factor

Inserting the following two lines of code in the previous DisplaySnoopy (void) function before the function glBegin()

```
glLineStipple(GLint sfactor, GLushort pattern);
glEnable(GL_LINE_STIPPLE);
```

will change the continuous lines to a broken line governed by the bit pattern stored in the parameter pattern. For pattern = 7939 the bit pattern is

$$0001 \; 1111 \; 0000 \; 0011$$

and the hexadecimal representation is   1   F   0   3

The stippled snoopy drawing is shown in Fig. 1.4.

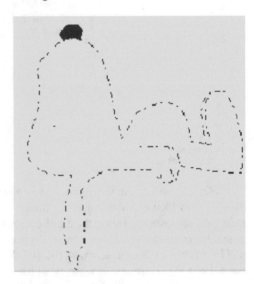

Fig. 1.4 Stippled lines

1.6.4 Surface Patterns and Polygon Stippling

We can extend the idea of line patterns based on the bit pattern occupying a byte to polygon filling of a shape with user-defined patterns. In this example we fill the outline of snoopy dog with polygons and fill it with circles or spots. In filling a general shape with polygons we need to remember that the parameter GL_POLYGON requires that the vertices define a convex polygon. Since the Snoopy in Fig. 1.4 has concavities, we partition the drawing into a series of convex polygons and build the complete image from the sum of these polygons. In Fig. 1.4 we must separate the ear from the face for drawing purposes since a concavity exists at the joining point of these two objects. Similar situations exist at other parts of the drawing and we use the concavity vertices to separate each convex component. We avoid drawing the outline of any internal triangles used to fill the drawing by checking for three point polygons and omitting the GL_LINE_STRIP drawing.

We can draw patterns on the polygons used to fill snoopy by use of the glPolygonStipple(const Glubyte *mask) function, where mask is a pointer to a 32×32 bit map. The bit map draws a pixel whenever a 1 is set on the polygon and nothing when a 0 occurs where four bytes represent each row of pixels in the mask. A byte containing 0×8003 is shown as

$$80 \mid 03$$

Bit pattern for one pixel drawn, five not drawn and two drawn

By a suitable choice of bytes we can draw a variety of shapes and repeat them over the area of any polygon after enabling stippling with glEnable (GL_POLYGON_ STIPPLE). The stippling is disabled using glDisable (GL_POLYGON_STIPPLE). In the following display function the data points defining the polygons that contribute to snoopy are stored in the file 'snoopy3polygon.txt' and the bit pattern for a ring is stored as integers in the file 'ringbytes.txt', both supplied on the web site. The data defines when a polygon vertex finishes at a point of concavity via the variable tfill and an extra closure point is added to complete the polygon. The additional point is not plotted when drawing the outline of the object snoopy in Fig. 1.5.

```
void DisplaySnoopy ( void ) {
char tfill;
GLfloat xaj[40], yaj[40]; //polygon data points
int j, no_of_pts, intring[128];
GLubyte ring[128];        //bit pattern store

fstream inRings;
fstream inStream;
inStream.open("c:\\rob\\Graphics\\cppgr\\snoopy3polygon.txt",ios ::in);
if(!inStream) { cout << "File would not open\n";
                return;
                }
inRings.open("c:\\rob\\Graphics\\cppgr\\ringbytes.txt",ios ::in);
if(!inRings) {cout << "File would not open\n";
                return;
                }

for (j=0; j<128; j++) { //i/p stipple pattern as integers->bytes
```

```
        inRings >> intring[j];
        ring[j] = (char) intring[j];
}

glClear ( GL_COLOR_BUFFER_BIT );
glScalef(5.0, 5.0, 1.0);
glEnable(GL_POLYGON_STIPPLE);
glPolygonStipple(ring);
do {
        inStream >> no_of_pts >> tfill;
        input polygon outline
        for (j=1; j<=no_of_pts; j++) inStream >> xaj[j] >> yaj[j];
        //draw polygon
        glBegin(GL_POLYGON);
                for (j=1; j<=no_of_pts; j++) glVertex2f(xaj[j],yaj[j]);
        glEnd();
        //draw outline & skip last point if internal to snoopy
        if(tfill == 'y') no_of_pts--;
        if(no_of_pts != 2) {
        glBegin(GL_LINE_STRIP);
                for (j=1; j<=no_of_pts; j++) glVertex2f(xaj[j],yaj[j]);
        glEnd();
        }
} while((no_of_pts = inStream.get()) != EOF);
glFlush();
}
```

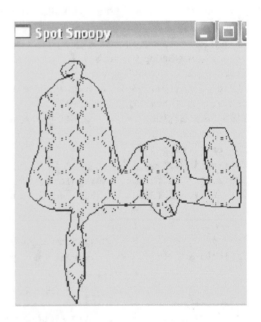

Fig. 1.5 Stipple pattern of rings

Readers may find it instructive to modify the data file 'ringbytes.txt' to make smaller filled in rings when the dog then appears as spotted.

1.6.5 Character Generation

OpenGL provides the capability for manipulating 1-bit pixels as used in drawing the various character sets. The following example simply demonstrates the drawing of a letter 'A', Fig. 1.6. There are imperfections in the bit map and readers should correct this in order to be familiar with mapping the 16×16 pattern and even consider developing their own fonts. Each row is 32 bits long in order to end on an even word boundary and as before we use hexadecimal (Ox) to represent the bit patterns (0–f) for each row of the character. The character 'A' is stored in an unsigned byte array and where a bit is set the screen location will be set to white with in this example a black background. If we consider one part of the array representing 8×8 pixels then

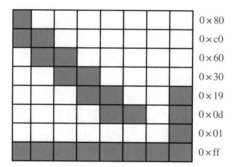

are the hexadecimal representations of each row of pixels. The bitmap byte array (letter A) is an argument in glBitmap() function used to draw a bitmap.

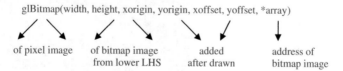

glBitmap(width, height, xorigin, yorigin, xoffset, yoffset, *array)

of pixel image | of bitmap image from lower LHS | added after drawn | address of bitmap image

The rendering function is as follows:

```
void Render(void)        /* A */
{
GLubyte letterA[] =
  {
0xe0, 0x07, 0, 0, /* ***          *** */
```

```
0xe0, 0x07, 0, 0, /* ***           *** */
0xe0, 0x07, 0, 0, /* ***           *** */
0xe0, 0x07, 0, 0, /* ***           *** */
0xe0, 0x07, 0, 0, /* ***           *** */
0xe0, 0x07, 0, 0, /* ***           *** */
0xff, 0xff, 0, 0, /* **************** */
0xff, 0xff, 0, 0, /* **************** */
0xe0, 0x0e, 0, 0, /* ***          *** */
0x70, 0x16, 0, 0, /* ***         *** */
0x38, 0x38, 0, 0, /*  ***        *** */
0x1c, 0x38, 0, 0, /*  ***        *** */
0x1c, 0x78, 0, 0, /*   ****     **** */
0x0f, 0xc0, 0, 0, /*    ********** */
0x0f, 0xc0, 0, 0, /*     ******** */
0x01, 0xc0, 0, 0 /*        ****     */
};
GLint i;

glClearColor(0.0, 0.0, 0.0, 1.0);
glClear(GL_COLOR_BUFFER_BIT);
glColor3f(1.0, 1.0, 1.0);

for (i = 0; i < 10; i ++) {
  glRasterPos2i(i * 15, i * 15);
  glBitmap(16, 16, 0, 0, 0, 0, letterA);
  }
}
```

Fig. 1.6 Drawing characters
from bitmap definitions

1.7 Parametric Representation of Curves

This chapter is all about getting started and although the examples are not particularly related, they are intended to give readers a taste of what is possible. Some we will come back to in later chapters and modify for other applications. Graphical rendering involves plotting pixels at (x, y) locations and while this has been convenient up to now, there are a number of geometric shapes where we can generate the (x, y) coordinates from equations. A parametric representation of a curve is a way of representing the curve or shape by one or more mathematical relations that also contain parameters, that when altered draw the object concerned. In this example we will construct a helical spring.

Consider the circle in Fig. 1.7

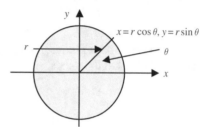

Fig. 1.7 Parametric representation of a circle

where a Cartesian point x, y is represented in polar coordinates with the angle θ being the parameter that we vary. If θ increases from 0 to 2π then for a line of constant length r, the point x, y will trace out a circle in 2D space. If we add a third dimension in the z-direction out of the plane of the paper and let z change incrementally as we rotate in the x-y plane, the locus of the curve becomes a helix.

Introducing the three dimensional view requires a different projection view matrix from the 2D views used so far and is discussed further in Chapter 5. For this example we create a viewing volume box using glOrtho(left, right, bottom, top, near, far) rather than the two dimensional rectangle used in previous sections. The parameters left, right, bottom, top, near and far refer to the clipping planes in the x, y and z directions.

```
void reshape (int w, int h)
{
  glViewport (0, 0, (GLsizei) w, (GLsizei) h);
  glMatrixMode (GL_PROJECTION);
  glLoadIdentity ();
  glOrtho(-11.0, 11.0, -11.0, 11.0, 11.0, -11.0);
  //projection volume
  glMatrixMode(GL_MODELVIEW);
  glLoadIdentity();
}
```

```
void Spring ( void ) {
GLfloat degtorads, theta, z;
degtorads=3.14159265/180.0;
z = 0.0;
glRotatef(20.0, 0.0f, 1.0f, 0.0f);
glBegin(GL_LINE_STRIP);
  for (theta=0.0; theta<=1500.0; theta +=1.0) {
    glVertex3f( 3.0* cos(theta*degtorads), 3.0
                * sin(theta*degtorads), z);
    z = z + 0.005;
}
glEnd();
glFlush();
}
```

Using the above code produces a result shown in Fig. 1.8 where we have rotated the helix by 20° about the y-axis.

Fig. 1.8 A spring

The relationship between Cartesian and polar coordinates is very useful in drawing a number of commonly occurring spirals.

The helical spring in Fig. 1.8 is a continuous line drawn by a small increase in z after every circle is completed. Clearly a more exact representation would require that we increment z with every angular increase in θ, although for display purposes the error is not easily resolved by eye. With practice such approximations are often used in games to speed up processing while not seriously distorting the visual effect. In applications where one is replicating real processes such as flight simulation, *approximation must be used with care and always documented.*

The same software can be modified to draw objects built from numbers of circles placed at different locations. A cone can be thought of as a number of circles in parallel planes with decreasing radii. The main difference from the spring in Fig. 1.8 is that after drawing each circle (θ increases from 0 to 2π), we start again with a decreased radius and repeat the process while the radius is greater that zero as illustrated in the following code and illustrated in Fig. 1.9.

```
void Cone ( void ) {
GLfloat degtorads, theta, z, radius;
degtorads=3.14159265/180.0;
radius = 3.0;
glRotatef(20.0, 0.0, 1.0, 0.0);
```

```
z = 0.0;
do {
glBegin(GL_LINE_STRIP);
   for (theta=0.0; theta<=360.0; theta +=1.0) {          //draw a
       //new circle
           glVertex3f( radius* cos(theta*degtorads), radius
                   * sin(theta*degtorads), z);
   }
   radius = radius - 0.3;     //next circle radius
   z = z + 0.5;               //move up the cone
} while(radius > 0.0);
glEnd();
glFlush();
}
```

Fig. 1.9 A cone built from
circles

1.7.1 The Growth or Logarithmic Spiral

Spirals occur throughout nature whether on a large scale in the form of galaxies, the intermediate size of organisms and fossils such as ammonite or in the very small building blocks of life such as the macro structure of DNA. The logarithmic spiral can be used to represent a number of naturally occurring systems where the polar distance r from the centre at any angle θ varies as log r. Bernoulli referred to this as 'the miraculous spiral' since it looks the same no matter how large or small it is. We shall return to the issue of 'self similarity' later in Chapter 9 when we consider the application of fractal systems. We illustrate construction of the logarithmic spiral in Fig. 1.10 where p_i are points on the spiral.

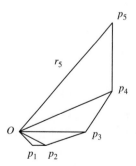

Fig. 1.10 The logarithmic
spiral

For a logarithmic spiral, the log of the distance r_i between the centre O and the point's p_i can be written as

$$\log r_{i+2} - \log r_{i+1} = \log r_{i+1} - \log r_i$$
$$\text{or} \quad r_{i+2}/r_{i+1} = r_{i+1}/r_i$$

which is a geometric series when the polar angle increases by a regular constant factor (equiangular) as we move from point p_i to point p_{i+1}. Thus we can represent our spiral in polar form as

$$\log r = b\,\theta$$

where b is some constant. Taking anti logs for both sides the equation becomes

$$r = e^{b\,\theta}$$

The following code draws the spiral in 2D and if we uncomment the line $//z = z + 0.005$; we draw an outline Fig. 1.11 approximating to that of a snails shell.

```
void LSpiral ( void ) {
GLfloat degtorads, theta, z, a , b, r;
degtorads=3.14159265/180.0;                    //degrees to radians
z = 0.0;
a = 0.5; b = 0.1;
glRotatef(20.0, 0.0f, 1.0f, 0.0f);
glBegin(GL_LINE_STRIP);
  for (theta=0.0; theta<=1500.0; theta +=1.0) {
    r = a * exp( b * theta*degtorads);
    glVertex3f( r * cos(theta*degtorads), r
    * sin(theta*degtorads), z);
    //z = z + 0.005;
}
glEnd();
glFlush();
}
```

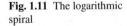

Fig. 1.11 The logarithmic spiral

Readers might like to experiment with values of b such that

$$b = 0$$
$$b < 0$$

and consider what this might mean say in relation to the navigation of an aircraft flying in a holding pattern. Small modifications to the program permit the drawing of an Archimedean spiral given by the relations

$$r = K * \theta;$$
$$x = r * \cos(\theta) \text{ and } y = r * \sin(\theta)$$

where $K = $ constant.

1.8 Approximation and Processing Efficiency

Drawing circles from a parametric definition makes for clear and simple code and for many purposes this is quite satisfactory. We have already alluded to the approximation in drawing the spiral by incrementing z every 2π radians and reducing the amount of processing, while not apparently corrupting the visual effect. The view is often taken that a faster processor will be available next year and these effects will not matter. For many applications this is probably true although in real time systems such as flight simulation or missile tracking, accuracy of approximation coupled with processing speed can be a vital consideration. It is always worth considering any mathematical representation when drawing and whether it may be simplified through the removal of floating-point operations or recast in an incremental form.

In the previous example we used to represent Cartesian coordinate values as $x = r \cos\theta$, $y = r \sin\theta$ from Fig. 1.7. Consider point's x_i, y_i around the circumference of a circle shown in Fig. 1.12.

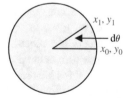

Fig. 1.12 Spacing points around a circle

We can represent successive points as

$$x_i = r \, \cos\theta, \, y_i = r \, \sin\theta \text{ and}$$
$$x_{i+1} = r \, \cos(\theta + d\theta), \, y_{i+1} = r \, \sin(\theta + d\theta)$$

Expanding the relationships for x_{i+1}, y_{i+1} we get

$$x_{i+1} = r \cos\theta \, \cos d\theta - r \sin\theta \, \sin d\theta$$
$$y_{i+1} = r \sin\theta \, \cos d\theta + r \cos\theta \, \sin d\theta$$

Substituting for $r \cos\theta$ and $r \sin\theta$ in terms of x_i, y_i

$$x_{i+1} = x_i \cos d\theta - y_i \sin d\theta$$
$$y_{i+1} = y_i \cos d\theta + x_i \sin d\theta$$

We now have relationships for the next point x_{i+1}, y_{i+1} in terms of the previous point x_i, y_i and the sine and cosine of a fixed incremental value $d\theta$. We have to only evaluate two floating-point calculations ($\cos d\theta$, $\sin d\theta$) and each point on the circle is found in terms of the previous point. Compared with evaluating the trigonometric functions at every angle this method offers a significant saving in processing for a real time application. Readers might note that the circle is a special case of an ellipse in terms of parametric representation and wish to perform a similar derivation for the figure.

1.8.1 Line Drawing

In the previous sections we have shown the value of considering the mathematical representation of points and whether any gains can be found from alternative representations. Drawing a line with OpenGL is apparently quite simple using the following code

```
glBegin(GL_LINES);
        glVertex2i(x0, y0);
        glVertex2i(x1, y1);
glEnd();
```

although some readers may wonder what processing is involved in moving from the point (x_0, y_0) to (x_1, y_1). We saw in Section 1.6.1 that the function glBegin() takes a number of parameters that govern the type of line and line connections that required. We now turn to the problem of displaying points often calculated from floating-point relationships on a screen with integer Cartesian locations. If we calculate that a point has the position (2.6, 7.1) then the best that can be represented on a screen is to plot the point at (3, 7). A series of points when plotted does not form a smooth line but rather a series of steps, sometimes called 'jaggies', Fig. 1.13, where the jagged

Fig. 1.13 Step effect when
plotting lines – jaggies

Steps are particularly noticeable on high-resolution graphics screens. A line is represented in two dimensions by the equation

$$y = mx + c$$

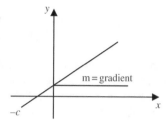

Fig. 1.14 Line drawing

If δy is the increment in y that occurs when we increment x by δx, then

$$\delta y / \delta x = m$$

On a raster display the increments in the x and y directions are constrained by the resolution of the display, which is the minimum pixel separation possible. In practice this is the distance that the electronics can move the electron beam in the case of a cathode ray tube or the size of the RGB cells in the case of a flat panel display. We can think of the problem as what is the smallest distance we can sample along any line in the x and y directions and find the best representation of the points to be plotted on the actual line concerned.

1.8.2 The Digital Difference Analyser

We can represent the slope of the line when using discrete coordinate values as

$$\delta y / \delta x = m = (y_n - y_0)/(x_n - x_0)$$

as shown in Fig. 1.14.

If we have the start and end points (x_0, y_0) and (x_n, y_n) of a line we can use the gradient m, to calculate all the intermediate points along the line if we assume either increment in the x or y directions is one (the minimum movement possible on a digital display). We might use the gradient of the line in Fig. 1.15 as a determiner of how best to draw the line with relationships

Fig. 1.15 Line drawing in
first octant

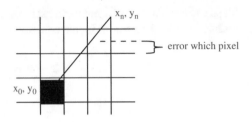

if $m \le 45°$ (1) then $x_{i+1} - x_i = 1$ and $y_i + 1 = m + y_i$
if $m > 45°$ (1) then $y_i + 1 - y_i = 1$ and $x_i + 1 = 1/m + x_i$

Such an algorithm avoids the multiplication and floating-point calculations in
directly evaluating the pixel positions of $y = mx + c$ as we move along the line.
At each point along the line a decision is required as to which pixel is closest to
the line and is to be illuminated. Between any two raster lines the measure of the
error is used to determine how close screen pixels are to the line being drawn. The
following code is an implementation in the first quadrant of a line generator from
pixels, which are scaled and twice normal size for purposes of visual clarity.

```
void DDA1 ( void ){
float m, error, x0, y0, xn, yn;
int x, y, i;
glClear ( GL_COLOR_BUFFER_BIT );
glPointSize(2.0);
glScalef(2.0, 2.0, 1.0);
x0 = 10; y0 = 10;
for( i=0; i<2; i++) {
                    if(i == 0) {     //2 sets of end points
                            xn = 100;
                            yn = 30;
                            } else {
                            xn = 30;
                            yn = 100;
                            }
m = (yn - y0) / (xn - x0);
x = (int) x0;
y = (int) y0;
glBegin(GL_POINTS);
glVertex2i(x, y);
error = 0.0;
do {
        error = error + m;
                            //slope>1 & increment y
                    while (error > 0.5) {
                            y++;
                            error = error - 1.0;
```

```
                              glVertex2i(x , y);
                              }
              x++;             //slope<1 & increment x
              glVertex2i(x , y);
} while (x < (int) xn);
glEnd();
}
glFlush();
}
```

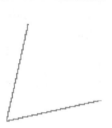

Fig. 1.16 Digital difference
analyser drawing

Figure 1.16 demonstrates the creation of lines from the individual pixel locations
normally implemented by glBegin(GL_LINES).

1.8.3 Bresenham's Algorithm

This is an algorithm that uses incremental integer calculations for raster generation
of lines. The horizontal x-axis represents the pixel column position and the vertical
y-axis represents the scan line position on a screen shown in Fig. 1.15. Bresenham
noted that the calculation of raster position could be further reduced to integer operations and used the error distance as a test for which pixel is nearest the line.

We know that the slope $m = (y_n - y_0) / (x_n - x_0)$, and by cross multiplying we get:

$$m (x_n - x_0) = (y_n - y_0)$$

making both sides of the equation integer since all raster coordinates are represented
by integers. By scaling the DDA by the end point values of the line we can introduce
integer only calculations, which facilitate testing the 'error' with zero. Bresenham's
algorithm is given in the following code fragment for the first quadrant.

```
void Bresn ( void ) {
int error, x0, y0, xn, yn, x, y, i, dx, dy;
glClear ( GL_COLOR_BUFFER_BIT );
glPointSize(2.0);
glScalef(2.0, 2.0, 1.0);
x0 = 10; y0 = 10;                    //end points
for( i=0; i<2; i++) {
```

```
                    if(i == 0) {
                            xn = 100;
                            yn = 30;
                            } else {
                            xn = 30;
                            yn = 100;
                            }
dx = xn - x0;
dy = yn - y0;
x = x0;
y = y0;
glBegin(GL_POINTS);
glVertex2i(x, y);
error = -dx / 2;                    // non zero intercept?
do {
        error = error + dy;
                //slope>1 & increment y
                while (error > 0) {
                        y++;
                        error = error - dx;
                        glVertex2i(x , y);
                        }
        x++;                    //slope<1 & increment x
        glVertex2i(x , y);
} while (x < xn);
glEnd();
}
glColor3f(1.0f, 0.0f,0.0f); //superimpose a line on point plot
glBegin(GL_LINES);
glVertex2i(10 , 10);
glVertex2i(30 , 100);
glEnd();
glFlush();
}
```

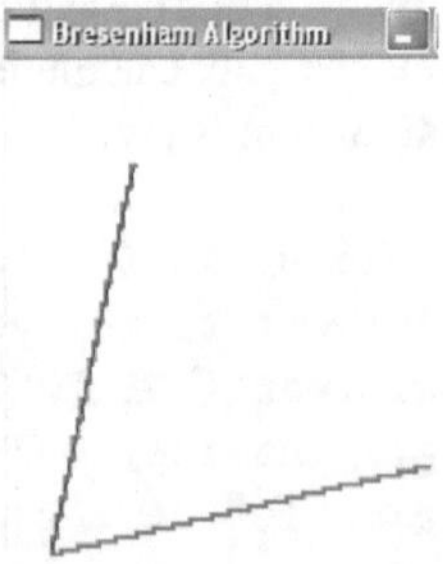

Fig. 1.17 Bresenham's
algorithm

Confirmation of the algorithm is provided by superimposing the line drawn using glBegin(GL_LINES) in the second case. Similar algorithms are required for the other six octants, testing whether the absolute value of the gradient is >1 when we increment y or < 1 when we increment x (see Appendix B).

1.8.4 Bresenham's Algorithm for a Circle

The equation of a circle is given by

$$x^2 + y^2 = r^2$$

centred at the origin with a radius r. Consider Fig. 1.18, where we have the first quadrant and some of the possible pixels shown near the circumference. If we move clockwise from the black pixel in Fig. 1.17 we have three possibilities to consider when deciding which pixel is to be lit on the circle: next right, right lower diagonal and directly beneath. The lighting of the appropriate pixel depends on where we are as we move around the circumference of the circle in the first quadrant.

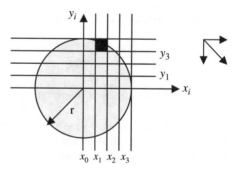

Fig. 1.18 Bresenham's circle algorithm

Clearly the best pixel to illuminate is the one, which is the least distance from the radius r of the actual circle. Written in terms of the circle equation it is the minimum of the three distances.

$$|x_2^2 + y_3^2 - r^2|$$
$$|x_2^2 + y_2^2 - r^2|$$
$$|x_1^2 + y_2^2 - r^2|$$

We generalise this to any point on the raster where each pixel is one unit square giving the distances.

$$|(x_i + 1)^2 + y_i^2 - r^2|$$
$$|(x_i + 1)^2 + (y_i - 1)^2 - r^2|$$
$$|x_i^2 + (y_i - 1)^2 - r^2|$$

If any of these distances is less than zero, then the corresponding pixel lies inside the circle. The variation of how much a pixel is inside or outside of the circle changes as we rotate clockwise from $(0, r)$ to $(r, 0)$ and in Fig. 1.19 there are five possible connection conditions for the tree pixels. The distance between the actual circle and the diagonal pixel at $(x_i + 1, y_i - 1)$ is

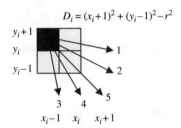

Fig. 1.19 Possible pixel illumination conditions

From the pixel positions illustrated Fig. 1.17 we can see that for the first two conditions

If $|(x_i + 1)^2 + y_i^2 - r^2| < |(x_i + 1)^2 + (y_i - 1)^2 - r^2|$ go to right hand pixel
If $|(x_i + 1)^2 + y_i^2 - r^2| > |(x_i + 1)^2 + (y_i - 1)^2 - r^2|$ go to diagonal pixel

The difference between the distances is

$$\delta_i = |(x_i + 1)^2 + y_i^2 - r^2| - |(x_i + 1)^2 + (y_i - 1)^2 - r^2|$$
$$\text{(right)} \qquad\qquad\qquad \text{(right diagonal)}$$

and δ_i provides a measure of which one to choose to illuminate i.e. the smallest distance.

If $\delta_i \leq 0$ and $D_i < 0$ then go to right hand pixel, else go to diagonal pixel. We can simplify the distances a little further by noting that the right hand pixel in Fig. 1.18 is largely outside of the circle and the diagonally connected pixel is largely inside the circle, which can be written as

$$(x_i + 1)^2 + y_i^2 - r^2 \geq 0$$
$$(x_i + 1)^2 + (y_i - 1)^2 - r^2 < 0$$
$$\delta_i = (x_i + 1)^2 + y_i^2 - r^2 + (x_i + 1)^2 + (y_i - 1)^2 - r^2$$
$$= 2\{(x_i + 1)^2 - r^2\} + y_i^2 + (y_i - 1)^2$$
$$= 2\{(x_i + 1)^2 + (y_i - 1)^2 - r^2\} + 2y_i - 1$$
$$= 2D_i + 2y_i - 1$$

Thus evaluating the distance to the diagonally connected pixel enables us to determine the *sign* of δ_i and the direction of the pixel to be illuminated.

The third and fourth possible conditions occur when the diagonal pixel is outside the circle as we move closer to $(0, r)$ when $D_i > 0$. In this case we move either to the right diagonal $(x_i + 1, y_i - 1)$ or vertically down position $(x_i, y_i - 1)$ for the next pixel.

$$(x_i + 1)^2 + (y_i - 1)^2 - r^2 \geq 0$$
$$x_i^2 + (y_i - 1)^2 - r^2 < 0$$

Using similar reasoning to that for the first two cases

$$\delta_i{}' = (x_i + 1)^2 + (y_i - 1)^2 - r^2 + x_i^2 + (y_i - 1)^2 - r^2$$
$$\delta_i{}' = 2D_i - 2x_i - 1$$

Again for the third and fourth cases the move vertically down or diagonally is determined by the sign of $\delta_i{}'$. If $\delta_i{}' \leq 0$ and $D_i > 0$ then go to diagonal pixel, else go to pixel below.

The final condition is $D_i = 0$, when we choose the diagonal pixel.

Each pixel is of unit size dimensions and thus as we move right $x_{i+1} = x_i + 1$. We remember that $D_i = (x_i + 1)^2 + (y_i - 1)^2 - r^2$ was the distance between the circle and a pixel at location $(x_i + 1, y_i - 1)$. Thus as we move right to the next location $(x_i + 2, y_i - 1)$, where $x_i + 2 = x_{i+1} + 1$, $y_{i-1} = y_i - 1$.

$$
\begin{aligned}
D_{i+1} &= (x_{i+1} + 1)^2 + (y_i - 1)^2 - r^2 \\
&= x_{i+1}^2 + (y_i - 1)^2 - r^2 + 2x_{i+1} + 1 \\
&= D_i + 2x_{i+1} + 1
\end{aligned}
$$

similarly if we move diagonally

$$D_{i+1} = D_i + 2x_{i+1} - 2y_{i+1} + 2$$

and moving down

$$D_{i+1} = D_i - 2y_{i+1} + 1$$

Implementation for the first quadrant of a circle, Fig. 1.20 is given in the following code fragment. Readers are encouraged to consider a reflection of this code and generalise to all four quadrants. As for the case of line drawing, the point size was increased only for reasons of visual clarity.

```
void BresnCir ( void ) {
int delta, deltadash, r;

glClear ( GL_COLOR_BUFFER_BIT );
glPointSize(3.0);
r = 150;                //circle radius
x = 0; y = r;           //start point in first quadrant
D = 2 * (1 - r);        //D= distance between pixel & actual circle
glBegin(GL_POINTS);
do {
        glVertex2i(x, y);
        if (D < 0) {  //go right horizontally - increase x
                delta = 2 * D + 2 * y - 1;
```

```
                    if (delta <= 0) {
                            x++;
                            Right(x);
                    }
                    else {  //diagonal move - increase x & decrease y
                            x++;
                            y--;
                            Diagonal(x, y);
                        }
            glVertex2i(x, y);
            }
            else {  //down vertically - decrease y
                    deltadash = 2 * D - 2 * x - 1;
                    if (deltadash <= 0) {
                            x++;
                            y--;
                            Diagonal(x, y);
                    }
                    else {
                            y--;
                            Down(y);
                            }
                    glVertex2i(x, y);
            }
            if (D == 0) {    //exact diagonal move
                    x++;
                    y--;
                    Diagonal( x, y);
                    glVertex2i(x, y);
            }
    } while (y > 0);
    glEnd();
    glFlush();
    }
```

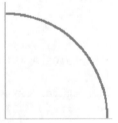

Fig. 1.20 Bresenham's circle
algorithm

1.9 Problem Solving Through Graphics

In getting started in graphics we have introduced the idea of simple visualisation to represent data in a pictorial form. We can extend this concept to use images to help us understand progress in solving a problem and to illustrate this, we consider geometric probability of how a needle might fall on the ground through a Monte Carlo simulation. Monte Carlo methods are probably named after the casino town of this name and involve solving problems using random numbers to statistically represent a problem by simulation. A widely known example was first articulated in 1733 by Count Buffon involved the finding the value of π by throwing a needle onto the floor where a set of ruled lines had been marked. This is not a method for finding π accurately, but rather illustrates a way of obtaining some natural constants by sampling when accurate measurements are difficult. The geometric layout is illustrated in Fig. 1.21 for a simple case.

Consider two lines drawn one unit apart and a needle of length L is thrown between the lines shown in Fig. 1.21, where the centre point of the needle is at location (x, y) and it is randomly orientated at an angle θ. The end points of the needle are (x_0, y_0) and (x_1, y_1) and will be used to graphically represent the needle as the simulation progresses, while the needle orientation lies between $0 \leq \theta \leq 2\pi$. From Fig. 1.21 when $y \geq 0.5$ the point (x_1, y_1) is likelier to cross the upper line while when $y \leq 0.5$ the point (x_0, y_0) is likelier to cross the lower line.

The needle crosses the line if and only if $d \leq L/2\sin\theta$.

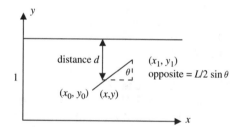

Fig. 1.21 Buffon's needle problem

The number of needle hits that obey this condition is a summation and this is represented by the integral

$$L/2 \int_0^\pi \sin\theta \; d\theta = L/2 |-\cos\theta \; |_0^\pi$$
$$= -L/2 |-1-1|$$
$$= L$$

The integral is shown in Fig. 1.22 as the area under the sine curve together with the total area where all needles must fall. The total area between the lines where all needles must fall is $\pi/2$.

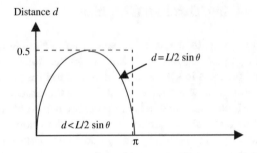

Fig. 1.22 Area where needles fall

The probability of a needle falling inside the sine curve is proportional to the area L, which occurs when the needle hits the line. The probability of a hit is given by the ration of the two areas

$$\frac{\text{Number of line crosses}}{\text{Total number of needle throws}} = \frac{L}{\pi/2}$$

$$\pi = \frac{2L \text{ Total number of needle throws}}{\text{Number of line crosses}}$$

These relations are implemented in the following code fragment:

```
void PositionAngle(void) {
float x, y, angle, dist, opposite, d2r;
float x0, y0, x2, y2;
d2r = 3.14159265 / 180.0;
x = (float) rand() / 32767 *3.14159265;
y = (float) rand() / 32767;
angle = rand() % 360;   // convert to radians
if(angle > 0.0 && angle< 90.0) {     //find which quadrant
        x2 = x + length * 0.5 * cos(angle*d2r);
        y2 = y + length * 0.5 * sin(angle*d2r);
        x0 = x - length * 0.5 * cos(angle*d2r);
        y0 = y - length * 0.5 * sin(angle*d2r);
        opposite = length * 0.5 * sin(angle*d2r);
}
if(angle > 90.0 && angle< 180.0) {
        x2 = x - length * 0.5 * cos(angle*d2r);
        y2 = y + length * 0.5 * sin(angle*d2r);
        x0 = x + length * 0.5 * cos(angle*d2r);
        y0 = y - length * 0.5 * sin(angle*d2r);
        opposite = length * 0.5 * sin(angle*d2r);
}
```

```
if(angle > 180.0 && angle< 270.0) {
        x2 = x - length * 0.5 * cos(angle*d2r);
        y2 = y - length * 0.5 * sin(angle*d2r);
        x0 = x + length * 0.5 * cos(angle*d2r);
        y0 = y + length * 0.5 * sin(angle*d2r);
        opposite = length * 0.5 * sin(angle*d2r);
}
if(angle > 270.0 && angle< 360.0) {
        x2 = x - length * 0.5 * cos(angle*d2r);
        y2 = y - length * 0.5 * sin(angle*d2r);
        x0 = x + length * 0.5 * cos(angle*d2r);
        y0 = y + length * 0.5 * sin(angle*d2r);
        opposite = length * 0.5 * sin(angle*d2r);
}
if(y2 > y) opposite = y2-y;              //+ve first & second quad
else opposite = y0-y;
dist =  y;
if(y > 0.5) dist = 1.0 - y;

if(dist <= opposite) {
    nthhit++;                           //line crossing occurs
}

glBegin(GL_LINES);                      //draw needle
    glVertex2f(x0,y0);
    glVertex2f(x2,y2);
glEnd();
}
```

Output from this code is shown in Fig. 1.23.

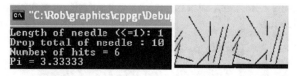

Fig. 1.23 Graphical progression of evaluation of π using Monte Carlo methods

Monte Carlo methods are widely used for solutions to complex problems in science and engineering either by reformulating a deterministic problem in statistical terms or by simulating complex physical systems. Graphical presentation of the progress of the simulation, for example the random walk of a particle passing through a material, enables us to modify a model to more closely resemble the actual physical system and so improve the model with time.

1.10 The Application Programming Interface (API)

The OpenGL API together with the GLUT library are made up from many functions and we shall only cover a small number in this book. The reader should refer to (Kilgard 1996, Shreiner 2004) for the operation all functions. The API and the GLUT library are intimately related for platform independent systems and provide functions, which may be categorised as follows:

1. The primitive functions for display of lines and points such as; glVertex
2. State functions which define what an object will look like such as; glColor
3. Viewing functions such as; glOrtho, gluPerspective
4. Transformation functions such as; glRotate, glTranslate
5. Mouse, pen and keyboard input such as through; glutSpecialFunc

The function libraries are included, as we have seen at the start of every program.

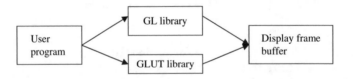

Within the user program the all of the above functions will provide input to the frame buffer, which is the rendered screen image.

In this chapter we have met simple OpenGL primitives used for rendering an image, used a subset of the GLUT library routines to create a window and process the event of displaying the complete image. We now consider several other glut functions that deal with events in programs that will be used in later chapters. These events are usually associated with movement and animation and involve use of the keyboard and mouse.

1.10.1 The OpenGL Utility Toolkit (GLUT) Library

The callback functions available from the GLUT library allow users to change images, either through movement, digitisation of screen locations or additional drawing. The particular action taken when a change occurs at any given peripheral depends on the requirements of the user program. In this section we describe some of the actions that are possible and give readers an introduction to interaction with a screen image. For a more detailed description readers should consult with Kilgard, 1996.

1.10.2 Mouse Interaction

```
void glutMouseFunc( void (*mouse)( int button, int state, int x, int y));
void glutMotionFunc( void (*motion)( int x, int y));
```

These functions operate whenever an event occurs as a result of using a mouse by calling the respective functions *mouse* and *motion*. The parameters used by mouse are as follows:

```
button-- takes possible values of GLUT_LEFT_BUTTON,
GLUT_MIDDLE_BUTTON, GLUT_RIGHT_BUTTON
state-- the mouse button is either pressed or not; GLUT_DOWN
or GLUT_UP
x, y-- Cartesian location of mouse
```

It should be noted that while the mouse moves on a 2D plane, most pictures are 3D in nature. Intuitively, moving the mouse right or left along an x-axis is akin to rolling an object about the y-axis, while an up and down movement of the mouse along the y-axis is equivalent to rotating an object about the x-axis. Rotation of an image about the z-axis out of the screen can be achieved by a combination of x and y motion producing a circular path for a mouse. Alternatively we can use a mouse button to provide a 'zoom' facility in the z-direction. Rotation of a screen image by a given number of degrees does not have a simple deterministic equivalent of linear mouse movement and so any relationship is empirical, such that the user interface is '*friendly*'. Writing for instance, code of the form

xrotation = new_mouse_y_position - previous_ mouse_y_position;
(degrees)   (centimetres)

has no mathematical validity, but rather reflects the intuitive hand movement a user might expect in order to rotate the image by some amount. If the rotation appears too quick, readers should introduce a scale factor until they are happy with the screen interaction. We control when rotation can occur by pressing one of the mouse buttons and testing the state variable for up or down as is illustrated in the following code.

```
void mouse(int btn, int state, int x, int y)
{
if (state == GLUT_DOWN){
        mouseState = state;
```

```
        mouseButton = btn;
        mouseX = x;
        mouseY = y;
}else{
        mouseState = 0;

}
}
```

With a mouse button pressed the coordinates of the position of the mouse cursor in the GLUT window are captured during this event.

The motion function void glutMotionFunc(void (*motion)(int x, int y)) is called when the mouse moves after a button is pressed, where the mouse state and which button has been pressed are defined in the preceding mouse() function. The linear movement of the mouse controlling an object specified by xrotation and yrotation changes determines the rotational movement of the screen object. Finally the function glutPostRedisplay() is used, as the rotation requires that the contents of the window be redrawn.

```
void motion(int x, int y)
{
if (mouseState == GLUT_DOWN){
        if (mouseButton == GLUT_LEFT_BUTTON){
                yrotation -= (mouseX - x); //about y-axis
                xrotation -= (mouseY - y); //about x-axis
        }
}
mouseX = x;
mouseY = y;
glutPostRedisplay();
}
```

The functions are all called through the loop in the main program using

```
glutMouseFunc(mouse);
glutMotionFunc(motion);
```

where xrotation and yrotation are variables used to represent the angular rotation in the display rendering function.

1.10.3 Keyboard Interaction

void glutSpecialFunc(void (*keysNA)(unsigned char key, int x, int y));

This function operates whenever an event occurs as a result of pressing a non-ASCII key by calling the function *keysNA*. The parameters used by keysNA are as follows:

key – takes any one of the non ASCII keys
x, y – current mouse position returned

The function is particularly useful for moving a screen object when the rest of a keyboard may be used for data input. In the following example we set up a function Arrowkeys (), for processing the use of the non-ASCII arrow keys to rotate an object about the x and y axes. This may be accomplished by incrementing a variable representing the angle of object orientation every time an arrow key is pressed.

```
void ArrowKeys(int key, int x, int y)
{    //rotation about x or y axis by ± 5 degrees
        if(key == GLUT_KEY_LEFT) xrotation += 5.0;
        if(key == GLUT_KEY_RIGHT) yrotation += 5.0;
        glutPostRedisplay();
}
```

As in the previous example, after peripheral movement the image has to be redrawn using glutPostRedisplay(). The function is executed in the GLUT main processing loop, which usually resides in the main program using glutSpecial-Func(ArrowKeys). All the non-ASCII key values are given in the OpenGL Reference Manuel, Shreiner, 2004 and a number of programs using these functions are described in later sections of this book.

A function with very similar characteristics, but using the ASCII keys is

    void glutKeyboardFunc(void (*keys)(int key, int x, int y));

1.11 Exercises

1. Develop the program given in Section 1.8.3 to implement Bresenham's Line-Algorithm in all quadrants.
2. Repeat exercise one for Bresenham's Circle Algorithm in Section 1.8.4.

1.12 Conclusion

In this chapter we have got started with some simple programs and hopefully begun to inspire enthusiasm to explore further what can be achieved with graphical systems. We have introduced Cartesian (x, y) representation of data, generated points from parametric representations and used OpenGL primitives to render a display. Drawings are often hand generated and we have set values within (x, y) data to indicate how the drawing process can be data driven. Further using a Monte Carlo method we have described how using a graphical system we can begin to visualise and follow the process of problem solving when exact answers may not be apparent. Using Bresenham's Algorithm as an example we have introduced the importance of analysing the mathematical representation of points and considering if there are alternative forms which make for more efficient processing. In the early stage of Computer Graphics this may not seem so important, but as we progress readers will become aware of the needs of real time processing systems. Finally we have introduced the OpenGL Utility Toolkit (GLUT) and used it to create the window in which object rendering tales place. A brief introductory discussion is presented of some functions of the toolkit, which will be used in later sections of the book.

Chapter 2
Image File Formats

2.1 Introduction

In this chapter we shall consider the bitmap (.BMP) and audio video (.AVI) binary files and their structure to provide a foundation for the understanding of pixel colour representation and the drawing of the information. We shall not consider every variation (and there are many) of these files but only those, which will be developed through later examples in the area of image processing. The file formats are an essential precursor to the study of image processing methods and this knowledge will also support the work on texturing.

2.2 The Bitmap File

Graphics files are stored in a variety of formats and a full description is given in (Miano 1999). We shall consider the bitmap file format as it is simple to use, easily obtained from scanners and digital cameras, useful in the understanding of audio visual output [AVI] from web cameras and forms a foundation for basic image processing and graphics systems.

Bitmap files are stored with the name extension .BMP and occasionally we also see bitmap files stored in a device-independent bitmap form with the name extension .DIB. Device-independent bitmap files are simply a list of pixels with values for the red, green and blue components and omit the header information associated with size and other descriptors. The bitmap image format originated in early versions of the Microsoft Windows and has stayed ever since through packages such as Paintbrush/Paint. While the Windows operating system supports images with 1, 4, 8, 16, 24 and 32 bits per pixel we shall largely focus on the use of monochrome and 24-bit colour in this text.

2.2.1 Bitmap-file Structure

The bitmap file structure is very simple and consists of a bitmap-file header, a bitmap-information header, a colour table, and an array of bytes that define the bitmap image. The file has the following form:

File Header Information
Image Header Information
Colour Table (if present)
Pixel values

BITMAPFILEHEADER

The bitmap file header contains information about the type, size, and layout of a bitmap file and permits a check as to the type of file the user is reading. The first two bytes of the file contain the ASCII character "B" followed by an "M" to identify the file type.

The next four bytes of the header contain the file size with the least significant bit first.

The next four bytes are unused and set to zero.

The final four bytes are an offset to the start of the image pixel data from the header and measured in bytes. Formally the structure is of the form:

BITMAPFILEHEADER {

uint	2 bytes	*file type*
dword	4 bytes	*file size in bytes*
uint	2 bytes	*reserved*
uint	2 bytes	*reserved*
dword	4 bytes	*offset to data in bytes*

} BITMAPFILEHEADER;

BITMAPINFOHEADER

The bitmap-information header specifies the dimensions, compression type, and colour format for the bitmap.

The first four bytes are the header size, usually 40 bytes, followed by the width and height of the image measured in pixels. The next two bytes contain 1 which is the number of planes. The next two bytes store the number of bits used to represent the colour intensities of a pixel, which in this text is usually 24 (referred to as true colour) as we frequently use such images. Twenty-four bit colour has over the years become more prevalent as memory has become cheaper and processor speeds have increased. The next four bytes store the compression (0 for 24 bit RGB) followed by the Image size (may be 0 if not compressed). The next eight bytes store the X and Y resolution (pixels/meter). The final entries in the bitmap information section are the number of colour map entries and the number of significant colours. Formally this is written as:

BITMAPINFOHEADER {

dword	4*bytes*	*needed for BITMAPINFOHEADER structuresize*
long	4 bytes	*bitmap width in pixels*
long	4 bytes	*bitmap height in pixel*
word	2 bytes	*1*
word	2 bytes	*bits/pixel (1 = monochrome)*
dword	4 bytes	*compression 0, 8, 4*
dword	4 bytes	*image size in bytes (may be 0 for monochrome)*
long	4 bytes	*pixels/metre*
long	4 bytes	*pixels/metre*
dword	4 bytes	*number of colour indexes used by bitmap in colour table*
dword	4 bytes	*number of colour indexes considered important*

} BITMAPINFOHEADER;

COLOUR TABLE

The colour table is not present for bitmaps with 24 bit files because each pixel is represented by the 8-bit blue-green-red (BGR) values in the actual bitmap data area.

IMAGE DATA

The bitmap data immediately following the colour table consist of BYTE values representing consecutive rows (scan lines) of the bitmap image in left-to-right order. A scan line must be zero-padded to end on a 32-bit boundary or rounded up to a multiple of four bytes. The scan lines in the bitmap are stored from bottom to the top of the image. This means that the first byte in the file represents the pixels in the lower-left corner or origin of the bitmap and the last byte represents the pixels in the upper-right corner.

The format of the file depends on the number of bits used to represent each pixel with the most significant bit field corresponding to the leftmost pixel. Details of formats using less that 24 bits can be found in the references given.

2.2.2 A Typical File Layout

The following file header information used for illustrative purposes is a 512×256 bit map image using 24-bit colour. The file type indicators of 'B' and 'M' are in the first two file locations. The file size is calculated from the double word of the next four bytes with the least significant byte occurring first (393,270 bytes). The author notes that this value can be found using the old 'dir' command in the DOS command window where Windows explorer will only give an approximation to this file size. The file size can be alternatively verified from the image size, bytes per pixel and the header offset.

$$512 \times 256 \times 3 + 54 = 393270 \text{ bytes}$$

66	B	Information Header	24	Bit colour
77	M		0	
54	File size		0	
0	"		0	
3	"		0	
0	"		0	
0			0	
0			0	
0			6	
0			0	
54	Offset to data from start of header		35	Resolution pixels / metre
0			11	
0			0	
0			0	
40	Image Header Size from here		35	Resolution
0			11	
0			0	
0			0	
0			0	
2	Image width (512 pixels)		0	
0			0	
0			0	
0			0	
1	Image height (256 pixels)		0	
0			0	
0			0	End of Header
1			245 234 212	Start of image pixel data
0			245 234 212	

2.2.3 Reading and Drawing a Bitmap File

The following program is for the purpose of understanding pixel data and 24 bit binary images. Later on we shall generalise the reading of the headers with the introduction of classes and functions to simplify the repetition of code but for now we will hard code some values for simplicity in understanding of the file structure. Many of the examples in the text together with data files are given on the web site supporting the book.

The image data file header is given in the preceding section where we know both the width and height of the image. This can be found from many Windows applications such as Paint in the Image Attributes part of the menu. Because most graphics and imaging applications will require the use of all bits in representing colours we characterise the input data files as binary and define the bytes for storing the red, green and blue (RGB) pixel colour components as unsigned bytes. Further we can skip the first 54 bytes, as we know this is defined for the header information of bitmap files, although in a real system we would check the various components of the header for verification of file type and the reading of the rest of the file. The size of the image is (512 × 256) pixels. Each byte of the image data is read as an *unsigned character* as all bits contribute to the colour level and were converted to integers to afford explanation of the file structure in the previous section and output to the file debug.txt. Pixels would be plotted as green-blue-red at each position on a scan line and there are 3 bytes per pixel for the 24-bit colour image.

```
void listing (void) {
unsigned char pixel;
int x, y, xs, xf, ys, i, pix, xpack;
ofstream debug("c:\\rob\\graphics\\lectures\\book\\programs
                \\debug.txt", ios::out);
ifstream inpaint( "c:\\rob\\images\\earth512256.bmp",ios::binary);
if(!inpaint) {
    cout << "File not opened\n";
    exit(1);
}
for(x=1; x<=54; x++) {
    inpaint.get(pixel);          //go to start of data after header stuff
    pix = pixel;
    debug << pix << endl;        //file data for explanation
    }
debug << "End of Header?" << endl;
xs = 1;
xf = 512;                        //will get x&y from header later
xpack = xf % 4;                  //multiples of 4 bytes/x line?
ys = 0;
for (y = ys; y<= 255; y++) {
    for (x = xf; x>= xs; x--) {
        for (i=0; i<=2; i++) { //3 bytes = 1 pixel in 24 bit colour
                        inpaint.get(pixel);
                        pix = pixel;
                        debug << pix << " ";
                        }
        debug << endl;
        }
if (xpack != 0) for (i=1; i<=xpack; i++) inpaint.get(pixel);
}                               // next raster line y
}
```

In this program example, output and input was via disc files and console screen. We are now going to modify the program to provide graphical output to gain a clearer understanding of the data in the file. Later on we shall provide a fuller explanation of OpenGL graphics but for the present we shall use a very simple subset of facilities in order to get started and further understand bit map files.

We can extend the file-listing program and plot the pixel colours at each location of the image using the included program (BMcol.cpp). The setting up, management and refreshing of the graphical window where the image is drawn is performed through using the GLUT library described in the previous chapter and using system defaults to reduce the number of functions for purposes of clarity.

```cpp
//Software to recreate 24 bit image from file

GLsizei wh = 256; // height of window
GLsizei ww = 512; // width of windo
void MyInit (void) {
  glPointSize(1.0);
  gluOrtho2D( 0.0, (GLdouble)ww, 0.0, (GLdouble)wh ) ;
}
void paint (void) {              //read and draw a bit map file
unsigned char pixel;
GLint x, y, xs, xf, ys, i, pix, xpack;
GLfloat pixtmp[3];
ofstream debug( "c:\\rob\\graphics\\lectures\\book\\programs
                \\debug.txt",ios::out);
glClear (GL_COLOR_BUFFER_BIT );
ifstream inpaint( "c:\\rob\\images\\earth512256.bmp", ios::binary);
                //w=640
if(!inpaint) {
        cout << "File not opened\n";
        exit(1);
}
for(x=1; x<=54; x++) {
        inpaint.get(pixel);    //go to start of data after header stuff
        pix = pixel;
        debug << pix << endl;  //file data for explanation purpose
          }
debug << "End of Header?" << endl;
xs = 1;
xf = 512;                    //should get x & y from header really
xpack = xf%4;                //multiples of 4 bytes/x line
ys = 0;
glBegin(GL_POINTS);
for (y=ys; y<= 255; y++) {
    for (x = xf; x>= xs; x--)     //earth_r.bmp
        for (i=0; i<=2; i++) {    //3 bytes = 1 pixel in 24 bit colour
                        inpaint.get(pixel);
                        pix = pixel;
                        debug << pix << " ";
                        pixtmp[i] = float(pix)/255.0;
              }
              debug << endl;
```

```
                glColor3f(pixtmp[2], pixtmp[1], pixtmp[0]); //G B R !
                glVertex2i(x,y);
        }
if(xpack != 0) for (i=1; i<=xpack; i++) inpaint.get(pixel);
}                              //next raster line y
glEnd();
glFlush();
}
```

The Program (BMcol.cpp)

int main(int argc, char **argv) {

Within our main routine the GLUT code
glutInitDisplayMode (GLUT_SINGLE | GLUT_RGB);
specifies the type of display used in the graphical window to be created. In this case
the display is using RGB colour mode (GLUT_RGB) and all graphics is performed
in the window; single buffered (GLUT_SINGLE).

2.2.4 Creating a Display Window

The window is created with the code

glutInitWindowSize (ww, wh);
glutCreateWindow ("24 bit BMP display");

and has the title in the top bar of the window with the size mapping directly to
the size of the image. The function MyInit ( ); initialises the pixel drawing size
and gluOrtho2D(0.0, (GLdouble)ww, 0.0, (GLdouble)wh); creates a matrix for
projecting the bitmap onto the screen clipped by the region (0.0, ww, 0.0, wh).
    The image of the bitmap file (earth512256.bmp) is reconstructed by the function
paint(); This function is called by GLUT when the window is drawn.

glutDisplayFunc(paint);

and is referred to as a 'callback'. The final GLUT function used is

glutMainLoop( );

which initiates the GLUT system display processes. For now that's all we need to
know about the display window.

2.2.5 Creating the Image for Display

We now have to read the binary bitmap and transfered the byte colour values to appropriate locations in the display window. Each pixel position is defined by a point with three bytes contributing to the resultant colour of the location. We plot one scan line (y) at a time and read the three bytes that contribute to the colour at each point (x) along the scan line. The colour is given by the green, blue and red components represented as floating point numbers using the code

```
glColor3f(pixtmp[2], pixtmp[1], pixtmp[0]); // G B R
glVertex2i(x,y);
```

at each (x, y) integer location. The colours can have 256 intensity levels stored in each byte and if we use floating-point representation, then this must be normalised between 0 (off) and 1 (maximum intensity). At the end of each scan line we check that we end on a 32-bit boundary and read dummy bytes out if required. Pixel plotting takes place using

```
glBegin(GL_POINTS);
glEnd();
```

to delimit the operations. The resultant image is shown in Fig. 2.1.

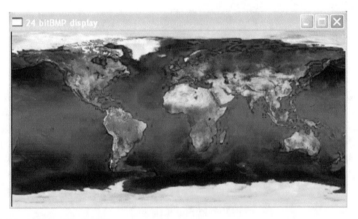

Fig. 2.1 Displaying a bit-map file

2.2.6 Monochrome Bitmaps

We shall briefly consider the monochrome bitmap since it is useful in the storage of line drawings and printed text where colour is not a requirement. The

BITMAPFILEHEADER and the **BITMAPINFOHEADER** are as already described with only the change in the information header where the bits / colour is now 1 as only black and white is present. Since we are working with a monochrome image each pixel ca be represented by 1 bit and each byte will store eight possible locations along each raster line. The code following is for an 800 × 600 pixel image where the colour black is represented by zero. If the whole byte is zero then we can draw a black line eight pixels long. If the byte is not zero indicating it is part of the edge of a shape or dots, then we must plot the individual bits that are zero that make up the byte. We accomplish this by using modulo 2 arithmetic; to test each bit position in the byte and plot depending on the value of the remainder. The code following, replaces the equivalent code in the paint function used to draw the 24-bit colour image already described.

```
for (y = 1; y<= 600; y++) {
      nx = 0;
      for (x = 1; x<= 100; x++) {
      //100 bytes = 800 pixels in monochrome BMP
            inpaint >> pixel;
            pixtmp = pixel;    //char to integer value
            nx = nx + 8;
            if (pixtmp == 0) { //8 pixel line
                  glBegin(GL_LINES);
                     glVertex2i(nx-8,y);
                     glVertex2i(nx,y);
                  glEnd();
            }
            else{
//whole byte is not black (>0 & < 255) near edges of image | spots etc!
            for (i = 1; i<= 8; i++) {
                     remain = pixtmp % 2;
                     if (remain == 0) {    // black - plot it
                           glBegin(GL_POINTS);
                              glVertex2i(nx-i,y);
                           glEnd();
                     }
            pixtmp = pixtmp / 2; //next pixel in byte
            }
            }
      }
} //next raster line y
```

2.2.7 A General Class for Input of Bit Map Files

We will now provide a class for the input of 24 bit map files used throughout this book, as it will save on space by repetitively using the same code where such files are required. The file (Read_bmp.cpp) is referenced in later programs by a #include "Read_bmp.cpp" throughout the text. The only input required to the class is the name of the bit map file and it will be read and stored in an array identified as a global variable by

static GLubyte Image[Height][Width][4];

where the RGB components of each pixel are captured as unsigned bytes. The class reads the header, calculates the width (ww) and height (wh) of the picture using binary to decimal conversion and the values to read the bytes into the above array. The function WidthHeight() converts the high and low pixels from the file to integers for defining the size of a window.

```
class ip_bmp_file
{
public:

long int WidthHeight(int pix1, int pix2) {
long int num=0, n=8 ,rem;
do {    //high byte only
 rem = pix2 % 2;
 num = num + rem * pow(2, n);
 pix2 = pix2 /2;
 n++;
} while(n <= 16);
num = num + pix1;
return(num);
}

void header_data ( void) {
unsigned char pixel;
char filename[25];
int i, j,x, pixlow, pixhigh, pix3, pix4, xpack, BMok;
cout << "Picture file name: ";
cin >> filename;
ifstream inpaint( filename, ios::binary);
if(!inpaint) {
        cout << "File not opened / found\n";
    exit(1);
}
BMok = 0;
inpaint >> pixel;
if(pixel == 'B') BMok++;
inpaint >> pixel;
if(pixel == 'M') BMok++;
```

```
if(BMok == 2) cout<<"is a valid bit map file\n";
        else exit(1);
for(x=3; x<=54; x++) {
    inpaint >> pixel; //go to start of data after header stuff
   if(x == 19) pixlow = pixel; //low
     if(x == 20) pixhigh = pixel; //high
     if(x == 23) pix3 = pixel; //low
     if(x == 24) pix4 = pixel; //high
}
xw = WidthHeight( pixlow, pixhigh);
yh = WidthHeight( pix3, pix4);
cout << "\nx width = " << xw << "y height = " << yh << endl;
xpack = ww  % 4; // multiples of 4 bytes/x line
for (j = 0; j < yh; j++) {
   for (i = 0; i < xw; i++) {
             Image[i][j][0] = inpaint.get( );
             Image[i][j][1] = inpaint.get( );
             Image[i][j][2] = inpaint.get( );
   }
   if (xpack != 0) for (i=1; i<=xpack; i++) inpaint.get(pixel);
}
}
};
```

Readers may like to generalise this class to include tests for the file type and output details such as file size.

The fourth component of each pixel location is set to 255 and initialises what is called the alpha channel and will be considered further when we come to consider texturing in Chapter 7.

2.2.8 Manipulating Bit Maps – Embossing

The image given in Fig. 2.1 is a typical picture of the world, which looks rather flat and uninteresting. We can provide the illusion of a three dimensional view through the simple method of embossing, by superimposing the original bit map image with an inverted version of the map that is slightly shifted or displaced in spatial coordinates. This produces an enhanced lightening a darkening at colour discontinuities that then appears to show highlights and give the impression of protrusions to a surface. For our example we shall use a bit map image of a brick wall and the colour levels (0–255) will be used to simulate a 'height' map at each location of the image. Using floating-point representation the corresponding colour values (0.0–1.0) are clamped between 0.0 and 0.5. We now make a second map of pixel values after subtracting the clamped values from 0.5. This in effect inverts the original colour

Fig. 2.2 Summation of
original and inverse bit map

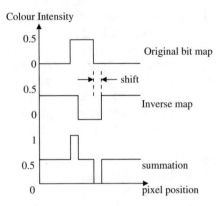

levels so that black becomes white and vise-versa. The final stage of the process is
to add the original clamped image to the inverse with a small positional shift, which
gives the effect of moving the inverse map slightly towards a light source in relation
to the original image. Another way to view this operation is that of finding the first
derivative of the image intensity. The addition of the pixel intensities after the shift
in x and y of the inverse map is shown in Fig. 2.2. The highlight and shadow effect
is seen in the pixel intensity after the summation in Fig. 2.2.

   The number of pixels specified for the shift should not be too large or distortions of the image occur when parts of the object (mortar joints in this case)
are missed. The method averages the summation about 0.5 and thus the embossed
result is a grey level image with highlights at the colour discontinuities as shown in
Fig. 2.3.

   The lower part of Fig. 2.3 is a plain bit map image of a brick wall, while the
upper part of the image results from the embossing process with a shift of two pixels
in both the x and y directions for each pixel. Implementation of this procedure is
supplied through the program emboss.cpp and readers can experiment using the data
file daniel.bmp and consider results for the embossing of letters. Similar results can
be obtained by performing the operations separately on each RGB component as
illustrated in the right hand image of Fig. 2.3.

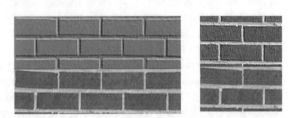

Fig. 2.3 Embossing using a
bit map of a brick wall

2.3 Audio/Video Interleaved (AVI) File Format

The AVI file format originated at the Microsoft Corporation and conceptually is a very flexible and simple structure for the storage and display video data and reproduction of sound from audio information. The format has continued to evolve over many years and what is developed in this section is but a small part of a very much larger system definition. Readers are cautioned that writing software for applications dependent on the large variety of AVI devices available is not always as straightforward as the file format definitions might imply. A number of different codes exist for the same field and this can be confusing; in writing software the collecting of all the codes can be time consuming and many are only documented on web sites of frequently asked questions! Further, files of the same type may have different information interspersed between the audio and video data dependent on device manufacturer. The files count16.avi and capture.avi used in developing AVI displays later in this section are provided to illustrate the issue. The following examples are designed to give readers an understanding and starting point, from which they can develop image-processing applications.

The AVI file format is part of what is known as the Resource Interchange File Format (RIFF) and is used for multimedia devices such as CDROM's, and Web cameras. We shall only be concerned with graphics/video files although mention will also be made of the sound component of the file. RIFF is a binary file *framework* within which existing and different file formats may be embedded and nested as data structures (chunks) *with no fixed positions* in the file. This results in a flexible vendor controlled file where one reads data according to the four character code chunk name. The data stored in a RIFF file is indicated by the file extension: Interleaved audio/visual (.AVI), Sound (.WAV), MIDI information (.RMI) etc.

The following is a typical example of the beginning of a RIFF file with the four character code (fcc) headers from a web camera producing frames of 160×120 with the three primary colours stored in 16 bits and read using a modification of the FileHeader.cpp program previously described. The user needs to check for the character sequences outlined above and use the appropriate structure/class to define the reading of the file.

82	R		0		0	0	
73	I		0		202 Ê	0	
70	F		104 h		8 €	1	//video
70	F		100 d		0	0	//only
32		//file size	114 r		0	0	
206	Î	// in bytes	108 l		0	0	
1 €			97 a	//avi	0	0	
0			118 v	//header	0	0	
65	A		105 i		16 €	//flags	0
86	V		104 h		0	0	
73	I		56 8	//size	1 €	160	//width
32			0		0	0	

76 L	0	2 € //no of	0
73 I	0---------------a	0 //frames	0
83 S	160	0	120 //height
84 T	134 †	0	0
92 \ //size	1 €	0 //no inter	0
1 €	0	0 //leave	0
0	0	0	0
0	0	0	0
0	0	115 s	0
0	0	116 t	118 v
0	0---------------a	114 r	105 i
0	76 L	108 l	100 d
0	73 I	115 s //stream	115 s
0	83 S	116 t //header	0
0	84 T	114 r	0
0	124 | // size	104 h	0
0	0	64 @ //size	0

The general form of the RIFF chunks is:

```
struct Chunk
{
DWORD ChunkID;                    //4 character identifier (fcc)
DWORD ChunkSize;                  //in bytes
BYTE ChunkData[ChunkSize];        //word aligned with NULL byte
};                                 //if odd (not in ChunkSize) pad with NULL
```

The RIFF identifier is the top-level chunk and the rest are sub chunks in an AVI file.

Chunks are identified by a 4 character name (RIFF, AVI, WAV, LIST, hdrl, avih, strl, strh, strf, ISFT, IDIT, JUNK, movi etc and if 3 characters then a NULL byte is added before the size which follows the chunk identifier. The size is the length of chunk in bytes (stored as a double word) and does not include any padding that may have been required. The data component is word aligned and a NULL byte is added if the data is of an odd byte length. Software to read a file requires we search through for the chunk types noting the length of what follows the chunk identifier. The JUNK chunk is used to pad out a file to fit special boundaries that exist on devices such as CD-ROM's (2048 byte boundaries). Each chunk is followed by a data length indicator and the data. The top level RIFF identifier is followed by the total file size less any padding bytes.

2.3.1 Chunk Hierarchy

The list of structures are of the following general form

```
RIFF - AVI                      //An AVI file
      LIST - hdrl               //Header list
             Avih               //main AVI header
             LIST - strl        //video stream list
                    strh        //video stream header
                    strf        BITMAPINFOHEADER
                    strd
JUNK
             LIST movi          //main data
                    00db        //Video frame
             . . . . . . . . . .
                    idx1        //Index
```

The first LIST chunk contains the AVI header (hdrl) chunk followed by the characters 'avih' and a structure of the form

```
structuretypedef struct {
       DWORD dwMicroSecPerFrame;       //Time between frames
       DWORD dwMaxBytesPerSec;         //AVI data rate
       DWORD dwReserved1;
       DWORD dwFlags;                  //type of data parameters
       DWORD dwTotalFrames;            //Number of frames
       DWORD dwInitialFrames;          //preview frames
       DWORD dwStreams;                //Number of data streams in chunk
       DWORD dwSuggestedBufferSize;    //Minimum playback buffer size
       DWORD dwWidth;                  //frame width in pixels
       DWORD dwHeight;                 //frame height in pixels
       DWORD dwScale;                  //time units
       DWORD dwRate;                   //playback rate
       DWORD dwStart;                  //Start time of AVI data
       DWORD dwLength;                 //Size of AVI data
} MainAVIHeader;
```

with the meaning of each variable given in the comment. The hdrl AVI header also contains one or more LIST chunks with the strl four character identifier. Each data stream will be associated with such a LIST chunk (1 for video, 2 for audio and video).

The second LIST chunk contains the AVI header (strl) chunk followed by the characters 'vids' or 'auds'. Three sub chunks are stored within the strl chunk: the stream header strh, the stream format strf and optionally another stream data

chunk strd. The length of the structure less any padding bytes follows each of the
character identifiers.

The following structure defines the stream header strh:

```
typedef struct {
  DWORD fccType;              //vids = video, auds = audio
  DWORD fccHandler;           //compressor used
  DWORD  dwFlags;
  DWORD  dwReserved1;
  DWORD  dwInitialFrames;  //if interleaved no of preview frames
  DWORD  dwScale;             //playback stream characteristics
  DWORD  dwRate;
  DWORD  dwStart;
  DWORD  dwLength;
  DWORD  dwSuggestedBufferSize;
  DWORD  dwQuality;
  DWORD  dwSampleSize;
} AVIStreamHeader;
```

The stream format (strf) is of the form used for storing bitmap files and contains the
following structure

```
typedef struct tagBITMAPINFOHEADER{
  DWORD biSize;             //40
  LONG biWidth;             //image width
  LONG biHeight;            //image height
  WORD biPlanes;            //1
  WORD biBitCount           //bits / pixel 1,4,8,16,24,32
  DWORD biCompression;      //0,1,2,3, CRAM etc
  DWORD biSizeImage;
  LONG biXPelsPerMeter;     //resolution
  LONG biYPelsPerMeter;
  DWORD biClrUsed;
  DWORD biClrImportant;
} BITMAPINFOHEADER;
```

For video this is the same as the BITMAPINFO structure described for bit maps.
For audio streams the data is defined in the WAVEFORMATEX or PCMWAVE-
FORMAT structure (http://msdn2.microsoft.com/en-us/library/ms712832.aspx).

The biBitCount specifies the number of bits used to illuminate a pixel and must be
used in conjunction with the biCompression. The values of biCompression govern
how the colour components are extracted from biBitCount.

BiCompression	BI_RGB	BI_RLE8	BI_RLE4	BI_BITFIELDS
	0	1	2	3

This field may also contain the character sequence 'CRAM' for BI_RLE8 from earlier systems. Pixel format depends on the number of bits per pixel. For single bit pixels each byte has eight fields, 4-bit pixels have two fields per byte while 8-bit pixels use the complete byte for the colour.

In the example which we will use to illustrate the display of AVI files on a frame by frame basis we shall use a web cam file where each pixel is represented by a 2-byte integer and BI_RGB = 0. With this definition the 16 bits are divided into three 5-bit colour components with the sixteenth bit being ignored. True colour uses 24 bits per pixel with one byte storing each of the RGB components and we shall also present this facility.

The optional stream data chunk strd may follow the stream format structure. The information is not needed to read and display AVI files and generally contains configuration information from the vendor.

Finally before we encounter the RGB colour values that make up each frame we may find a JUNK or other named chunks used to pad out data to device specific boundaries. We need to read past this information when we encounter the characters 'JUNK' in the file. The JUNK structure is of the form

```
typedef struct {
    DWORD   JunkID;              //four characters JUNK
    DWORD   JunkSize;            //Padding Size bytes
    BYTE    Padding[JunkSize];
} JUNKHeader
```

The final component is the movi chunk, which contains the image colour data for each pixel. Uncompressed RGB data is identified by four characters '**db' (abbreviation for DIB) followed by the size in bytes of the chunk. The '**' represents the stream identifier (00 for the first hdrl). Both the JUNK and 'db' chunks may be found in video and audio data and must be tested for and separated from the image bytes, which contribute to the display.

In general when processing the image data readers are advised to search for any possible four character headers. It is to be noted that the supplied files (capture.avi and count16.avi) have quite different information stored between each frame and in the authors experience this is device manufacturer dependent. The situation where the number of frames as indicated in the file header (BITMAPINFOHEADER) is not the same as the image data sometimes occurs due to frames not being captured because the computer was busy. The file capture.avi was included to demonstrate the effect of lost frames. Attention to detail in searching, correcting removing non-image data is essential for image processing applications.

2.3.2 An Example of Web Cam Display

The Web Camera is a low cost device for image capture which students can use as an introductory tool for image processing. Readers of this text will be aware of a number of systems such as the 'Real Player' which display AVI files and in this section we explore some of the construction that went into such software to provide frame by frame access for image processing applications. Data from cameras is provided via a USB port and stored as bytes in a binary file. A small file of half a dozen frames (capture.avi) is supplied on the Web site to aid the development of this example. The file was collected with BI_RGB set to zero and 16 bits per pixel location, giving 5-bit colour resolution for each RGB component. A second file (capframe.avi) containing two frames in 24-bit colour is also supplied for test purposes while a third test data file count16.avi came with my XP system.

Extraction of the 5-bit components is achieved by setting each byte to an unsigned integer so as not to omit the sign bit in the low order byte and finding the binary representation of each by repeated division by 2.

```
struct bytecolour          //RGB colour components (0->1)
{           float r;
            float g;
            float b;
};

bytecolour byte2int( unsigned char bchar[2] ) {
int  rem[16], i, i1, i2, j, ip, byte2;
unsigned int value;
double temp[3];
bytecolour subytecol;
bytecolour *addrsbcol;
addrsbcol = &subytecol;
value = int(bchar[0]);              //get sign bit also!
for(i=0; i<16; i++) rem[i] = 0;
byte2 = 0;
i = 0;
while(byte2 < 2) {                  //binary values of each byte
        while( value != 0) {       //rem[0] m sig bit
                rem[i] = value % 2;
                value = value / 2;
                i++;
        }
        i = 8;
        byte2++;
        value = int(bchar[1]);   //now the second byte
}
i1 = 0;             // red = rem[14-10] green = rem[9-5] blue = rem[4-0]
for(j = 0; j< 3; j++) {          //colour components
    i2 = i1 + 5;
    temp[j] = 0.0;
    ip = 0;
    for(i=i1; i<i2; i++) {
```

```
                    temp[j] = temp[j] + double(rem[i]) * pow(2.0, double(ip));
                    ip++;
              }
              i1 = i1 + 5;                    // next 5 bits for next colour
        }
        addrsbcol->r = temp[2]*0.03125;
        addrsbcol->g = temp[1]*0.03125;    // levels 1/32 = 0.03125 for 5 bits
        addrsbcol->b = temp[0]*0.03125;
        return (subytecol);
        }
```

The function byte2int() takes as argument two bytes read from a file generated by the web camera and returns through the structure definition of bytecolour, the three RGB colour components. Readers should note the order of the byte colours as this changes with different compressions.

Software to display an AVI file now requires two further components; the decoding of the RIFF header and the search and removal of any four character chunks within the display data. Formally AVI display software is described in Fig. 2.4.

Display only takes place for data, which follows the four character code 'oodb', and the following four bytes, which indicate the size in bytes of the data. The display data comes in different forms defined by the biBitCount field of the BITMAPINFO-HEADER structure. The 5-bit colour extraction from two bytes has already been described. For 24-bit colour extraction the issue is simpler in that we used three consecutive bytes to represent the RGB values. Code fragments for the two conditions is as follows

```
//16 bit display
  if(biBitCount == 16) {
      if(dbcharcount != 4 && jcharcount != 4) {  //junk & db fcc's ok?
            inpaint.get(chari[3]);
            for (j=0; j<2; j++) {                     //get RGB
                    for (i=0; i<2; i++) pixels8[i] = chari[i+j*2];
                    bytecols = byte2int( pixels8 );
                    red = cols->r;
                    green = cols->g;
                    blue = cols->b;
                    glColor3f(red, green, blue );
                    glVertex2i(x,y);
                    x++;
            }
      }
  }
// 24 bit colour
          if(biBitCount == 24) {
                  if(dbcharcount == 3) {     // first 3 of db fcc ok?
                      inpaint.get(pixel); // b
```

Fig. 2.4 Decoding AVI files

Read and decode AVI
file header information

Read and display image
data for each image frame

Check for chunks containing
non-image data

Next image frame

```
                if(pixel =='b') {
                        dbcharcount++;
                        chari[3] = pixel;
                }
        }
        if(dbcharcount != 4 && jcharcount != 4) {
                glColor3ub(chari[0], chari[1], chari[2]);
                glVertex2i(x,y);
                x++;
        }
}
```

and a complete program (AVIASCII2.cpp) together with the AVI test files is provided on the accompanying Web site.

2.3.3 Compression

The preceding example is software that is 'in progress' and provides a basis for readers to start further work. A useful student exercise may be based on the discussion in this section. The bitmap format supports run-length encoding (RLE) of four and eight bit per pixel images and implementation of this facility will expand the range of files that can be processed.

RLE is a form of encoding suitable for images where large numbers of pixels are all the same as might occur for instance in an engineering drawing. In this case the background paper colour is white with black lines making up the geometry of an object and type written text aiding the description. Considering the image on a line by line basis we can represent a line by alternate counts of the numbers of white and black pixels as we move from left to right along the line as illustrated in Fig. 2.5 where

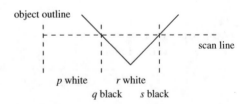

Fig. 2.5 Black and white
pixels along a scan line

p, q, r and s are the corresponding number of black or white pixels that contribute to the image along the scan line. The applicability of the method depends upon the nature of the image concerned, where for example an image exhibiting a lot of colour variation or detail will provide little compression.

RLE8

This form of run length encoding is stored in two-byte pairs where the second byte gives the value of the pixel intensity to be repeated by the number of times stored in the first byte. For an eight bit pixel image

$0A_{16}$ 66_{16} represents 66_{16} 66_{16} 66_{16} 66_{16} 66_{16} 66_{16} 66_{16} 66_{16} 66_{16} 66_{16}

A 00_{16} in the data indicates a new line and follows at the end of each scan line.

2.4 Exercises

1. Using the program AVIASCII2.cpp as a starting point integrate software to display files where 4 and 8-bit RLE encoding has been performed.
2. Using the programs provided for display of bit maps, provide additional mouse interaction (see Chapter 3) to develop a freehand drawing system.

2.5 Conclusion

In this chapter we have described two commonly available file structures, which are widely used in texturing (see Chapter 7), for imaging (see Chapter 3) and for data capture. Understanding the bitmap file structure is a prerequisite for image processing systems where we will filter and enhance images base on individual pixel distributions. Pixel maps in OpenGL generally require a size in x and y to be a power of 2 and it is convenient to scale all images to this size prior to processing. We have processed images using 24-bit and 16-bit colour demonstrating the division of two bytes into three 5-bit colour components.

Building on our knowledge of bitmaps we describe the AVI file structure and this understanding will facilitate later activities in image processing. Because this is a real time capture system, the frames have been separated so that readers will be able to perform tracking and timing measurements from images. It is not the purpose of this text to develop the processing of the audio component of AVI files. Where such data occurs it has been separated out and for those interested in these 'WAV' parts of the file, it may be processed separately.

Chapter 3
Image Processing

3.1 Introduction

At a first glance finding objects in a picture may not seem too much of a problem because the human brain is well practiced at recognition through many years of trial and error. Humans are also good at looking for major features and only looking for detail if that is needed. Present day computer systems have very little experience stored and we still have a long way to go to understand the human visual processing system from pixel to understanding – let alone implement such a model in software!

In this chapter we shall introduce some basic image processing techniques and their implementation. We shall consider how to find objects in a given image and suggest some approaches to situations where object capture is less than perfect. A knowledge of the file structures given in Chapter 2 will help in understanding the processing and enhancement of images. We attempt to present both theory and implementation to aid student development using OpenGL in a platform independent manner.

3.2 Finding Objects

The problem of finding objects can be approached in a number of ways, which ideally need to be integrated so that each augment or help each other in the overall search and recognition process. Thus edge finding is very valuable when there is a clear edge of say a silver aeroplane superimposed on a blue sky. If the aeroplane begins to enter wispy cloud the problem begins to become more difficult both for static frames and more so between frames for real time processing. Similarly if the colour changes around the edge of an object we have to adjust our threshold values. There are further problems associated with the apparent resolution (pixels/metre) of the image as shown in Fig. 3.1 and whether that is captured by eye or machine sensor.

Fig. 3.1 Apparent resolution
and image edge
determination

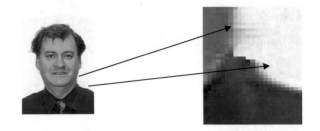

We observe that both the colour changes and the pixel resolution present problems that are not apparent when looking at the original left hand image by eye.

3.2.1 Edge Detection

An edge is defined as a local change in pixel intensity and we can envisage two types of edge; the step and the ramp edge. Clearly any change between adjacent pixels is a step change while if we consider a change over several pixels this may be a ramp of varying degrees of steepness depending on the intensity changes at the edge.

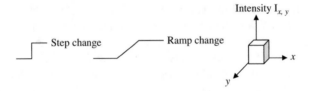

Intensity variation is generally different in the x and y directions where an edge is associated with a local peak in the intensity gradient **G**, a *vector* since variation is in a 2D scene.

$$\mathbf{G}[f(x, y)] = \begin{pmatrix} G_x \\ G_y \end{pmatrix} = \begin{pmatrix} \dfrac{\partial I}{\partial x} \\ \dfrac{\partial I}{\partial y} \end{pmatrix}$$

The vector **G** points in direction of maximum rate of intensity change G, where

$$G = \sqrt{G_x{}^2 + G_y{}^2}$$

and this takes in the direction θ given by

$$\tan\theta = G_y/G_x$$

3.2.2 Numerical Implementation

The simplest intensity approximation is between adjacent pixels

$$G_x \cong I(i+1, j) - I(i, j)$$
$$\text{and} \quad G_y \cong I(i, j+1) - I(i, j)$$

where i and j address pixels in the x and y directions of the image. G_x and G_y can be written as masks

$$G_x = 1 - 1 \text{ and } G_y = 1 - 1$$

However we should always measure the gradient at the 'centre of a pixel' if the partial derivatives are to be at the same position in the image and thus 2×2 or greater masks are usually used for purposes of accuracy. A general 3×3 operator is of the form

g_0	g_1	g_2
g_7	i,j	g_3
g_6	g_5	g_4

3.2.3 Sobel Operator

The Sobel operator is a first derivative edge finder in that it uses the intensity differences between a set of pixels surrounding a central pixel. The operator weights the contribution of each pixel according to how close it is to the central pixel. The intensity changes δI for a Sobel operator using a 3×3 neighbourhood of pixels using previous notation is given by

$$G_x = (I_2 + 2I_3 + I_4) - (I_0 + 2I_7 + I_6)$$
$$G_y = (I_6 + 2I_5 + I_4) - (I_0 + 2I_1 + I_2)$$

with masks

$$G_x = \begin{matrix} -1 & 0 & 1 \\ -2 & 0 & 2 \\ -1 & 0 & 1 \end{matrix} \qquad G_y = \begin{matrix} -1 & -2 & -1 \\ 0 & 0 & 0 \\ 1 & 2 & 1 \end{matrix}$$

called **convolution masks**. The weighting constant of 2 at the centre of the mask is because we place greater emphasis on the contribution of pixels closest to the central pixel when finding an edge.

3.2.4 Convolution

Many image-processing systems are modelled as being linear where the raw data image $I(x, y)$ is convolved with a mask (sometimes referred to as the impulse response) $G(x, y)$ to produce an output image $h(x, y)$.

Input Image $\longrightarrow$ Linear System $g(x, y)$ $\longrightarrow$ Output image
$f(x, y)$ $g(x, y)$ $h(x, y)$

The impulse response $g(x, y)$ can be considered as a form of scaling factor. The output $h(x, y)$ of convolving $I(x, y)$ with $g(x, y)$ is

$$h(i, j) = \sum_{k=1}^{n} \sum_{l=1}^{m} I(k, l)g(i - k, j - l)$$

We illustrate this operation with our grid of pixels $I(k, l)$ and our convolution mask $g(i, j)$

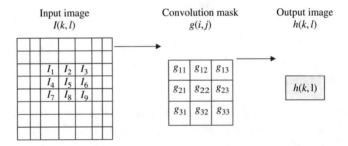

Input image
$I(k, l)$

Convolution mask
$g(i, j)$

Output image
$h(k, l)$

$$h(k, l) = g_{11}I_1 + g_{12}I_2 + g_{13}I_3 + g_{21}I_4 + g_{22}I_5 + g_{23}I_6 + g_{31}I_7 + g_{32}I_8 + g_{33}I_9$$

3.2.4.1 An Example

The following example is the application of a Sobel operator on data from a bitmap file of an X-ray image and stored as floating point grey level values in a 2D grid-array. The data is processed using the Sobel operator and the final result of the edge finding stored in an array FinalGrid. The original image is shown in Fig. 3.2 and we see the affect of the operator particularly on the skull surface where we clearly discern the bone. Where there are slowly varying grey levels due to similar material density in the brain few edges are found. The sensitivity of first derivative operators to noise is clearly apparent and for processed grey levels less that 10 we set these to black to reduce the effect. Students are encouraged to experiment with different values here and on different images to see the different effects of this operator.

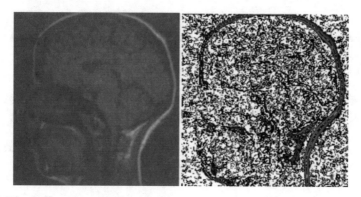

Fig. 3.2 Edge finding using a Sobel operator

```
void Sobel (void)    //sobel.cpp
{
 glClear ( GL_COLOR_BUFFER_BIT ) ;
 ifstream inpaint( "c:\\rob\\images\\sk24256.bmp", ios::binary);
 if(!inpaint)
 {
         cout << "File not opened\n";
         exit(1);
 }
 for(x=1; x<=54; x++) inpaint >> pixel; //skip header stuff

 for (y = 0; y <= wh-1; y++)
 {
         for (x = 0; x <= ww-1; x++)
         {
                 intens = 0;
                 for (i=0; i<=2; i++)
                 {
                         inpaint.get(pixel);
                         pix = pixel;
                         pixtmp[i] = float(pix) / 255.0;
                         intens = intens + float(pix);
                 }
                 Grid[x][y] = ((intens/3.0));
         }
 }
         //convolution
 for (int x = 0; x <ww-1; x++)
 {
         for (int y = 0; y <wh-1; y++)
```

```
                      {
      XPass = (Grid[x][y] + 2 * Grid[x][y+1] + Grid[x][y+2])-
      (Grid[x+2][y] + 2 * Grid[x+2][y+1]+
      Grid[x+2][y+2]);

      YPass = (Grid[x][y+2] + 2 * Grid[x+1][y+2] + Grid[x+2]
     [y+2])- (Grid[x][y] + 2 * Grid[x+1][y] + Grid[x+2][y]);

                  Result = sqrt((XPass * XPass) + (YPass * YPass));
                  Result = abs(Result/2); //Sobel scaling
                  FinalGrid[x][y] = Result;
                  }
      }

glBegin(GL_POINTS);
for(x = 0; x <= ww-1; x++)
{
                  for(y=0; y<= wh-1;y++)
                  {
                          if (FinalGrid[x][y] < 10.0) FinalGrid[x][y]
                            = 255.0;
                          FinalGrid[x][y] = FinalGrid[x][y]/255.0;
                            // normalise
                          glColor3f(FinalGrid[x][y], FinalGrid[x][y],
                            FinalGrid[x][y]);
                          glVertex2i(x,y);

                  }
}
glEnd();
glFlush();
}
```

3.2.5 Laplacian Operator

The Sobel operator is a first derivative operator, where if a difference occurred then an edge is considered to be found. The method works well where there are large image areas of the same colour and little noise. An alternative method for edge detection is to find local maximal grey level gradient changes, where the second derivative of the intensity changes is zero (a peak in first derivative is when second derivative = 0). We now derive the Laplacian operator from first principles followed by implementation.

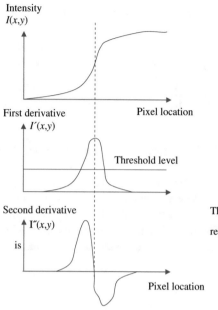

Intensity
$I(x,y)$

First derivative
$I'(x,y)$

Pixel location

Threshold level

Second derivative
$I''(x,y)$

is

Pixel location

The second derivative Laplacian is

represented as

$$\nabla^2 I = \frac{\delta^2 I}{\delta x^2} + \frac{\delta^2 I}{\delta y^2}$$

Second derivatives are found from the differences in the first derivatives.

$$\frac{\delta^2 I}{\delta x^2} = \frac{\delta[\delta I_x]}{\delta x}$$
$$= \frac{\delta[I(i+1,j) - I(i,j)]}{\delta x}$$
$$= \frac{\delta I(i+1,j)}{\delta x} - \frac{\delta I(i,j)}{\delta x}$$
$$= [I(i+2,j) - I(i+1,j)] - [I(i+1,j) - I(i,j)]$$
$$= I(i+2,j) - 2I(i+1,j) + I(i,j)$$
$$= I(i+1,j) - 2I(i,j) + I(i-1,j)$$

Similarly in the y direction

$$\frac{\delta^2 I}{\delta y^2} = I(i,j+1) - 2I(i,j) + I(i,j-1)$$

Now

$$\nabla^2 I = \frac{\delta^2 I}{dx^2} + \frac{\delta^2 I}{dy^2}$$
$$= [I(i+1,j) - 2I(i,j) + I(i-1,j)] + [I(i,j+1) - 2I(i,j) + I(i,j-1)]$$
$$= I(i+1,j) + I(i-1,j) + I(i,j+1) - 4I(i,j) + I(i,j-1)$$

which can be represented on a 3×3 grid of pixels centred on the middle point (i, j) as

0	1	0
1	−4	1
0	1	0

with each square on the grid containing the coefficient for each of the (i, j) terms of the Laplacian.

We have derived the Laplacian from first principles and depending on the nature of the original image, it may be necessary to adjust the weights to give more importance to the central pixel or to give some value to the diagonal pixels. Image processing is still something of art! The following implementation uses the Laplacian mask with a data file (edgetest1.dat) to illustrate the operation of the mask.

```
#define lsize 3
#define ylines 11
#define xpoints 19

void laplace ( void ) {     //laplace.cpp
ifstream indata("edgetest1.dat", ios::in);
int x, y, xpos, ypos, xpt, ypt, ix, xblk;
float sum, Lap[lsize][lsize], Data[xpoints][ylines];
cout << " Laplacian\n";
   for (y=0; y< lsize; y++) {
     for (x=0; x< lsize; x++) {
     indata >> Lap[x][y];
     cout << Lap[x][y] << " ";
     }
   cout << endl;
  }
cout << " Raw data\n";
  for (y=0; y< ylines; y++) {
    for (x=0; x< xpoints; x++) {
    indata >> Data[x][y];
    cout << Data[x][y] << " ";
    }
  cout << endl;
  }
cout << " Edge finding\n";
  xblk = xpoints - lsize + 1; //7
  for (ypos=0; ypos<= ylines - lsize ; ypos++) {//next y line
    xpos = 0;
```

```
for (ix=1; ix<=xblk; ix++) { //next x pixel block
    sum = 0.0;
    for (y=0; y< lsize; y++) {
        for (x=0; x< lsize; x++) {
        xpt = x + xpos;
        ypt = y + ypos;
        sum = sum + Lap[x][y] * Data[xpt][ypt];
        }
    }
    xpos++;
    cout << setw(3) << sum << " ";
}
cout << endl;
}
}
```

```
0 1 0
1 -4 1
0 1 0
3 7 7 7 7 7 7 7 7 7 7 7 3 3 3 3 3 3 3
3 3 7 7 7 7 7 7 7 7 7 3 3 3 3 3 3 3 3
3 3 3 7 7 7 7 7 7 7 3 3 3 3 3 3 3 3 3
3 3 3 3 7 7 7 7 7 3 3 3 3 3 3 3 3 3 3
3 3 3 3 3 7 7 7 3 3 3 3 3 3 3 3 3 3 3
3 3 3 3 3 3 7 3 3 3 3 3 3 3 3 3 3 3 3
3 3 3 3 3 3 3 3 3 3 3 3 3 3 3 3 3 3 3
3 3 3 3 3 3 3 3 3 3 3 3 3 3 3 3 3 3 3
3 3 3 3 3 3 3 3 3 3 3 3 3 3 3 3 3 3 3
3 3 3 3 3 3 3 3 3 3 3 3 3 3 3 3 3 3 3
```

Edge finding
```
8 -8  0  0  0  0  0  0 -8  8  0  0  0  0  0  0
0  8 -8  0  0  0  0 -8  8  0  0  0  0  0  0  0
0  0  8 -8  0  0 -8  8  0  0  0  0  0  0  0  0
0  0  0  8 -8  0 -8  8  0  0  0  0  0  0  0  0
0  0  0  0  8 -12 8  0  0  0  0  0  0  0  0  0
0  0  0  0  0  4  0  0  0  0  0  0  0  0  0  0
```

This simulation hides the fact that the above data is very clean while in reality noise is prevalent to most situations and must be ameliorated.

3.2.6 Smoothing and Edge Finding

Both the Sobel and Laplacian edge finders suffer from the same problem of being locally sensitive to noise. What is needed in the convolution process is a means of smoothing out the noise and possibly using a mask over a larger pixel grid. It should be noted that if we use a larger pixel mask we not only smooth out noise but also small features that may be of interest and are subsequently lost. We introduce a method due to Marr and Hildreth, which combines Gaussian filtering with the Laplacian edge detector, called the Laplacian of Gaussian (LoG).

The resulting image $h(x,y)$ is a result of the convolution

$$h(x, y) = \nabla^2[g(x, y) * I(x, y)]$$

where the Gaussian $g(x,y) = c e^{-(x^2+y^2)/2\sigma^2}$ and $I(x,y)$ is the original intensity image. For clarity we shall consider a 1D version of the Gaussian distribution $g(x)$ and generalise for an actual 2D convolution later. Let

$$g(x) = c\, e^{-(x^2)/2\sigma^2}$$

$$g'(x) = \frac{-c\,x\,e^{-x^2}}{\sigma^2}$$

$$= \frac{-x\,g(x)}{\sigma^2}$$

$$g''(x) = \frac{-c\,e^{-x^2}}{\sigma^2} + \frac{x^2\,c\,e^{-x^2}}{\sigma^4}$$

$$g''(x) = \frac{x^2 - \sigma^2}{\sigma^4}\,g(x)$$

If the Gaussian is uniform in both x and y then we would have used

$$g(x,\,y) = c\,e^{-(x^2+y^2)/2\sigma^2}$$

and partially differentiated with respect to x and y when the result would be

$$g''(x,\,y) = \frac{x^2 + y^2 - \sigma^2}{\sigma^4}\,g(x,\,y)$$

This is commonly called the Mexican Hat operator and the characteristics of the filter depend on the value of the spread σ. Using the 5×5 mask gives the outline edges shown in Fig. 3.3.

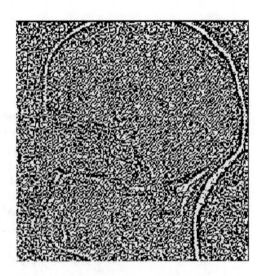

Fig. 3.3 Effect of filtering using Mexican Hat operator

3.3 Histogram Equalisation

Many images have grey level intensities occupying only a small number of the possible grey values available and this leads to limited contrast as shown in the original image of the skull in Fig. 3.2. An intensity histogram is a count of the number of pixels at each grey level within any image and Fig. 3.4 illustrate this where most pixels in the possible range of values lie at the low (blacker) intensities.

One can improve the look and contrast of such an image by spreading the grey levels out across all possible values in a more equitable fashion rather than just using the limited number in the original spectrum of the image. This redistribution is called Histogram equalisation and features in many commonly available picture processing systems.

Consider a picture with an area of N×N pixels where the object is to spread the M intensities evenly throughout the whole area of N^2 pixels. Ideally each grey level would occupy N^2/M pixels with lowest grey level in original image placed at lowest grey level available in new processed image. If a processed grey level is short of a fair share of pixels we add those from next grey level up in original image.

From Fig. 3.4 let

$$n_g = \text{number of pixels at grey level intensity } g \qquad 0 \le g \le M-1$$
$$\text{and} \quad t_g = \Sigma \, n_j \text{ number of pixels at intensity } g \text{ or less}$$
$$j = 0$$

For an even distribution of the pixels using all possible grey levels we need the number of pixels at intensity g or less to be a multiple of N^2/M (or as close as possible) so as to equalise the spectral distribution of intensities over all possible grey levels.

If the number of pixels in the processed image with some intensity s is f_s then

$$f_s = \max\left(0, \; \text{round}\left\{\frac{M \, t_g}{N^2}\right\}^{-1}\right)$$

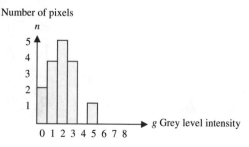

Fig. 3.4 An image with a bias towards being darker

Number of pixels

This is a mapping of original grey level g to processed grey levels f_s rounded to the nearest integer. From the graph in Fig. 3.4 and assuming a 4×4 image ($N^2 = 16$ and the number of intensities $M = 6$) then

Intensity g	n_g	t_g	Round($6t_g/16$) -1
0	2	2	0
1	4	6	1
2	5	11	3
3	4	15	5
4	0	15	5
5	1	16	5

We can now interpret the processed image f_s in relation to the original image g, where we see a shift from the old input intensity g to the new processed value f_s. Examples are where intermediate grey levels 2 and 4 are moved to other bands of grey intensity giving a contrast enhancement (old 2 becomes new 3 and old 3,4,5

Fig. 3.5 Intensity redistribution of histogram equalisation

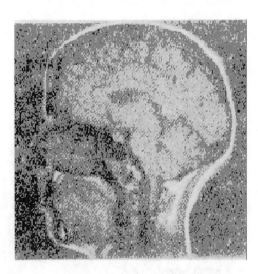

Fig. 3.6 Effect of histogram equalisation

moves to new 5 etc.). Histogram equalisation does not *add* information to an image but rather spreads the information over the whole spectrum of intensities providing a clearer view of the image shown in Fig. 3.5.

A program for Histogram equalisation operating on the image in Fig. 3.2 as original data, results in the image in Fig. 3.6 and is supplied on the accompanying web site.

3.4 Component (object) Labelling

A requirement of many image processing systems is to identify or label objects by connecting all the pixels that belong to an object in the correct *order*. Typically the linking occurs where all pixels are the same as occurs at the edge of an object. The task is much more complex when edges have different colours and also belong to the same single object, as illustrated in Fig. 3.1. We will assume in this section that we have a well-defined edge and develop methods to track around the edge of the object. Consider the following grid of pixels where the black pixels are the edge of an object. The number of objects depends on how we defined the connectivity of pixels.

If we permit a 4-way connection path of North, South, East and West then we have 4 individual square objects with a hole in the middle. If we permit 8-way connectivity by including North East, North West etc. then we have a single object through the joining at the corners of the pixels. The size of objects is also an important criterion when labelling as 'noise' pixels (perhaps due to dirt on a camera lens or scanning surface) can distort object shape. Care must be exercised in the removal of a small number of pixels as in the shown in Fig. 3.7 where it would be easy to remove the dot above the letter 'i' when removing small numbers of pixels that otherwise might be considered noise.

The importance of context in noise removal cannot be over emphasised. Similar issues arise in removal of dots and commas as sentence delimiters and generally noise reduction must not occur alone but as part of a wider software architecture in any image processing system.

Fig. 3.7 Problems associated
with noise removal

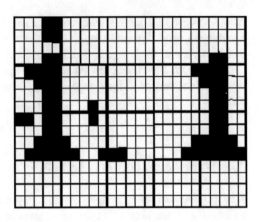

3.4.1 Exploring Connectivity (1)

The first algorithm is a simple search scan line by scan line for pixels equal to or
above some threshold and if they exist, label them as belonging to an object. The
pixels

```
0 0 0 0 0 0 0 0 0 0
0 0 0 0 0 0 1 1 0 0
0 0 0 0 1 1 1 1 0 0
0 0 0 0 0 1 1 1 0 0
0 0 0 0 0 0 1 1 0 0
0 0 0 0 0 0 1 1 0 0
0 0 0 0 0 0 1 1 0 0
0 0 0 0 0 0 1 1 0 0
0 0 0 0 1 1 1 1 1 0
0 0 0 1 1 1 1 1 1 1
0 0 0 0 0 0 0 0 0 0
```

belonging to the object of concern are shown in the data file as being 1 or greater
opposite. We can think of these as being from scan lines of an image where the
pixels are greater than some threshold. We can scan the lines starting at 0 from the
top and moving from left to right across the image. The first object pixel is found on
scanline 1 with the x-coordinate 6. Similarly scanline 2 will have an x-coordinate
of 4. The top or bottom of an object with no concavities is found when there is only
white space across the whole image. At this point we reverse the process searching
back up from the lowest point to the top of the object storing (x,y) coordinates as
we traverse the object. The logic of the process is as follows –

1. Scan image left –> right line by line
2. At each pixel search above and left adjacent neighbours for touching pixels – extend label
3. If separated enter new pixel label into a table
4. If different labels 'join' on bit map – relabel second/third etc. pixel labels to first label

The following function implements these ideas.

```cpp
void outline ( void ) {      //rleoutline.cpp
ifstream indata("outline.txt", ios::in);
int i, ii, points, x, y, white, xwide, ylines;
float Data[10][20], pixelpos[100];
ylines = 10;
xwide = 9;
for (y=0; y<=ylines; y++) {
   for (x=0; x<=xwide; x++) {
   indata >> Data[x][y];
   cout << Data[x][y] << " ";
   }
cout << endl;
}
cout << "End of data pixel file\n";
i = 0;
for (y=0; y<=ylines; y++) { //LHS search
white = 0;
         for (x=0; x<=xwide; x++) {
    if(Data[x][y] == 1) { // found black pixel
    pixelpos[i] = x;
    i++;
    pixelpos[i] = y;
    i++;
    break;
    }
    else {
    white++;
    }
 } // x
 if( white == xwide && i !=0) break; //all white bottom
 of object
} // y
for (y=ylines; y>=0; y--) { //RHS search
white = 0;
         for (x=xwide; x>=0; x--) {
    if(Data[x][y] == 1) { // found black pixel
```

```
      pixelpos[i] = x;
      i++;
      pixelpos[i] = y;
      i++;
      break;
      }
       else {
       white++;
       }
      }
      if( white == xwide && i!=0) break; //all white top of object
    }
  points = i /2 - 1;
  ii=0;
  for (i=0; i<=points; i++) {
  cout << pixelpos[ii] << " " <<pixelpos[ii+1] << endl;
  ii=ii+2;
  }
}
```

The very simple search technique illustrated above works for a limited set of object shapes, but what is needed is a more generalised search for labelling objects.

3.4.2 Exploring Connectivity (2)

The boundary of an object is a set of connected pixels x_i on edge of the object $\mathbf{O}$. The search is at boundary of $\mathbf{O}$ where p_i belong to $\mathbf{O}$ ($p_i \in \mathbf{O}$). We select an origin for our search and then follow an 8-way search clockwise from last direction of the previous search point.

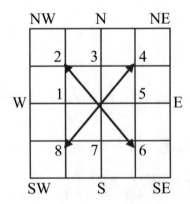

1. Find start pixel from top to bottom (y-scan line) and left to right x-position
2. Current pixel is p_i and move next pixel west (in **O**)

3. Search clockwise 8 nearest neighbours to find next pixel in **O** | Repeat until
4. Reset p_i to new current position and store previous p_i | reach origin

Sample code for this 8-way search algorithm is provided on the accompanying web site together with a sample test data file to illustrate the operation.

3.4.3 Multiple Regions

An extension of the 8-way search is required in situations where there are disjoint regions, which belong to a single object as illustrated in Fig. 3.8 of an aircraft in haze.

Fig. 3.8 The problem of disjoint regions from a single object

Instead of searching one-pixel distances, we specify a pixel distance threshold in order to join the areas into a single object outline. The choice of threshold distance will introduce errors in outline and is dependent on the nature of the image being investigated. One way to minimise this problem is to vary the connectivity threshold and compare the resultant shape with a database of known aircraft shapes looking for the best match.

3.5 Drawing on the Screen and Data Capture

In this section we shall develop a facility whereby we can interact with the position of the mouse pointer and either draw the position or use it to locate objects for later processing. To illustrate this process we will develop software to simulate the mouse behaving as a pen and allow the storage of handwriting. It is worth noting that there are a number of low cost devices, which can be used in place of a mouse that will add realism to this application – for example the WACOM 0405 pen and tablet. Such devices provide most of the facilities of a mouse and if plugged into the mouse port permit an alternative user interface and platform for hand input, although a little practice is required for the user to feel totally comfortable.

The GLUT kit provides callback functions to handle interrupts from the mouse via glutMouseFunc and glutMotionFunc. Using glutMouseFunc sets mouse callbacks to the current window and pressing or releasing the mouse buttons generates the interrupt or callback. The state parameter (GLUT_ UP or GLUT _DOWN) indicates whether the callback was due to a release or press respectively of a mouse button. The x and y callback parameters indicate the window relative coordinates when the mouse button state changed. The motion callback for a window is called when the mouse moves within the window using glutMotionFunc while one or more mouse buttons are pressed. The x and y callback parameters indicate the mouse location in window relative coordinates.

The function glutMouseFunc (Mouse) requires a user written function Mouse, that requires a button be pressed or released in order to perform some function at the current relative window coordinates (x,y) – in this example will draw the location with a coloured square. Our function looks like

```
void Mouse ( int btn, int state, int x, int y ) {
        if ( GLUT_LEFT_BUTTON == btn && GLUT_DOWN == state )
        DrawSquare ( x, y ) ;
        if ( GLUT_RIGHT_BUTTON == btn && GLUT_DOWN == state )
        exit ( 0 ) ;
        }
```

where DrawSquare(x, y) gets and stores the position cordinates from

```
glutMotionFunc(DrawSquare) as the mouse moves across the
window.
```

```
void Display ( void ) {
  glClear ( GL_COLOR_BUFFER_BIT ) ;
}
```

```
void DrawSquare ( int x, int y ) {  //Mouselnp.cpp
//convert y from Windows convention to OpenGL
    y = wh - y ;


    //set up random colour for illustration purposes
    glColor3ub ((GLubyte)rand( ) % 256,
                       (GLubyte)rand( ) % 256,
                       (GLubyte)rand( ) % 256 ) ;
    drawfile << x << " " << y << endl;  // maybe store colour
                                    //as well?
```

```
    glBegin ( GL_POLYGON ) ;
      glVertex2f ( x + size, y + size ) ;
      glVertex2f ( x - size, y + size ) ;
      glVertex2f ( x - size, y - size ) ;
      glVertex2f ( x + size, y - size ) ;
    glEnd ( ) ;
    glFlush ( ) ;
}

void Mouse ( int btn, int state, int x, int y ) {
      if ( GLUT_LEFT_BUTTON == btn && GLUT_DOWN == state )
      DrawSquare ( x, y ) ;
      if ( GLUT_RIGHT_BUTTON == btn && GLUT_DOWN == state )
      exit ( 0 ) ;
}

void Reshape ( int w, int h ) {

  glMatrixMode    ( GL_MODELVIEW ) ;
  glLoadIdentity ( ) ;
  glViewport      ( 0, 0, w, h ) ;
  glClear         ( GL_COLOR_BUFFER_BIT ) ;
  glutPostRedisplay ( ) ;
  // update globals
  ww = w ;
  wh = h ;
}
```

Mouse coordinates are plotted in random colours, Fig. 3.9 and stored in a disk file (mtest.txt). The author has found that on some systems duplicate points occasionally occur due to a lack of smooth hand movement, at pen down or pen up and should be filtered out if further processing of data is required.

Fig. 3.9 Freehand data input via the mouse port

3.5.1 Outlining of Areas of Interest on Images

The previous program needs only a small modification in order to be used for data
capture and the outlining of objects for image presentation. Instead of using the
mouse for input and display we can replace the blank background with an image of
the object we wish to digitise. Consider the scan of a section of a brain in Fig. 3.10
where we have superimposed grid lines for measurement purposes.

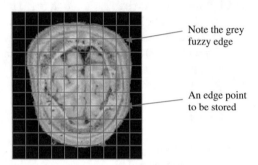

Note the grey
fuzzy edge

An edge point
to be stored

Fig. 3.10 Brain scan section

The grid lines have been superimposed on the scan to indicate where we are
in Cartesian space and each press of the left hand mouse button interrupts at the
coordinates of the cursor location, which can then be stored on disk. For this
example the grid lines are 16 points apart in x and y directions for a 256×256
bit map image and can also be used as a data check from time to time. All that
is required to modify the previous program is a function to input and display
the image of interest in Fig. 3.6 and then we are ready to digitise any image.
The following code is a slight revision to that already met in chapter 1, will suffice.

```
void paint (void) {
unsigned char pixel;
int x, y, xs, xf, ys, i, pix, xpack;
float pixtmp[3];
glClear\index{glClear} ( GL_COLOR_BUFFER_BIT ) ;

ifstream inpaint( "c:\\rob\\images\\head\\Image8.bmp",
                                    ios::binary);
if(!inpaint) {
        cout << "File not opened\n";
   exit(1);
```

```
}
for(x=1; x<=54; x++) {\{}
inpaint.get(pixel); //go to start of data after header stuff
pix = pixel;
}
xs = 0;
xf = 256;                   // should get x&y from header really
ys = 0;
glBegin\index{glBegin}(GL_POINTS);
for (y = ys; y<= 255; y++) {
  for (x = xs; x<= xf; x++) {
    for (i=0; i<3; i++) { // 3 bytes = 1 pixel in 24 bit colour
    inpaint.get(pixel);
    pix = pixel;
    pixtmp[i] = float(pix) / 255.0;
    }
  glColor3f(pixtmp[2], pixtmp[1], pixtmp[0]); // G B R !
  glVertex2f(x,y);
  }

}
glEnd();
glColor3f(1.0, 0.0, 0.0);
glBegin(GL_LINE); //grid lines
for(y=0; y< 256; y=y+16) {
        glVertex2f(0.0, (float) y); glVertex2f( 256.0,
                                            (float) y);
        glVertex2f((float) y, 0.0); glVertex2f( (float)
                                            y, 256.0);
}
glEnd();
glFlush();
}

void Display ( void ) {
   glClear\index{glClear} ( GL_COLOR_BUFFER_BIT );
   paint();
}
```

This code provides a simple method of data capture although laborious and inappropriate for large numbers of points. Duplication of data points will occur if when clicking the mouse at the edge points of the image, the mouse also moves slightly due to 'shake' in the operators hand. This can easily be corrected in *either* the *x* or *y* directions since we have a fixed line spacing, but not in both directions! We shall use this program in a later chapter to provide data for a simple 3D construction of a head from CAT scans. A useful modification which some of my students have implemented is to add a colour value to scan lines to differentiate objects at display time.

3.5.2 An Approach to Automating Edge Detection

We have explored in this chapter methods of enhancing an image, which visually appear to provide clearer information. Further we introduced a simple method of capturing coordinate values along the edge of a CAT scan for subsequent processing. The question naturally arises as to how efficiently can we capture outlines automatically and the answer is somewhat ambiguous. The scan in Fig. 3.10 appears to have a well delineated edge yet on careful examination we notice that there are also artefacts inside the main body of the image, which will also be captured if we use edge finding alone. In general recognition is a multi-faceted problem requiring the input of higher level knowledge to improve data capture. In this simple case we might assume the skull has no concavities and just two sides. This knowledge will allow us to ignore data captured in the brain area and get a better set of $x-y$ data by using only the minimum and maximum values of x along any given scan line. Thus our first assumption is that we know something about the shape of a skull in performing the edge finding.

A second area of useful knowledge is how sharp are the edges? Edge finding around the flesh background interface is quite different from the top of the skull where it is an interface between grey hair and background with a less well defined edge as is evident with careful examination of the original scans. We might thus find it advantageous to compare blocks of pixels rather than adjacent ones in order to define a more *fuzzy* edge although this will introduce a variation in the edge position of $\pm$ the pixel block size. Smaller block sizes can be used with sharp clearly defined edges although this will increase the risk of finding spurious edges due to noise within the scan data.

Determination of an appropriate threshold at the scan edge requires a knowledge of the RGB values and some initial pre-processing of the image. In Fig. 3.6 one might assume that the RGB values of the black background are zero or that the cream coloured brain matter has values near to 255 and this would prove erroneous. Typically the eye cannot resolve these variations and in practice the edge finder must have a knowledge of the RGB range before an effective threshold can be defined and a histogram of these values across the image is often a useful starting point. Such pre-processing can lead to a dynamically varying threshold across the scan.

The context of the scan has led us to consider three knowledge components that can be used to improve the edge finding:

- constraints of object shape
- constraints due to nature of edges
- constraints of RGB variability

In general, knowledge beyond the edge finding algorithm operating at the pixel level alone is essential to enhance performance. The knowledge is usually specific to the problem concerned and also dependent on the nature of the data collection.

The code that follows illustrates some of these principles in a modified form by replacing the edge finding using the mouse with thresholding. One should not implement such code in the display function as it is very inefficient, but we use this as an illustration developed from previous programs for purposes of clarity. The coordinates of the edge are output in

```
if(fabs (xsum1 - xsum2) > threshold) cout << "x="<< x1+xblock_size
   <<"y="<<y<<"\n";
```

where a suitable threshold was found from scanning the RGB variation and plotting a histogram of values. The averaging of the pixels (xblock_size = 8;) was the result of looking at the edge in a number of locations and comparing it with visual capture using the mouse.

```
void paint (void) {
unsigned char pixel;
int x, y, xs, xf, ys, i, pix, xpack, threshold;
int pixsum, xblock_size, yline[256], x1, x2, ix, xsum1, xsum2;
float pixtmp[3];
glClear ( GL_COLOR_BUFFER_BIT ) ;

ifstream inpaint( "c:\\rob\\images\\head\\ Image8.bmp",
                                          ios::binary);
if(!inpaint) {
        cout << "File not opened\n";
        exit(1);
}
for(x=1; x<=54; x++) {
inpaint.get(pixel); //go to start of data after header stuff
pix = pixel;
}
xs = 0;
xf = 256;          // should get x&y from header really
threshold = 450;   //from histogram analysis
xblock_size = 8;
ys = 0;
glBegin(GL_POINTS);
for (y = ys; y< 256; y++) {
   for (x = xs; x< xf; x++) {
```

```
        pixsum = 0;

        for (i=0; i<3; i++) { // = 1 pixel in 24 bit colour
                    inpaint.get(pixel);
                    pix = pixel;
                    pixtmp[i] = float(pix) / 255.0;
                    pixsum = pixsum + pix;
        }
        yline[x] = ((float) pixsum) / 3;
        glColor3f(pixtmp[2], pixtmp[1], pixtmp[0]); // G B R !
        glVertex2f(x,y);
}
    if (y%16==0) {
            x1 = 0;
            for (x = 0; x< 30; x++) {
                        x2 = x1 + xblock_size * 2;
                        xsum1 = 0;
                        xsum2 = 0;
                        for (ix = x1; ix< x2; ix++) {
                                    if( ix < (x2-xblock_size))
                                    xsum1 = xsum1 +yline[ix];
                                    else xsum2 = xsum2 +yline[ix];
                        } //ix
                        if(fabs ( xsum1 - xsum2) > threshold)
                        cout << "x= "<< x1+xblock_size
                        <<"y="<<y<<"\n";
                        x1 = x1 + xblock_size;

                    }
                }

}
glEnd();

glColor3f(1.0, 0.0, 0.0);
glBegin(GL_LINE);
for(y=0; y< 256; y=y+16) {
        glVertex2f(0.0, (float) y); glVertex2f( 256.0,
        (float) y);
        glVertex2f((float) y, 0.0); glVertex2f( (float)
        y, 256.0);
}
glEnd();
glFlush();
}
```

3.6 Exercises

1. Using the mouse drawing software, develop a system for measuring handwriting characteristics such as closed loops, height of ascending and descending strokes, diacritical marks, gaps in writing etc. Use your software for recognition and conversion to typescript.
2. Using the mouse drawing software, digitise and outline some of the main anatomical features from the CAT scan images provided.
3. Using Fig. 3.4 or a similar image of your own, experiment with some of the image processing operators described, to enhance an image so that edge detection can be considered. Suggest how noise may be removed prior to any edge detection.

3.7 Conclusion

In this chapter we have explored some of the issues around finding edges and capturing the coordinates that make up an edge. Algorithms have been implemented that demonstrate limitations with indicators for solutions that are still application specific. Comparing edges to a shape database is alluded to, although the task is a significant project with imperfect data where gaps in the edge may vary over a number of image frames. Finally we have created simple image data capture software for still images that with modification can be adapted for a number of student problems.

Chapter 4
Transformations

4.1 Introduction

One of the aims of this text is to introduce mathematics where it is needed and *implement* it in software. Transformations are fundamental to graphics and animation since we often need to look at things in different ways. We could treat all the OpenGL functions as black boxes with no understanding of how they work but hiding theory does not inform the user of the limitations of, or aid the development of software to overcome limitations. As in Chapter 3 where we illustrated some of the weaknesses of image processing when working at the pixel level alone, so we will develop mathematics in relation to applications. We introduce some key ideas in how we store and manipulate points and vectors, which facilitate graphical operations.

For the graphics in this text we shall be concerned with scalars, points and vectors in a general 3D space defined by the x, y, z directions. The definitions we shall use are:

Point: a location in space plus its colour
Scalar: a number that we multiply other variables by
Vector: a line that has magnitude, direction and a colour

From these three items we shall build and manipulate objects for graphical display. Readers unfamiliar with matrix and vector operations are referred to Appendix C for a brief introduction together with references for further reading.

4.2 Representing Points and Vectors

A line in computer graphics is represented by two end points (x_1, y_1, z_1) and (x_2, y_2, z_2) in 3-D space. Although the computer monitor is flat and in 2 dimensions we represent depth (z) by making objects smaller the further they are from the eye viewpoint. This is a simulation of how humans actually see, since our eyes are a small distance apart and we are able to almost simultaneously look at objects and comprehend depth through stereopsis.

A line in space is referred to as a *vector* in that it has magnitude (length) and direction (orientation) in relation to some origin. Although we are all familiar with 3-D space we should be aware that there are other dimensions than distance. If we were graphically representing a problem of an objects mass, velocity and energy then our dimensions might be represented by these quantities to produce a new surface and understanding of the object characteristics.

Consider a line with end points P_1 and P_2 in Fig. 4.1. The size or magnitude of this vector is the Euclidian distance between the points specifying the line

$$|P_1 - P_2| = \sqrt{(x_1 - x_2)^2 + (y_1 - y_2)^2 + (z_1 - z_2)^2}$$

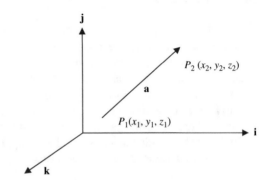

Fig. 4.1 Cartesian space representation

The vector *a* to represent the line is

$$a = P_1 - P_2$$
$$= (x_1 - x_2)\mathbf{i} + (y_1 - y_2)\mathbf{j} + (z_1 - z_2)\mathbf{k}$$

where $(\mathbf{i}, \mathbf{j}, \mathbf{k})$ are the unit vectors representing the axes of the coordinate frame of reference in which we are working. A vector has both magnitude and direction and thus in the above definition $P_2 - P_1 = $ -**a**, that is in the opposite direction. If the vector **a** were written as $\mathbf{a} = (3, 3, 3)$, the numbers would the size of each component in the unit vector directions. It should be noted that this is different from a point in Cartesian space $P_1 = (1, 2, 3)$ where the numbers are the coordinate values of the location in 3D space. If we place our second point P_2 at $(4, 5, 6)$, then vector **a** representing the line is $(3, 3, 3)$ and $|\mathbf{a}| \approx 5.2$. The unit vector or normalised vector of

$$\mathbf{a} = \mathbf{a}/|\mathbf{a}| = (3/5.2, 3/5.2, 3/5.2)$$

The direction of a vector that is normal to a surface can be used as a means of representing how much light is reflected to the eye-point of a viewer. We shall investigate later on how to use this fact to develop shading models and provide the illusion of shape on a flat screen monitor.

4.2.1 Vector Dot Products

The dot product of two vectors **a** and **b** is defined as

$$\mathbf{a} \cdot \mathbf{b} = \sum_{i=1}^{n} a_i b_i$$

where a_i and b_i are the components of each vector.

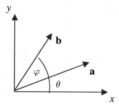

Now

$$
\begin{aligned}
\mathbf{a} &= (|\mathbf{a}| \cos \theta, |\mathbf{a}| \sin \theta) \\
\mathbf{b} &= (|\mathbf{b}| \cos \varphi, |\mathbf{b}| \sin \varphi) \\
\mathbf{a} \cdot \mathbf{b} &= |\mathbf{a}||\mathbf{b}| \cos \theta \cos \varphi + |\mathbf{a}||\mathbf{b}| \sin \theta \sin \varphi \\
&= |\mathbf{a}||\mathbf{b}| \cos(\varphi - \theta)
\end{aligned}
$$

Thus when the vectors are perpendicular or **orthogonal** ($\varphi - \theta = 90°$), the dot product is zero. If the vectors lie in two different planes then we refer to the planes as being **normal** to each other.

It is also to be noted that $\mathbf{a} \cdot \mathbf{b} / |\mathbf{a}| = |\mathbf{b}| \cos (\varphi - \theta)$ which is the length of the orthogonal projection of **a** onto **b**.

4.2.2 The Vector Cross Product

Two vectors in space will define a plane and three vectors, which intersect, will form a triangle.

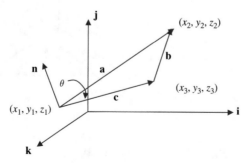

We can use any two of the above vectors to define a third, which is orthogonal to the plane of the triangle by using the cross product, which is defined as

$$\mathbf{a} \times \mathbf{c} = \mathbf{n}\,|\mathbf{a}||\mathbf{c}|\sin\theta$$

where θ is the angle between $\mathbf{a}$ and $\mathbf{c}$ and $\mathbf{n}$ is the unit vector normal to the plane defined by the triangle. Using the Cartesian coordinates we can represent the vectors $\mathbf{a}$ and $\mathbf{b}$ as

$$\mathbf{a} = \mathbf{i}(x_2 - x_1) + \mathbf{j}(y_2 - y_1) + \mathbf{k}(z_2 - z_1)$$
$$\mathbf{c} = \mathbf{i}(x_3 - x_1) + \mathbf{j}(y_3 - y_1) + \mathbf{k}(z_3 - z_1)$$

$$\mathbf{a} \times \mathbf{c} = \begin{vmatrix} \mathbf{i} & \mathbf{j} & \mathbf{k} \\ (x_2 - x_1) & (y_2 - y_1) & (z_2 - z_1) \\ (x_3 - x_1) & (y_3 - y_1) & (z_3 - z_1) \end{vmatrix}$$

$$= \mathbf{i}\{(y_2 - y_1)^*(z_3 - z_1) - (y_3 - y_1)^*(z_2 - z_1)\}$$
$$- \mathbf{j}\{(x_2 - x_1)^*(z_3 - z_1) - (x_3 - x_1)^*(z_2 - z_1)\}$$
$$+ \mathbf{k}\{(x_2 - x_1)^*(y_3 - y_1) - (x_3 - x_1)^*(y_2 - y_1)\}$$

If we were to patch a surface with triangles then a knowledge of the surface normal gives the orientation of each triangular patch which then may be used to adjust the colour level for shading purposes. To smooth out the edges of each triangle we can average the value of the normals between adjacent triangles (see Chapter 7).

4.2.2.1 A Worked Example

Consider 3 vertices at (0, 10, 0), (11, 60, 11) and (22, 10, 22)

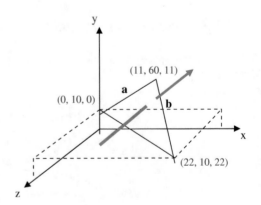

Fig. 4.2 The vector cross product

Now $\mathbf{a} = (-11, -50, -11)$ and $\mathbf{b} = (-11, 50, -11)$

$$\mathbf{a} \times \mathbf{b} = \begin{matrix} \mathbf{i} & \mathbf{j} & \mathbf{k} \\ -11 & -50 & -11 \\ -11 & 50 & -11 \end{matrix} = 1100\mathbf{i} - 0\mathbf{j} - 1100\mathbf{k}$$

and

$$\mathbf{b} \times \mathbf{a} = \begin{matrix} \mathbf{i} & \mathbf{j} & \mathbf{k} \\ -11 & 50 & -11 \\ -11 & -50 & -11 \end{matrix} = -1100\mathbf{i} - 0\mathbf{j} + 1100\mathbf{k}$$

From this example we deduce that $\mathbf{a} \times \mathbf{b} \neq \mathbf{b} \times \mathbf{a}$.

We notice from the normal $\mathbf{a} \times \mathbf{b}$ that the x-component is positive, the y-component is zero (parallel with the x-z plane) and the z-component is negative. This is shown in Fig. 4.2. Normalising the normal vector

$$= 1100/\sqrt{242 \times 10^4}\mathbf{i} - 1100/\sqrt{242 \times 10^4}\mathbf{k}$$
$$= 0.7071\mathbf{i} - 0.7071\mathbf{k}$$

where 0.7071 is the direction cosine in x-y and y-z planes (45°) and zero in the x-z plane (orthogonal to the plane of the triangle). We now follow up with an implementation of all this theory and observe how we can use it to provide an impression of shape.

4.2.3 Using the Cross Product to Provide Colour Variation to a Cylinder

In this implementation the triangular patches that we are going to use to cover our cylinder are stored in the file "inptent.dat" which is supplied on the web site. Each patch has three vertices with the corresponding values for x, y, z at each vertex.

Reading the file by eye may not seem very instructive and for more complex shapes very little could be learnt from the coordinate values alone. We now define a data structure to represent the triangles, which contains vertices (v) with (x, y, z) values plus a normal to the surface of the triangle. The definition is

```
struct polygon3 {
        float v[100][3];
        float normal;
};
```

This structure will permit us to define a new data type appropriate for operating on triangles and allow the use of colour in our model. Thus in the example we have 50 triangles of data type polygon3.

```
polygon3 triangle[50];
```

For the purposes of this example we shall imagine we are looking at the front of the cylinder and the light is behind the viewer. In this position the front of the cylinder will be brightest while as we move to the sides it will appear progressively darker.

The reader should not conceive of this as a real illumination model as that will come later, but only as an illustration of the use of a normal to give an impression of reality.

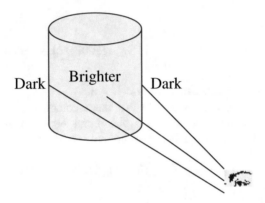

The function Normal is used to calculate the normal components for each of the (**i**, **j**, **k**) directions. In this example we have considered the normal only in the z-direction for purposes of simplicity. Each vector defining the triangle is calculated from the vertices

vect[vi][coord] = tridata[ith].v[j][coord] – tridata[ith].v[j+1][coord];

and then the z component of the normal is stored in data type representing the triangle of concern

tridata[ith].normal = abs(normz)/res;

We have normalised this component so that it always takes a value between 0 and 1. OpenGL provides the function glColor3f(red, green, blue); for drawing in a given colour where using floating-point numbers 1 is fully on and 0 is off (black). We use the blue colour component only to colour the triangular patches with the value of the normal to define the blueness of each triangle.

```
struct polygon3 {//-----MESHtent.cpp
  float v[100][3];
  float normal;
  };

void DisplayMesh ( void ) {
glClear ( GL_COLOR_BUFFER_BIT );
ifstream inptri("inptent.dat", ios::in);
int t, nt, tmax;
float red, green, blue;
polygon3 triangle[50];                    // up to 50 triangle patches
```

```
glTranslatef(50.0, 30.0, 0.0);
glBegin(GL_TRIANGLES);
  tmax = 21;   //26!;                    //read in points
  for (nt=1; nt<=tmax; nt++) {      //for each triangle
        for (t=nt-1; t<=nt+1; t++) {  //3 vertices
                inptri >> triangle[nt].v[t][0];
                inptri >> triangle[nt].v[t][1];
                inptri >> triangle[nt].v[t][2];
        }
  Normals(triangle, nt);
    // Illustrate mesh shape
  blue = triangle[nt].normal; red=0.0; green=0.0;
  glColor3f(red, green, blue);
  for (t=nt-1; t<=nt+1; t++)  glVertex2f(triangle[nt].v[t][0],
  triangle[nt].v[t][1]);
}
glEnd();
glFlush();
}


void Normals( polygon3 tridata[], int ith)
{
int vi, coord, j, vst, vfin;
float vect[100][3], normx, normy, normz, res;
vst = 2 * ith - 2;
vfin = vst + 1;
if (ith > 40) cout << "Too many triangles - increase vect size\n";
j=ith-1;
for(vi=vst; vi<=vfin; vi++) {
  for (coord=0; coord<=2; coord++) {
vect[vi][coord] = tridata[ith].v[j][coord]
- tridata[ith].v[j+1][coord];
  }
  j++;
}
normx = vect[vst][1] * vect[vfin][2] - vect[vst][2] * vect[vfin][1];
normy = vect[vst][0] * vect[vfin][2] - vect[vst][2] * vect[vfin][0];
normz = vect[vst][0] * vect[vfin][1] - vect[vst][1] * vect[vfin][0];
res = normx * normx + normy * normy + normz * normz;
res = sqrt(res);
tridata[ith].normal = abs( normz )/ res;
return;
}
```

We shall return to the use of the normal when we consider Gouraud shading in Chapter 7.

4.3 Coordinate Systems

Up to this point we have considered vertices and vectors in a fixed and rather inflexible manner and some readers will have noticed that the output in the preceding section was translated to a location (50, 30) with no apparent explanation! While simplicity aids our initial understanding we will now move to a more general representation that will fit the vectors into a frame of reference that will later permit animation, magnification and all round viewing. We also need to clearly distinguish between points (x, y, z) and vectors that we found from subtracting points. Points have a location in space with no magnitude or direction while vectors are characterised by magnitude and direction but not a particular location.

The spatial coordinate system we are all familiar with is our seemingly three-dimensional world. For most of the time this concept works well with three directions specified by the axes frequently denoted by the shorthand (x, y, z) but more correctly by $(\mathbf{i}, \mathbf{j}, \mathbf{k})$, the axis unit vectors. Although we write the origin as (0, 0, 0), it should be remembered that this frame of reference resides somewhere in the universe and our reference frame is always relative to some other location in space. To manipulate points and vectors using the same objects of direction $(\mathbf{i}, \mathbf{j}, \mathbf{k})$ and position (0, 0, 0), we homogenise the representation of points and vectors.

A vector $\mathbf{a}$ requires three scalars and is represented as

$$\mathbf{a} = (x_1 - x_2)\mathbf{i} + (y_1 - y_2)\mathbf{j} + (z_1 - z_2)\mathbf{k}$$

where as a point P is any offset (x, y, z) from the origin as shown in Fig. 4.1. We can rewrite our representations in the form of row and column vectors as

$$\mathbf{a} = (\mathbf{i}, \mathbf{j}, \mathbf{k}, w) \begin{pmatrix} x_1 - x_2) \\ y_1 - y_2) \\ z_1 - z_2) \\ 0 \end{pmatrix} \quad \text{and} \quad P = (\mathbf{i}, \mathbf{j}, \mathbf{k}, w) \begin{pmatrix} x \\ y \\ z \\ 1 \end{pmatrix}$$

where w is our origin. This is called a **homogenous representation** and the fourth component enables graphical operations to be performed. Although the data structure for points and vectors is the same they transform very differently and students should always use the homogenous representation in order to avoid major errors occurring.

4.4 Transformations

A transformation T is the process of moving a point in 3D space from one position to another. If a number of points are involved all belonging to the same object then we will have moved the object in some fashion. Consider two points P and Q in Fig. 4.3

Now in our homogenous representation

$$P = \begin{pmatrix} x_1 \\ y_1 \\ z_1 \\ 1 \end{pmatrix} \quad \text{and} \quad Q = \begin{pmatrix} x_2 \\ y_2 \\ z_2 \\ 1 \end{pmatrix}$$

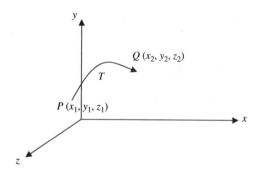

Fig. 4.3 Moving points in space

The transformation from P to Q is

$$\begin{pmatrix} x_2 \\ y_2 \\ z_2 \\ 1 \end{pmatrix} = T \begin{pmatrix} x_1 \\ y_1 \\ z_1 \\ 1 \end{pmatrix}$$

where T is the required transformation function. Typical *linear transformations* used in graphics and imaging include object rotation, translation and scaling are referred to as **Affine Transformations**. If we wished to move an object a distance (d_x, d_y, d_z) then the point Q is

$$
\begin{pmatrix} x_2 \\ y_2 \\ z_2 \\ 1 \end{pmatrix} = \begin{pmatrix} x_1 + d_x \\ y_1 + d_y \\ z_1 + d_z \\ 1 \end{pmatrix}
$$

To achieve this use a matrix containing values (d_x, d_y, d_z) to multiply the *vector representation* of P.

$$
\begin{pmatrix} x_1 + d_x \\ y_1 + d_y \\ z_1 + d_z \\ 1 \end{pmatrix} = \begin{pmatrix} 1 & 0 & 0 & d_x \\ 0 & 1 & 0 & d_y \\ 0 & 0 & 1 & d_z \\ 0 & 0 & 0 & 1 \end{pmatrix} \begin{pmatrix} x_1 \\ y_1 \\ z_1 \\ 1 \end{pmatrix}
$$

The glTranslate* (d_x, d_y, d_z)[1] function provides this facility. Scaling permits the magnification of an image in the same way by multiplying the point P by some scale are intuitive but we will need a little more effort to develop the rotational matrices. If the scale parameters are set negative, we will develop a reflection about an axis. factor to transform it to point Q.

$$
\begin{pmatrix} x_2 \\ y_2 \\ z_2 \\ 1 \end{pmatrix} = \begin{pmatrix} s_x & 0 & 0 & 0 \\ 0 & s_y & 0 & 0 \\ 0 & 0 & s_z & 0 \\ 0 & 0 & 0 & 1 \end{pmatrix} \begin{pmatrix} x_1 \\ y_1 \\ z_1 \\ 1 \end{pmatrix}
$$

The glScale*(s_x, s_y, s_z)[1] provides this facility. The matrices for translation and scaling.

4.4.1 Rotation

Consider the point $P (x_1, y_1, z_1)$ to be rotated to point $Q (x_2, y_2, z_2)$ in Fig. 4.4.

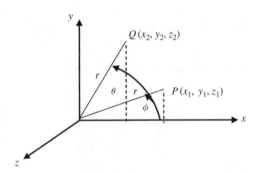

Fig. 4.4 Rotating points in space

---

[1] * denotes the data type of the function arguments

Now $\qquad x_1 = r \cos\phi$ and $y_1 = r \sin\phi$

similarly $\qquad x_2 = r \cos(\theta + \phi) = r \cos\theta \cos\phi - r \sin\phi \sin\theta$

and $\qquad y_2 = r \sin(\theta + \phi) = r \sin\theta \cos\phi + r \cos\theta \sin\phi$

We can eliminate reference to ϕ since we know the initial position of P at (x_1, y_1, z_1) by substituting for $\sin\phi$ and $\cos\phi$, therefore

$$x_2 = x_1 \cos\theta - y_1 \sin\theta$$
$$y_2 = x_1 \sin\theta + y_1 \cos\theta$$

which in matrix notation is

$$\begin{pmatrix} x_2 \\ y_2 \end{pmatrix} = \begin{pmatrix} \cos\theta & -\sin\theta \\ \sin\theta & +\cos\theta \end{pmatrix} \begin{pmatrix} x_1 \\ y_1 \end{pmatrix}$$

From Fig. 4.4 it is noted that as θ increases the rotation is counter clockwise about the *origin*. For the general case of rotation about the z-axis in any plane parallel to the x–y plane the matrix representation of rotation is

$$\begin{pmatrix} x_2 \\ y_2 \\ z_2 \\ 1 \end{pmatrix} = \begin{pmatrix} \cos\theta & -\sin\theta & 0 & 0 \\ \sin\theta & \cos\theta & 0 & 0 \\ 0 & 0 & 1 & 0 \\ 0 & 0 & 1 & 1 \end{pmatrix} \begin{pmatrix} x_1 \\ y_1 \\ z_1 \\ 1 \end{pmatrix}$$

In OpenGl this represented by glRotate*(θ, 0, 0, 1); where the angle θ is in radians[2] and the z parameter is set to 1 to indicate rotation about the z-axis.

The rotational matrices about the x (in y-z plane)and y (in x-z plane) axes can be defined from the symmetry requirements of operations.

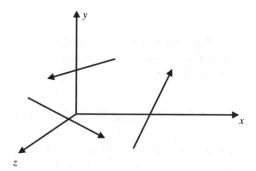

Fig. 4.5 Symmetry associated with rotational matrices

----

[2] $180° = \pi$ (3.14159265) radians

Since positive angular increases are counter clockwise, the y coordinates in the x-plane become z coordinates in the y-z plane and the x coordinates become the corresponding y coordinates.

$$
\begin{array}{ll}
\left[\begin{array}{l} x_2 = x_1\cos\theta - y_1\sin\theta \\ y_2 = x_1\sin\theta + y_1\cos\theta \end{array}\right. & \text{In } x\text{-}y \text{ plane} \\[2em]
\left. \begin{array}{l} y_2 = y_1\cos\theta - z_1\sin\theta \\ z_2 = y_1\sin\theta + z_1\cos\theta \end{array}\right] & \text{In } y\text{-}z \text{ plane}
\end{array}
$$

The matrix representation about the x-axis that is in the y-z plane is similar

$$
\begin{pmatrix} x_2 \\ y_2 \\ z_2 \\ 1 \end{pmatrix} =
\begin{pmatrix}
1 & 0 & 0 & 0 \\
0 & \cos\theta & -\sin\theta & 0 \\
0 & \sin\theta & \cos\theta & 0 \\
0 & 0 & 0 & 1
\end{pmatrix}
\begin{pmatrix} x_1 \\ y_1 \\ z_1 \\ 1 \end{pmatrix}
$$

which is glRotate*$(\theta, 1, 0, 0)$;

The symmetry for the x-z plane is perhaps a little more obscure. The counter clockwise rotation above means that moving from the x-y plane to the y-z plane, the coordinates $x \to y$ and $y \to z$ in the rotational matrix as shown in Fig. 4.5. In the same way in moving from the y-z plane to the x-z plane $y \to z$ and $z \to x$ and thus

$$
z_2 = z_1\cos\theta - x_1\sin\theta
$$
$$
x_2 = z_1\sin\theta + x_1\cos\theta
$$

The corresponding matrix rotation in the z-x plane is

$$
\begin{pmatrix} x_2 \\ y_2 \\ z_2 \\ 1 \end{pmatrix} =
\begin{pmatrix}
\cos\theta & 0 & \sin\theta & 0 \\
0 & 1 & 0 & 0 \\
-\sin\theta & 0 & \cos\theta & 0 \\
0 & 0 & 0 & 1
\end{pmatrix}
\begin{pmatrix} x_1 \\ y_1 \\ z_1 \\ 1 \end{pmatrix}
$$

which is glRotate*$(\theta, 0, 0, 1)$ in OpenGl.

It should be noted that all of the rotations discussed so far are about the *origin* of the frame of reference.

4.4.2 A Simple Example of Rotation

In the following example we have drawn a rectangle and rotated it at 30 increments about the z-axis (in green) followed by three more rotations about the x-axis (in red). The question of just what has been rotated about the origin is now apparent and Fig. 4.6 does not provide an intuitive understanding.

Fig. 4.6 An illustration of
rotation about the z-axis
followed by the x-axis

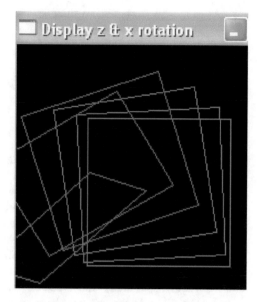

```
void Display ( void ) { // rotate.cpp
glClear ( GL_COLOR_BUFFER_BIT );
glColor3f(0.0, 1.0, 0.0);
glMatrixMode    ( GL_MODELVIEW ) ;
glLoadIdentity ( ) ;
for(angle=0; angle <18; angle=angle + 3) {
glRotatef( angle, 0.0, 0.0, 1.0);
if (angle > 8) {
        glRotatef( angle*2, 1.0, 0.0, 0.0);
        glColor3f(1.0, 0.0, 0.0);
}
glBegin(GL_LINE_LOOP);
    glVertex2f(0.25, 0.25);
    glVertex2f(0.75, 0.25);
    glVertex2f(0.75, 0.75);
    glVertex2f(0.25, 0.75);
glEnd();
}
glFlush();
}
```

4.4.3 General Rotations About Any Point

In the previous example Fig. 4.6, the green square is initially rotated about the z-axis. It was noted however that the bottom left hand corner does not stay in the fixed position expected. To perform a general rotation the reader must first remember that

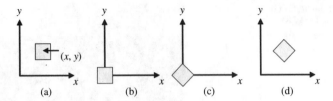

Fig. 4.7 Process of rotation of points

all the rotational matrix derivations were defined from rotation about the origin. In
general we will require rotations about arbitrary points that are of interest to users.
To achieve this requirement we translate the axis of rotation to the origin, perform
the rotation and translate the axis back to the original position using matrices already
defined for translation (Section 4.1). By specifying the point on the object in this
manner through which the axis of rotation passes we get a much clearer picture of
what to expect as a result of rotation. In the following example, rotation is about the
top right hand corner of the square and 4 increments, each of 3° are implemented.
The sequence of operation is illustrated in Fig. 4.7.

In (a) we illustrate the original object position and in (b) the translation to the
origin of the location in the object where rotation is to be applied. Rotation is applied
(c) and we then translate back to an appropriate position in the window. In matrix
notation this is represented as

$$\mathbf{T}(x, y)\mathbf{R}_z(\theta)\mathbf{T}(-x, -y)$$

where in OpenGl the functions used are

glTranslate*(x, y, 0.0);
glRotate*(θ, 0, 0, 1);
glTranslate*(−x, −y, 0.0);

In the following example the rectangle is from bottom left (0.25, 0.25) to top right
(0.75, 0.75) and rotated in 3° increments.

```
// rotateaboutvertex.cpp
void Display ( void ) {
glClear ( GL_COLOR_BUFFER_BIT );
glColor3f(0.0, 1.0, 0.0);
for(angle=0; angle <10; angle=angle + 3) {
glTranslatef(.75f, 0.75f, 0.0f);
glRotatef( angle, 0.0, 0.0, 1.0);
glTranslatef(-0.75f, -0.75f, 0.0f);
   glBegin(GL_LINE_LOOP);
     glVertex3f(0.25, 0.25, 0.0);
     glVertex3f(0.75, 0.25, 0.0);
```

```
      glVertex3f(0.75, 0.75, 0.0);
      glVertex3f(0.25, 0.75, 0.0);
   glEnd();
}
glFlush();
}
```

We have used floating-point representation of the square where in our 250×250 pixel window the top right hand corner of the square is $\sim(188,188)$.

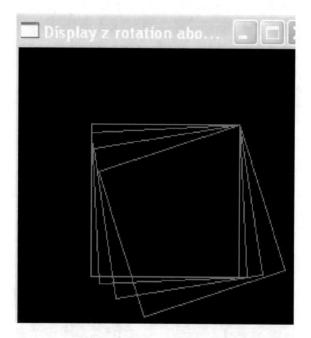

It is informative to develop this program by experimenting with combinations of rotations about all three axes to confirm ones visual expectation. Visual expectation can be erroneous and experimenting at an early stage, will frequently aid the understanding of more complex views later on. In the following code for the display function we have allowed the square to rotate about two axes and change colour with each rotation.

```
void Display ( void ) {
GLfloat red;
glClear ( GL_COLOR_BUFFER_BIT );
glColor3f(0.0, 1.0, 0.0);
red = 0.3;
for(angle=0; angle < 25; angle=angle + 3) {
if( angle < 10 ) {
```

```
glTranslatef(.75f, 0.75f, 0.0f);
glRotatef( angle, 0.0, 0.0, 1.0);
glTranslatef(-0.75f, -0.75f, 0.0f);
}
if( angle > 9 ) {
          red = red + 0.1;
          glColor3f(red, 0.0, 0.0);
          glTranslatef(.75f, 0.75f, 0.0f);
          glRotatef( angle, 1.0, 0.0, 0.0);
          glRotatef( angle/2.0, 0.0, 0.0, 1.0);
          glTranslatef(-0.75f, -0.75f, 0.0f);
          }
  glBegin(GL_LINE_LOOP);
    glVertex3f(0.25, 0.25, 0.0);
    glVertex3f(0.75, 0.25, 0.0);
    glVertex3f(0.75, 0.75, 0.0);
    glVertex3f(0.25, 0.75, 0.0);
  glEnd();
}
glFlush();
}
```

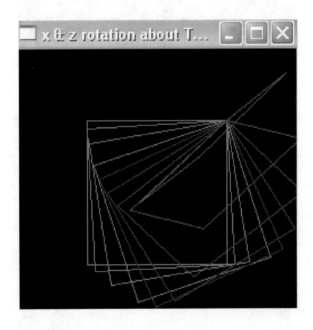

4.5 The Model View Matrix

The three operations of translation, rotation and scaling enable us to manipulate the vertices of an object and in combination are referred to as the **current transformation** (4×4) **matrix**. These are the matrix operations that combine to give the model or view of the object we see on the screen. We shall also include projection and the effect of perspective a little later, but for now concentrate on the modelling orientation of the object.

Up to this point we have discussed the three modelling operations while treating where the matrix they result from as a bit of a 'black box'. In order to perform the modelling operations we require space for the matrix and because there may be many operations of different parts of an artefact such as a robot, we may need to stack them up for purposes of animation. The function glMatrixMode (GL_MODELVIEW); specifies that we require space for a 4×4 matrix to be used for setting up the view of the model and in common with all the derived matrices we initialise the model view matrix to the identity matrix with glLoadIdentity( );. Schematically this is written as

Object vertices ⟶ MODELVIEW ⟶ Model vertices

In the preceding examples the model view matrix was initialised in function MyInit() and the matrix operations were formulated in the function Display() together with the object vertices.

4.6 Adding Some Movement

We introduced some simple movement in this chapter when we looked at transformations and now we will generalise this motion with control both by the keyboard and mouse. We must first however consider movement in a little more detail and how we may make a series movements, which in total may result in a quite complex trajectory. The projection and model view matrices are the mathematical representation of some movement (viewer or object). Thus any movement is the result of a number of separate matrix operations that individually contribute the to total object movement that is required. A useful way to think of movement is as a stack of homogenous (4×4) matrix operations. If we wanted to move between two points we might use a single function glTranslate(), but if there was an obstacle in the way might have to use glTranslate() several times as we feel our way around the obstacle. In other words, there is a stack of matrix operations for motion depending on the nature of the movement required and this may well include a combination of rotation and translation used in a non-deterministic manner. Earlier in this chapter we noted that the rotation matrix was defined about the origin and if we were at some point away from this, then we first had to translate to the origin, perform the rotation and move back to where we were. What is needed is some way of separating these activities so that we know where we are and when to come back there! The stack is a means of storing and discarding matrix operations associated with movement and we use the functions glPushMatrix() and glPopMatrix() to achieve the operations.

glPushMatrix() copies or adds the last matrix operation on to a stack and this represents where we currently are in the progression of the object movement.

glPopMatrix() pops or destroys the last matrix on the stack, which is equivalent to going from where we are in the object movement back to the previous situation.

Object movement can be considered as a number of simple movements that are combined through the use of glPushMatrix() and glPopMatrix() to produce the resultant movement. The first matrix in the stack is the identity matrix, which is used for initialisation. In general movement may be written as

```
do {
   glPushMatrix()
      move the object to new position
      display the object
   glPopMatrix()
} while( more movement is required)
```

If the object is made up of several moving components operating independently (e.g. a robot animation) then a number of sections of code, each bracketed by glPush-Matrix() and glPopMatrix() will be required for each of the moving components contributing to the total object movement.

4.6.1 Movement of Composite Objects

So far we have moved a simple object such as a square in a predictable manner. Objects in every day life are much more complex and made up from a number of differing components with different functions which combine to form the resulting action. Examples that we might consider are a robot arm with joints and fingers; an internal combustion engine with pistons, valves, crankshaft and connecting rods or an Orrery demonstrating planetary motion. Each component acts for purposes of display independently of all others even when connected by joints or acted upon by external forces (e.g. gravity, friction). In order to model behaviour we need to define the components, organise the linkages between components and provide some means of specifying movement of each component. We shall consider the three examples in a little more detail and develop these functions.

4.6.2 The Orrery

An Orrery is a mechanical model representation of the motion of the planets in our solar system and was very popular in Victorian times. The solar system we shall develop will be simplified since the physics is complex and we are finding that new planets and moons are being discovered, particularly with the use of the Hubble telescope (see www.nasa.gov). The Orrery will allow us to examine facilities to

move objects using the OpenGl routines of glPushMatrix(); glTranslatef(......);
glRotatef(.........); and glPopMatrix();
What follows is a simple model of a sun, planets and moons with simplification in
respect of the following:

– all planets orbit in the same plane
– linear scaling is not possible for all planets simultaneously if we wish to distinguish each, including moons on one screen
– we shall not include orbit variation with time and effects of precession

In the example we rotate a blue sphere (Planet) around a yellow sphere (Sun) in
an elliptical orbit. Since this is the only matrix operation, there is no need for
the glPushMatrix();/glPopMatrix(); operations as there are no other independent
movements that require matrix manipulation. The elliptical movement of planets
is described by a point in the x-y plane.

where $x = 120.0^* \sin(\theta)$ and $y = 40.0^* \cos(\theta)$
with the semi major and semi minor axes being 120 and 40 respectively.
The blue sphere (planet) is moved to this position by

glTranslatef(120.0* sin(thetar), 40.0 *cos(thetar), 0.0);

in the x-y plane ($z = 0$). The examples being considered all have some real time
motion which will vary with the processor speed of your computer and readers
will have to adjust timing parameters accordingly. In this example we shall use
the glutTimerFunc(param1, TimerFunc, 1) function where param1 is a time delay
(milliseconds) before the callback function TimerFunc is called.
    One of the blue spheres has a green sphere representing a moon rotating about
it in a circular orbit. Since the moon has a center of rotation about the planet they
have a combined motion, which in turn rotates about the sun. This combined activity
means that the modelview matrix describing the moons motion must be separated
from the matrix describing the planet rotation about the sun using glPushMatrix()
and glPopMatrix().

```
void DrawIt(void)          //sunellipsemoon.cpp
{
float d2r;
// Angle of revolution around Sun
static float theta = 0.0, thetar, phi = 0.0, phir = 0.0;
        d2r = 3.14159265 / 180.0;
```

```
            thetar = theta * d2r;
            phir = phi * d2r;

            glClear(GL_COLOR_BUFFER_BIT | GL_DEPTH_BUFFER_BIT);
            glMatrixMode(GL_MODELVIEW);
            glLoadIdentity();

            glTranslatef(0.0, 0.0, -10.0);
            glColor3ub(255, 255, 0);   // yellow Sun
            glutSolidSphere(30.0f, 15, 15);

// Planet Orbit
glPushMatrix();
     glColor3ub(0,0,255);              // blue Planet
            // Translate from origin to orbit distance
     glTranslatef(50.0 + 120.0* sin(thetar), 40.0 *cos(thetar), 0.0f);
     glutSolidSphere(6.0f, 15, 15);

//moon orbit
     glColor3ub(0, 255,255);      // Green moon (cheese!)
     glTranslatef(-120.0* sin(thetar), -40.0 *cos(thetar), 0.0f);
     glTranslatef(20.0* sin(phir*0.75), 20.0 *cos(phir*0.75), 0.0);
     //move moon
     glTranslatef(120.0* sin(thetar), 40.0 *cos(thetar), 0.0);
     glutSolidSphere(3.0f, 15, 15);
     phi +=20.0;
glPopMatrix();
//second planet
glPushMatrix();
     glColor3ub(0,0,255);              // Blue Planet
     // Translate from origin to orbit distance
     glTranslatef(40.0* sin(thetar*0.5), 40.0 *cos(thetar*0.5), 0.0);
     glutSolidSphere(7.0f, 15, 15);
glPopMatrix();

//Third planet
glPushMatrix();
   glColor3ub(255,0,255);              // Pink Planet
               // Translate from origin to orbit distance
   glTranslatef(60.0* sin(thetar*0.25), 60.0 *cos(thetar*0.25), 0.0);
   glutSolidSphere(5.0f, 15, 15);
glPopMatrix();

   theta += 10.0;
   glutSwapBuffers(); // motion=swap+redraw
}
```

```
void TimerFunc(int value)
{
  glutPostRedisplay();
  glutTimerFunc(50, TimerFunc, 1);
}
```

Output from this program is given in Fig. 4.8.

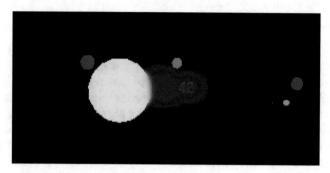

Fig. 4.8 An example of planetary motion

4.6.3 The Internal Combustion Engine

We now develop an example of cyclical motion involving the components of the engine – particularly the crank, connecting (con) rod and piston. An engine works on 4 cycles: induction (fuel input), compression (mixture of fuel + air compressed), ignition (power output from burning mixture) and exhaust (removal of burnt products, CO, CO_2 etc from cylinder).

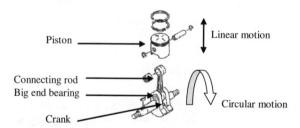

Diagrammatically the main components of an engine are illustrated where the linear motion of the piston is converted to circular motion by means of the crank. The four strokes (phases) of the complete engine cycle will be animated graphically.

4.6.3.1 The Internal Combustion Engine – Component Motion

A single cylinder engine may be considered to be composed of three motion components: the piston, the connecting rod and the crank each with different motion profiles. While the piston moves linearly in an up and down motion, the crank rotates

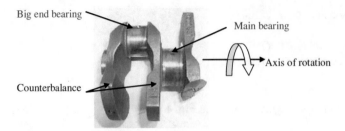

Fig. 4.9 Crank component showing big end connection

circularly about the axis of the crankshaft. This is achieved by having the big end bearings offset from the axis of rotation running through the centre of the main bearings of the crankshaft. These features on part of a crankshaft are shown in Fig. 4.9.

The final component, the connecting rod, moves linearly at one end and in a circular locus at the other end by means of the offset big end bearing. We represent this motion inside each matrix manipulation (Push → Pop) for each engine component with the corresponding rotation, scaling and translation operations that define the movement of the respective components.

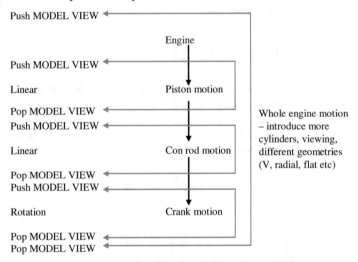

Internal combustion engines operate by converting the linear motion of one end of the connecting rod (piston) to rotary motion of the other end by means of the crankshaft and drive to the gearbox via a clutch. This motion is shown in Fig. 4.10

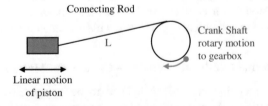

where L is the length of the connecting rod. We redraw the geometry of motion.

Fig. 4.10 Animating the con
rod motion

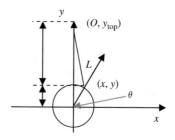

If the crank radius is denoted by r, then from Fig. 4.10 the position of the top of
the connecting rod y_{top} is

$$y_{top} = y + \sqrt{L^2 - x^2}$$
$$= r\,\sin(\theta) + \sqrt{L^2 - r^2 \cos^2(\theta)}$$

while $x = 0$ for linear motion at the top end of rod. The locus of the motion for the
lower end of the connecting rod is determined by the connecting point of the big
end of the crankshaft at

$$(r\,\cos(\theta), r\,\sin(\theta))$$

with the angle of rotation θ moving through complete rotations of 0–2π radians.
The following program is a simple implementation of one cylinder operation and
if modified to be an object, readers will be able to build multi cylinder engines of
different designs. Students have also added cylinders and varied the colour depending on which part of the cycle the piston is operating (inlet, compression, power and
exhaust).

```
static GLfloat xRot = 0.0;              //pist_lit.cpp
static GLfloat yRot = 0.0;
char thetachar[3];
float theta = 0.0, degtorads = 0.0174532925;

void DisplayPiston ( void );
void MyInit     ( ) ;
void Bang();
void Int2Char(int );

void Bang( void)
{
glColor3f(1.0, 0.0, 0.0);
glBegin(GL_POINTS);
 glVertex2f(0.0,12.0);
glEnd();
glFlush();
```

```
glPointSize(10.0);
}


void Int2Char(int number)
{      //integer -> char for graphics o/p
char charnum[10] = {'0','1','2','3','4','5','6','7','8','9'};
int n1, n2, n3;
n1 = number % 10;
n2 = number - n1;
n2 = n2 % 100;
n3 = number - n2 - n1;
n2 = n2 / 10;
n3 = n3 / 100;
thetachar[0] = charnum[n1];
thetachar[1] = charnum[n2];
thetachar[2] = charnum[n3];
}


void DisplayPiston( void ) {
char xang[9] = {'T','h','e','t','a','='};
int i;
GLfloat x, y, xtop, ytop, crank_rad, crank_rad2, con_lenth;
GLUquadricObj *cylobj;
glClear( GL_COLOR_BUFFER_BIT);
Int2Char( (int) theta);
xang[6] = thetachar[2];
if( xang[6] == '0') xang[6] = ' ';
xang[7] = thetachar[1];
xang[8] = thetachar[0];
glColor3f(1.0, 0.0, 0.0);
for(i=0; i<9; i++) {
 glRasterPos3f(3.1+i*0.8, 0.0, 0.0);
 glutBitmapCharacter(GLUT_BITMAP_HELVETICA_18, xang[i]);
}
//  rotation of whole systen
glPushMatrix();
        glRotatef(xRot, 1.0, 0.0, 0.0);
        glRotatef(yRot, 0.0, 1.0, 0.0);
        glPushMatrix();       //ignition
                if(theta >75.0 && theta <95.0) Bang();
   glPopMatrix();

   glPushMatrix();   //Rectf axes centred on origin
     glColor3f(0.0, 1.0, 0.0);
     glTranslatef( 0.0, -2.0, 0.0);
```

```
      glRectf(5.0, 0.2, -5.0, -0.2);
      glRotatef(90.0, 0.0, 0.0, 1.0);
      glRectf(5.0, 0.2, -5.0, -0.2);
    glPopMatrix();

glPushMatrix();      //con rod
  crank_rad = 2.0;
  con_lenth = 6.0;
  xtop = 0.0;
  glColor3f(1.0, 0.0, 0.0);
  glBegin(GL_LINES);
    x = crank_rad *  cos(theta*degtorads);
    y = crank_rad *  sin(theta*degtorads);
    ytop = y + sqrt(con_lenth*con_lenth - x*x);
    glVertex2f(x, y-2.0);
    glVertex2f(xtop, ytop+1.0);
  glEnd();
glPopMatrix();

  cylobj = gluNewQuadric();
  gluQuadricDrawStyle(cylobj, GLU_FILL);
  gluQuadricNormals(cylobj, GLU_FLAT);
  glColor3f(0.6, 0.6, 0.6);
glPushMatrix();      // piston
  glRotatef(-90.0, 1.0, 0.0, 0.0);
  glTranslatef( xtop, 0.0, ytop); //z now in y direction
  gluCylinder(cylobj, 1.0, 1.5, 3.0, 10, 8);
glPopMatrix();
glPushMatrix();    //line crank
  crank_rad2 = crank_rad * 0.5;
  glColor3f(0.0, 0.0, 1.0);
  glTranslatef( 0.0, -2.0, 0.0);
  glRotatef(theta , 0.0, 0.0, 1.0);
  glTranslatef( crank_rad2, 0.0, 0.0);
  glRectf(-crank_rad2, 0.1, crank_rad2, -0.1);
                  glColor3f(1.0, 1.0, 0.0);
        glPushMatrix();  //solid crank
              glScalef (1.5, 0.6, 0.5);
              glutSolidCube (1.0);
        glPopMatrix();
  glPopMatrix();
glutSwapBuffers();
glPopMatrix();
}
```

```
void MyInit ( void ) {
  glClearColor    ( 1.0, 1.0, 1.0, 0.0 ) ;
  glColor3f(1.0, 0.0, 0.0);
  glLineWidth(5.0);
  glShadeModel(GL_FLAT);
}

void ArrowKeys(int key, int x, int y)
{
        if(key == GLUT_KEY_UP) xRot-= 5.0;
        if(key == GLUT_KEY_DOWN) xRot += 5.0;
        if(key == GLUT_KEY_LEFT) yRot -= 5.0;
        if(key == GLUT_KEY_RIGHT) yRot += 5.0;
        if(key > 356.0) xRot = 0.0;
        if(key < -1.0)  xRot = 355.0;
        if(key > 356.0) yRot = 0.0;
        if(key < -1.0)  yRot = 355.0;
  glutPostRedisplay();
}

void wo_wo_wo()
{
int i, j;
for(i=0; i<900000; i++) j=0; //slow dowm!
  theta = theta + 0.5;
  if(theta>=720.0) theta-=720;
  glutPostRedisplay();
}
void reshape (int w, int h)
{
 glViewport (0, 0, (GLsizei) w, (GLsizei) h);
 glMatrixMode (GL_PROJECTION);
 glLoadIdentity ();
 glOrtho(-11.0, 11.0, -11.0, 13.0, 11.0, -11.0);
 glMatrixMode(GL_MODELVIEW);
 glLoadIdentity();
}
```

In this example, Fig. 4.11 we have also provided running output of the variation of θ with piston position and an indicator of when to ignite the mixture before top dead centre of the compression stroke.

There is also a facility to rotate the whole scene to view from different positions using the arrow keys. Readers should note that double buffering is used as the amount of change between each redisplay is such that single buffering would cause a very unstable picture.

Fig. 4.11 Elementary engine
display

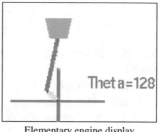

Elementary engine display

4.6.4 Arms, Robots, Actuators and Movement

In this example, which is developed from the example in (Shreiner, 2006), a robot
arm may be considered as composed of an upper arm connected to a main body at
the shoulder; a lower arm connected at the elbow to the upper arm; a hand connected
at the wrist to the lower arm; fingers made up from three sections connected to
the hand. We can use the functions glutWireCube or glutSolidSphere, glTranslate,
glRotate, glScale, glPush/PopMatrix to construct and move each component making
up the arm.

The physical structure might be represented as a tree like structure where each
node represents both the component and the code associated with movement control.

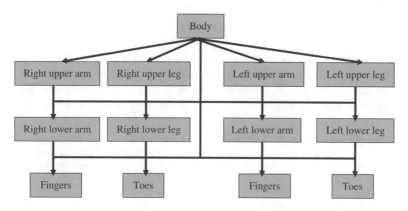

The arrows indicate the possible movements being either localised (say fingers
only) or more complex to include arm and finger movement. It must be remembered that when constructing the model, each component can move independently
of all others and the modelview matrices used to encapsulate the total movement
must be separate. We achieve this by use of a stack where the matrix associated
with any given movement is put on or taken off the stack as and when movement
control is required for the component. The stack operations facilitating independent
movement are

              glPushMatrix();
              // Surround each independent moving object

```
                    // glPushMatrix and glPopMatrix functions
                    glPopMatrix();
```

The order of tree traversal governs the type and complexity of the movement being modelled.

Earlier in this chapter we drew a square at different orientations but all was fixed and static. The present applications are cyclical in that they repeat over time in much the same way, generally only changing a little with time and for this we use the glutIdleFunc(IdleCallback) and glutPostRedisplay() functions. The glutPostRedisplay() function redraws with window contents as a result of some changes. The glutIdleFunc(IdleCallback) enables a new display after global variables have been changed which is ideal for animating a process. In the first example we develop the idea of a walking robot using only the legs so as to shorten the program for purposes of clarity. Our first task is to capture the data associated with leg movement for later use in the animation and readers should note that this process has a wider applicability for robotic control and analysis of motion. While many applications are repeatable this is not always the case and the process described also has application where for example there is disability with walking and replacement artificial limbs are required.

4.6.5 Data Capture of Limb Movement

In practice limb movement would be captured from camera images by noting either Cartesian coordinates or angular movement through a series of the frames. We will simulate this by using ASCII keys to move each upper and lower leg by 5-degree intervals and store that motion by means of a character as shown in the following table.

	Upper left leg	Lower left leg	Upper right leg	Lower right leg
Forward 5°	L	K	R	E
Backwards 5°	l	k	r	e

By writing these movements as characters to file we are storing the trajectory of movement for later use.

```
ofstream movement("movetest.txt");

void savemoves(unsigned char move)
{
    movement.put(move);
}
```

```
void keyboard (unsigned char key, int x, int y)
{
switch (key) {
   case 'l':
     luleg = (luleg + 5) % 360;
     savemoves(key);
     glutPostRedisplay();
     break;
   case 'L':
     luleg = (luleg - 5) % 360;
     savemoves(key);
     glutPostRedisplay();
     break;
   case 'k':
     llleg = (llleg + 5) % 360;
     savemoves(key);
     glutPostRedisplay();
     break;
   case 'K':
     llleg = (llleg - 5) % 360;
     savemoves(key);
     glutPostRedisplay();
     break;
   case 'r':
     ruleg = (ruleg + 5) % 360;
     savemoves(key);
     glutPostRedisplay();
     break;
   case 'R':
     ruleg = (ruleg - 5) % 360;
     savemoves(key);
     glutPostRedisplay();
     break;
   case 'e':
     rlleg = (rlleg + 5) % 360;
     savemoves(key);
     glutPostRedisplay();
     break;
   case 'E':
     rlleg = (rlleg - 5) % 360;
     savemoves(key);
     glutPostRedisplay();
     break;
   case 27:  // esc
     movement.put('Z');
```

```
      exit(0);
      break;
   default:
      break;
 }
}
```

The file will be a string of characters depending on the motion of each limb. The writing of the character 'Z' at the end of the string is to indicate End of File as the author has experienced system inconsistencies when using EOF between various flavours of UNIX / Linux and Windows and this has proved more robust!

4.6.6 Animation – A Walking Robot

Animation is the reverse of the data collection process and in this example we have added linear movement across the screen to give the impression of walking – perhaps down a hill. A similar effect could be achieved by moving scenery objects past the robot. All we need to do is read the file of characters that define the movement and rather than pressing keys to move the robot limbs, we use the character sequence to control the motion. The test file used in the following example is:

ReReReReRerErErErErELkLkLkLkLklKlKlKlKlK
Z

where the characters define the movement in the keyboard() function. In the Idle-Callback function we have slowed the motion down using a couple loops. We could have used the time() function but this varies with systems and loadings. Users can vary the loop size in order to get a reasonable speed of movement. The animation moves shown in Fig. 4.12 are stored in the array amoves[40] and for more complex movement this array should be increased in size.

```
//robot2.cpp
ifstream movement("movetest.txt");

unsigned char amoves[40];
static int luleg = -90, llleg = 0, ruleg = -90, rlleg = 0;
float xpos = -3.0, ypos = 3.0;
int cycle=0;

void definemove (unsigned char key)
{
 switch (key) {
```

```
  case 'l':
    luleg = luleg + 5;
                    glutPostRedisplay();
    break;
  case 'L':
    luleg = luleg - 5;
                    glutPostRedisplay();
    break;
  case 'k':
    llleg = llleg + 5;
                    glutPostRedisplay();
    break;
  case 'K':
    llleg = llleg - 5;
                    glutPostRedisplay();
    break;
  case 'r':
    ruleg = ruleg + 5;
                    glutPostRedisplay();
    break;
  case 'R':

                    ruleg = ruleg - 5;
                    glutPostRedisplay();
    break;
       case 'e':
    rlleg = rlleg + 5;
                    glutPostRedisplay();
    break;
       case 'E':
    rlleg = rlleg - 5;
                    glutPostRedisplay();
                    break;
  }
}

void readmoves()
{
unsigned char move;
int i;
i=0;
while((move=movement.get()) != 'Z') {
       amoves[i] = move;
       i++;
}
}
```

```
void IdleCallback(void)
{
long int i, j;

for(j=1; j<500; j++)     //slow down
        for(i=0; i<30000; i++) {
        }

        definemove(amoves[cycle]);

        cycle++;
        if(cycle >40) {    //repeat animation
                cycle = 0;
                xpos = xpos + 0.2;
                ypos = ypos - 0.1;
        }
        if (xpos > 3.0) {
                xpos = -3.0;
                ypos = 3.0;
        }
        glutPostRedisplay();
}

void init(void)
{
 glClearColor (0.0, 0.0, 0.0, 0.0);
 glShadeModel (GL_FLAT);
 readmoves();
}

void reshape (int w, int h)
{
 glViewport (0, 0, (GLsizei) w, (GLsizei) h);
 glMatrixMode (GL_PROJECTION);
 glLoadIdentity ();
 gluPerspective(65.0, (GLfloat) w/(GLfloat) h, 0.0, 20.0);
 glMatrixMode(GL_MODELVIEW);
 glLoadIdentity();
 glTranslatef (0.0, 0.0, -7.0);
}

void display(void)
{
 glClear (GL_COLOR_BUFFER_BIT);
 glPushMatrix();
 glColor3f(1.0f, 1.0f, 1.0f);
```

```
glTranslatef (xpos, ypos, 0.0);  //position object
glRotatef (60.0, 0.0, 1.0, 0.0); //whole object rotate
 glPushMatrix();   //body
 glScalef (0.5, 1.0, 0.5);
 glutWireCube (1.0);
 glPopMatrix();
glPushMatrix();
 glTranslatef (-0.5, 0.0, 0.0); //pivot point left upper leg
 glRotatef ( -90.0, 0.0, 0.0, 1.0);
 glRotatef ( 90.0, 0.0, 1.0, 0.0);
 glRotatef ((GLfloat) luleg, 0.0, 1.0, 0.0);
 glTranslatef (1.0, 0.0, 0.0);   //back to cube edge
 glPushMatrix();
 glScalef (2.0, 0.4, 0.7);
 glutWireCube (1.0);
 glPopMatrix();

 glTranslatef (1.0, 0.0, 0.0);      //pivot point lower leg
 glRotatef ( (GLfloat) llleg, 0.0, 1.0, 0.0);
 glTranslatef (1.0, 0.0, 0.0);
 glPushMatrix();
 glScalef (1.5, 0.3, 0.5);
 glutWireCube (1.0);
 glPopMatrix();
glPopMatrix(); // disconnected object = start again
glPushMatrix();
 glTranslatef (0.5, 0.0, 0.0);      //right upper leg
 glRotatef ( -90.0, 0.0, 0.0, 1.0);
 glRotatef ( 90.0, 0.0, 1.0, 0.0);
 glRotatef ((GLfloat) ruleg, 0.0, 1.0, 0.0);
 glTranslatef (1.0, 0.0, 0.0);
 glPushMatrix();
 glScalef (2.0, 0.4, 0.7);
 glutWireCube (1.0);
 glPopMatrix();

 glTranslatef (1.0, 0.0, 0.0);      //pivot point lower leg
 glRotatef ( (GLfloat) rlleg, 0.0, 1.0, 0.0);
 glTranslatef (1.0, 0.0, 0.0);
 glPushMatrix();
 glScalef (1.5, 0.3, 0.5);
 glutWireCube (1.0);
 glPopMatrix();
glPopMatrix(); // disconnected object = start again for further
              //objects/limbs
```

```
 glPopMatrix();
 glutSwapBuffers();
}

int main(int argc, char** argv)
{
 glutInit(&argc, argv);
 glutInitDisplayMode (GLUT_DOUBLE | GLUT_RGB);
 glutInitWindowSize (250, 250);
 glutInitWindowPosition (100, 50);
 glutCreateWindow (argv[0]);
 init ();
 glutIdleFunc(IdleCallback);
 glutDisplayFunc(display);
 glutReshapeFunc(reshape);
 glutMainLoop();
}
```

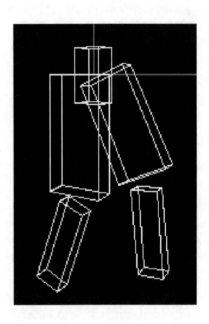

Fig. 4.12 Robot animation

4.7 Collision Detection

In everyday life we avoid collisions by observation and taking detours around obstructions, while at other times in the case of aggression we deliberately seek collisions. Collisions involve a 3D measurement between the two bodies involved

Fig. 4.13 Pyramid and plane
intersection

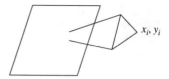

which superficially may seem trivial but at the lowest and most accurate would require a lot of calculations on pixel values. There are a number of ways we can simplify the problem which involve approximations but avoid the detail of looking at every pixel overlap between objects. In Fig. 4.13 we illustrate the interaction between a pyramid and a plane surface.

In the diagram, the apex of the pyramid has touched and passed through the plane indicating a collision between objects. If we know the equation* of the plane and the coordinates of the vertices of the pyramid then we can calculate the distance apart. This reasoning leads us to require a data structures that represent objects and is simple to manipulate in terms of object movement. Clearly in Fig. 4.13 we know nothing about the intersection points between the pyramid vertices but this error can be reduced depending on the resolution of vertex points x_i, y_i stored in the data structure. In general it is unlikely that each vertex will exactly intersect with the plane and so we calculate a minimum distance at which we say contact has occurred. The general equation* of the plane is

$$Ax + By + Cz + D = 0$$

and the perpendicular distance of a point (x_i, y_i, z_i) from the plane is given by

$$\frac{Ax_i, +By_i + Cz_i + D}{\pm\sqrt{A^2 + B^2 + C^2}}$$

If the sign of this relation is positive when D is positive, both (x_i, y_i, z_i) and the origin lie on the same side of the plane and if negative when D is negative then they lie on opposite sides of the plane. For those in need of familiarisation with relevant coordinate geometry, see also Chapter 7 and Appendix D for further details. All we need now is to capture the details of the model view matrix and apply this to each vertex of our object to give the new vertex location (see Section 5.4.2).

In this example we construct a pyramid with vertices $(-15, 0, 0)$, $(0, 30, 0)$ and $(30, 30, -60)$ and set up a plane $z = -45$ ($A = B = 0$, $D = -45$ and $C = 1$). Rotation of the pyramid will be about the x and y-axes. The initial conditions in the x-z plane with the model view matrix set to the identity matrix are shown in Fig. 4.14.

The y-axis in this view is vertically out of the plane of the paper. We can see that initially one vertex is hidden if viewed from along the positive z-axis in front of the plane and by suitable rotation about either the x or y axes it will come into view.

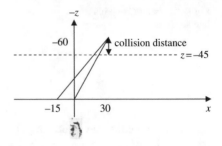

Fig. 4.14 Plan view of initial orientation of one face of pyramid

A convenient data structure for the pyramid is an array of four triangular faces, each with three vertices, specified by their Cartesian coordinates.

```
struct vertex {
        float v[3][4];
};
vertex face[4];
```

The dimension of matrix v[][] is 4 since we are using homogenous coordinate to facilitate general motion of the pyramid using the model view matrix. We store the model view matrix in a 1D vector, array[16] using.

```
glGetFloatv(GL_MODELVIEW_MATRIX, array);
```

Up to this point we have only concerned ourselves with object movement and taken little interest in the Cartesian locations of the points that define the object, except in terms of ensuring they lie within the viewing volume. We now are to consider interaction between the pyramid object in this example and a plane in z and for purposes of clarity place the 1D array containing the model view matrix in a 2D temporary array tempmv[][]. We now perform the normal 4×4 matrix multiplication operation associated with object movement as

$$sum = sum + tempmv[r][c] * face[k].v[c][ic];$$

where face[k].v[c][ic] is the vertex location associated with the k_{th} face of the pyramid. The result of these operations is stored in a collision matrix collmt[4][4], which contains the Cartesian coordinates of each vertex after movement. A collision matrix will exist for each face of our object and can be stored in a similar structure to that already defined.

```
struct mvmatrices {
        float collmt[4][4];
};
mvmatrices allfaces[4];
```

For a collision to occur we now determine the distance between the face defined by the coordinates stored in collmt[4][4] and any plane of another object. In practice we use a threshold distance between the points in the collision matrix and the other planes of interest. The action taken when the threshold condition is met depends on the application: whether exploding a missile, car crash or walking around an obstruction! In this example a message is given with the object orientation using the z-plane $z = -45$ for simplicity while rotating about the y-axis. The calculation of the collision matrix and collision detection is found in the function matrixmultiply() following.

```
void matrixmult(float a[16]) {
float tempmv[4][4], sum, colldist, threshold;
int k, r, c, ic;

struct mvmatrices {
    float collmt[4][4];
    };
mvmatrices allfaces[4];

for(r=0; r<4; r++) {
    k=0;
    for(c=r; c < 16; c=c+4) {
        tempmv[r][k] = a[c];
        k++;
    }
}
for(k=0; k<4; k++) {
    for(r=0; r<4; r++) {
        ic = 0;
        while (ic < 4) {
            sum = 0.0;
            for(c=0; c<4; c++) {
                sum = sum + tempmv[r][c] * face[k].v[c][ic];
}
        allfaces[k].collmt[r][ic] = sum;
        ic++;
        }
    }
}

//collision specific to z plane only
threshold = 5.0;
                for(k=0; k<4; k++) {
                    for(c=0; c<3; c++) {
                        for(r=0; r<4; r++) {
```

```
colldist = fabs(allfaces[k].collmt[2][c]
- 45.0);
if(colldist < threshold) cout <<"yrotation
= "<<yRot<< endl;
        }
    }
}
}
```

4.8 Exercises

1. Write a program to simulate the operation of an analogue clock with an hour, minute and second hand. Ensure that the timing of each rotation is correct in relation the hand and compare the operation with your own clock or watch.
2. Write a program to simulate the operation of a pendulum where the period of each oscillation is given by the relation

$$T = 2\pi [l/g]^{0.5}$$

where l = length of pendulum in metres and $g = 9.8$ m sec^{-2}
3. Using the software developed in Section 4.6.6, create a track and animate two or more robots racing around the track. By building the robots with different length legs (strides) you can set up winners and losers. If this choice is done randomly you can have great fun with other students developing this game.

4.9 Conclusion

In this chapter we have considered the mathematics associated with object movement and with a number of connected objects provided an introduction to robotic animation. These operations are described in OpenGl by what are called the MODELVIEW matrices. Readers unsure of the mathematics should also consult the appendices of this book to refresh their knowledge and will be adequately rewarded later as graphics applications are developed. Sample data files are discussed in relation to a walking motion and this concept can be expanded to simulate other system behaviours. The separation of the matrices providing the movement of each object has been described using the push/pop concept of the stack of operations required to illustrate the operation of a total system.

Finally we have introduced collision detection between objects as a means of considering object motion within a larger environmental framework.

Chapter 5
Viewing and Projection

5.1 Introduction

Readers may have noticed that we have included functions such as glMatrix-Mode(GL_PROJECTION) and glMatrixMode(GL_MODELVIEW) in a number of programs and treated them as 'black boxes' with little explanation. We will now begin to explore the viewing process in a little more detail as a combination of actions associated not only with movement of the object or the viewer discussed in Chapter 4, but also the space in which the object resides and how this is projected onto the screen monitor of the computer. The space in which an object resides is called the viewing volume and specified through projection view matrices, which map this space onto the screen. Projection is either parallel or perspective depending on how we wish to image the viewing volume and clipping takes place if any part of the object lies outside of the volume. A screen is by nature a two-dimensional display, while most objects are solid and three-dimensional. In this chapter we establish how to bring together these representations together to display objects.

The object to be displayed is defined by the modelview matrices, which govern object movement, position and orientation (see Chapter 4) within a viewing volume. Object vertices may be moved through rotation and translation activity in relation to the eye or camera position, which is usually considered to be at the origin. Object vertices are drawn within a viewing volume and any points outside this volume are clipped or not drawn. The projection view may be either orthographic, which is akin to viewing an object from a long distance or perspective, where a perception of depth is achieved by defining a viewing volume as part of a truncated pyramid.

5.2 Vertex Pipeline

The complete process of moving from the real world object to the corresponding screen image is accomplished by what is called the **vertex pipeline**.

The vertex pipeline is the conversion of real world coordinates (x_i, y_i, z_i) to the normalised screen view image using 4×4 matrix operations.

The Modelview matrix (4×4) multiplies object vertex coordinates and transforms to the orientation required on the screen. The projectionview matrix maps the

R. Whitrow, *OpenGL Graphics Through Applications,*
© Springer-Verlag London Limited 2008

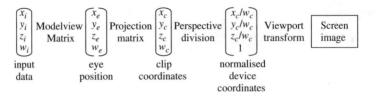

$$
\begin{pmatrix} x_i \\ y_i \\ z_i \\ w_i \end{pmatrix} \text{Modelview Matrix} \begin{pmatrix} x_e \\ y_e \\ z_e \\ w_e \end{pmatrix} \text{Projection matrix} \begin{pmatrix} x_c \\ y_c \\ z_c \\ w_c \end{pmatrix} \text{Perspective division} \begin{pmatrix} x_c/w_c \\ y_c/w_c \\ z_c/w_c \\ 1 \end{pmatrix} \text{Viewport transform} \boxed{\text{Screen image}}
$$

input   eye   clip   normalised
data   position   coordinates   device
                                 coordinates

results of the Modelview orientation into a viewing volume and after normalisation based on the window size, the image is rendered on to the screen.

5.3 The Viewing Process

Up to this point we have been concerned only with the two dimensional object and paid little attention to where the viewer is when looking at an object. The 'solidity' of an object and size with respect to the nearest and furthest points from the viewer have either been assumed or not considered. For many everyday artefacts these issues may not seem significant but when looking further, say at railway lines seemingly coming together at infinity or the size of stars in relation to their distance from earth, then viewer position is not only optically important but can also be used to make extrapolations with respect to physical measurements. The 'infinity' where the railway lines appear to join together is much less than that of the distance to the nearest stars which clearly do not appear to join together. The relative sizes of the different objects (stars and railway lines) leads us to conceive of the idea of a viewing volume in which all relevant objects may be displayed.

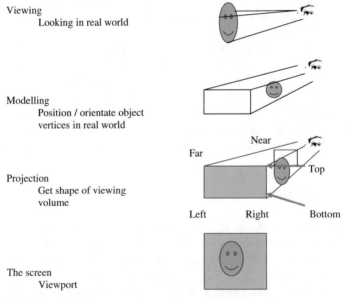

Viewing
    Looking in real world

Modelling
    Position / orientate object
    vertices in real world

Projection
    Get shape of viewing
    volume

The screen
    Viewport

Fig. 5.1 Visualising an object

Objects are viewed through the eye or by a camera usually considered the centre of projection and the image is projected onto a viewing plane as illustrated in Fig. 5.1. If the distance of the camera to the object is very large, the centre of projection is at infinity and we have what is called a parallel view with the projection plane at the viewpoint origin. A view with a finite distance between the camera and object gives rise to the perspective view. In the first case depth is not apparent due to the large camera-object distance, while in the latter depth perception and size may be inferred. OpenGl supports both types of viewing.

The last image in Fig. 5.1 treats the complete screen as the viewport although this is not a necessity and OpenGL provides a function glViewport(), which lets the user draw pictures in different parts (viewports) of the screen. As an example we will draw a sine function at various positions on the screen. All we need is to define a number of viewports at different locations and draw the sine curve in each as illustrated in Fig. 5.2. We have generated the start location of each viewport randomly and altered the colour as we progress along the sine wave.

```
void Displaysinex ( void ) {
GLfloat degtorads, x;
int i;
degtorads=3.14159265/180.0;         //degrees to radians
glClear( GL_COLOR_BUFFER_BIT);
for(i=0; i<5; i++) {         //5 different viewports
glViewport ( rand() % 100,rand() % 50, 100 , 50 );
glBegin(GL_LINE_STRIP);
   for (x=0.0; x<=360.0; x +=1.0) { //sine curve between 0 and 2π
          glColor3f(1.0f, (1.0- (float) x /360.0), 0.0f);
          glVertex2f(x, sin(x*degtorads));
     }
glEnd();
}
glFlush();
}
```

Fig. 5.2 Sine waves in multiple viewports

5.3.1 Engineering Drawings

The ability to use multiple viewports has an important application in engineering drawing where objects are often represented in either first or third angle projection. Each system provides three views of an object viewed from the front, side and plan elevations, which are usually sufficient to completely, determine and construct the object concerned. Each of the elevations are views of an object as seen from three orthogonal points and any hidden features represented as dotted lines in one view, can be seen in the other views. In Fig. 5.3 we represent a solid letter 'N' in *first angle* projection with the corresponding viewpoints. Textual and dimensioning information is usually required to remove any ambiguities that may be inherent in the geometric representation but that is not part of our consideration here. Using multiple viewports and suitably orientating the engineering artefact in each viewport allows a better comprehension and understanding of the object concerned.

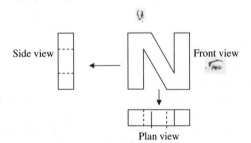

Fig. 5.3 First angle projection

For this example we will use a pyramid with differently coloured faces to illustrate the application of the glViewport () function. Each view is presented in a different viewport and this is accomplished by placing each at three convenient locations on the screen while the pyramid is defined by four faces each of a different colour, and four vertices, centred about the origin with a base on the plane $y = 0$. Additionally we have provided a rotational capability of each view showing the differences in a simultaneous manner as viewed from infinity (orthographic parallel view).

```
#include <windows.h>          //EngDraw.cpp
#include <gl/glut.h>

static GLfloat xRot = 0.0;
static GLfloat yRot = 0.0;

void DrawScene(void)
{
int i;
glClear(GL_COLOR_BUFFER_BIT | GL_DEPTH_BUFFER_BIT);
for(i=0; i<3; i++) {
        if(i == 0) glViewport  ( 0,200, 100 , 50 );
```

```
        if(i == 1) {  //side
                glViewport  ( 100,200, 100 , 50 );
                glPushMatrix();
                glRotatef(90.0, 0.0, 1.0, 0.0);
        }
        if(i == 2) { //plan
                glViewport  (0,100 , 100 , 50 );
                glPushMatrix();
                glRotatef(90.0, 1.0, 0.0, 0.0);
        }

    glPushMatrix();
    glRotatef(xRot, 1.0, 0.0, 0.0);
    glRotatef(yRot, 0.0, 1.0, 0.0);

        // Coloured pyramid + vertices
    glColor3ub(0, 255, 0);
    glBegin(GL_TRIANGLES);
        glVertex3f(0.0, 0.0, 15.0);
        glVertex3f(15.0,0.0, -15.0);
        glVertex3f(-15.0, 0.0, -15.0);
    glEnd();
    glColor3ub(255, 0, 0);
    glBegin(GL_TRIANGLES);
                glVertex3f(15.0,0.0,-15.0);
        glVertex3f(0.0, 15.0, 0.0);
        glVertex3f(0.0, 0.0, 15.0);
    glEnd();
    glColor3ub(255, 255, 255);
    glBegin(GL_TRIANGLES);
                glVertex3f(0.0, 0.0, 15.0);
        glVertex3f(0.0, 15.0, 0.0);
        glVertex3f(-15.0,0.0,-15.0);
    glEnd();
        glColor3ub(0, 0, 255);
    glBegin(GL_TRIANGLES);
                glVertex3f(15.0, 0.0, -15.0);
        glVertex3f(0.0, 15.0, 0.0);
        glVertex3f(-15.0,0.0,-15.0);
    glEnd();
        glPopMatrix();
glPopMatrix();
}
glutSwapBuffers();
}
```

```
void Init()
{
     glEnable(GL_DEPTH_TEST);        // Hidden surface removal
     glClearColor(1.0, 1.0, 0.5, 1.0);
}

void ArrowKeys(int key, int x, int y)
{     //rotation about x & y
     if(key == GLUT_KEY_UP) xRot-= 5.0;
     if(key == GLUT_KEY_DOWN) xRot += 5.0;
     if(key == GLUT_KEY_LEFT) yRot -= 5.0;
     if(key == GLUT_KEY_RIGHT) yRot += 5.0;
     glutPostRedisplay();            //new image
}

void ChangeSize(int w, int h)
{
GLfloat nRange = 20.0;            //view volume
     if(h == 0) h = 1;
     glMatrixMode(GL_PROJECTION);
     glLoadIdentity();
   if (w <= h)
     glOrtho (-nRange, nRange, -nRange*h/w, nRange*h/w,
     -nRange, nRange);
   else
     glOrtho (-nRange*w/h, nRange*w/h, -nRange, nRange,
     -nRange, nRange);
     glMatrixMode(GL_MODELVIEW);
     glLoadIdentity();
}

int main(int argc, char* argv[])
{
     glutInit(&argc, argv);
     glutInitDisplayMode(GLUT_DOUBLE | GLUT_RGB | GLUT_DEPTH);
     glutCreateWindow("3 rd angle projection");
     Init();
     glutReshapeFunc(ChangeSize);
     glutSpecialFunc(ArrowKeys);
     glutDisplayFunc(DrawScene);
     glutMainLoop();
     return 0;
}
```

Fig. 5.4 Use of glViewport()
for engineering drawings

In principle computer graphics systems dispense with the need for three views although unless complete automation of object building is possible, the traditional engineering practice on site is for the three view displays as given in Fig. 5.4.

The OpenGl **projection matrix** scales the vertices of our artefacts so that they can exist with a viewing volume in function ChangeSize(). Visualisation may be thought of as four processes: Vertices of the actual real world object; Required orientation of object; Specify viewing volume; Put object onto screen.

The projection matrix allows us to put the real world object vertices into a volume centred on the origin, which we display on the 2D screen. It is the projection transformation that after all model view transformations are complete, translates the object to the image seen on a screen. After the projection transformation we return to the modelview matrix in function ChangeSize() for any object movement that may take place. In this example we rotate the object using the arrow keys in 5° intervals inside the glut loop. OpenGL provides two forms of projection display that come from ideas used in engineering drawings.

Orthographic projection of an object is where there is a one to one correspondence between the units of measurement of the vertex coordinates in the real world and the pixel positions of the screen. Using the example of railways lines, the lines appear parallel.

In engineering, orthographic drawings are widely used, usually with plan and side elevations to encapsulate the whole object. There is no distortion due to distance since it is equivalent to viewing an object from infinity or in practice where the view distance is sufficiently large that the front and rear vertices can be considered as having the same z coordinate (Fig. 5.5).

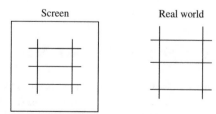

Screen   Real world

Fig. 5.5 Orthographic
projection of railway lines

Perspective projection of an object is where we look at a scene on the large scale and in order to comprehend the whole image we must foreshorten the image so that

Fig. 5.6 Perspective
projection of railway lines in
distance

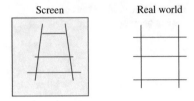

objects on a distant horizon appear much smaller than we know they are in reality
(Fig. 5.6).

Perspective views are typical of what we see in drawings and observe with our
eyes in large scenic views. The distortion due to distance away from the viewpoint
is referred to as foreshortening. OpenGL permits both orthographic and perspective
viewing with the viewpoint at the origin and looking in the negative z direction
along the z-axis.

5.4 Orthographic or Parallel Projection

The default x–y plane for images on the screen is the plane $z = 0$ and this will have
been observed in the examples given in Chapter 4 of this book where projection view
matrices were used with default values. Consider the viewing volume in Fig. 5.7
with the eye looking along the z-axis in the negative direction. The computer screen
lies in the x-y plane at $z = 0$ and all points of the object inside this volume will be
projected onto the screen.

All points on the real world cylinder are mapped onto the screen viewport at
$z = 0$ forming a rectangular shape defined in pixels by the corresponding x-y
coordinates.

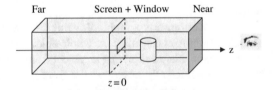

Fig. 5.7 Orthographic
viewing volume

5.4.1 From Real World to Screen Window

We will now derive the transformation of our real world object modelview to the
screen view orthographic projection which we see as an image. The real world will
be governed by actual object dimensions while we will normalise our computer
screen window to have maxima and minima of ± 1 in each of the x and y directions
Fig. 5.8.

Fig. 5.8 Real to screen
coordinate transformation

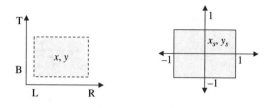

In moving from the real world measurements to the image world of the screen and in order not to distort the image there must be a proportionality such that

$$\frac{x - L}{R - L} = \frac{x_s + 1}{2}$$

and $\quad \dfrac{y - B}{T - B} = \dfrac{y_s + 1}{2}$

where T, B, R, L are the top, bottom, right and left maxima and minima of the real world object reference frame.

rearranging $\quad 2(x - L) = (R - L)(x_s + 1)$

$$\therefore \; x_s = \frac{2x}{R - L} - \frac{R + L}{R - L}$$

and similarly $\; y_s = \dfrac{2y}{T - B} - \dfrac{T + B}{T - B}$

The equations have two terms of recognizable functions; scaling and translation where $2/(R - L)$ and $2/(T - B)$ are scaling factors between the two frames of reference in x and y and $(R + L)/(R - L)$ and $(T + B)/(T - B)$ are the corresponding translation distances. The orthographic view is a translation and scaling of a real world object coordinates to the screen window which we can represent in homogenous coordinates.

$$
\begin{array}{c}
\text{Orthographic} \\
\text{view}
\end{array}
=
\begin{array}{c}
\text{Translation} \\
\text{matrix}
\end{array}
\times
\begin{array}{c}
\text{Scaling} \\
\text{matrix}
\end{array}
$$

$$
=
\begin{pmatrix}
1 & 0 & -\dfrac{R + L}{R - L} \\[2ex]
0 & 1 & -\dfrac{T + B}{T - B} \\[2ex]
0 & 0 & 1
\end{pmatrix}
\begin{pmatrix}
\dfrac{2}{R - L} & 0 & 0 \\[2ex]
0 & \dfrac{2}{T - B} & 0 \\[2ex]
0 & 0 & 1
\end{pmatrix}
$$

$$
= \begin{pmatrix} \dfrac{2}{R-L} & 0 & -\dfrac{R+L}{R-L} \\[2ex] 0 & \dfrac{2}{T-B} & -\dfrac{T+B}{T-B} \\[2ex] 0 & 0 & 1 \end{pmatrix}
$$

Thus we can map values for x and y between the real word coordinates and the image screen coordinates x_s, y_s, which we can write in matrix form

$$
\begin{pmatrix} x_s \\ y_s \\ 1 \end{pmatrix} = \begin{pmatrix} \dfrac{2}{R-L} & 0 & -\dfrac{R+L}{R-L} \\[2ex] 0 & \dfrac{2}{T-B} & -\dfrac{T+B}{T-B} \\[2ex] 0 & 0 & 1 \end{pmatrix} \begin{pmatrix} x \\ y \\ 1 \end{pmatrix} \tag{5.1}
$$

where the scale factors are on the diagonal and the translation distance is the last column of the orthographic projection matrix. In 3D similar terms will be included in the third row of the matrix using the *far* and *near* real world coordinates. The orthographic projection matrix in OpenGL is provided through the function glOrtho(left, right, bottom, top, near far).

5.4.2 Inside the Matrix

It is now worth looking at the values of the elements in the matrices used in transformations and orthographic projection that subsequently contribute to the view seen on the monitor screen. Students should experiment with the sample program with scaling and translation in order to gain confidence with how changes seen on the screen are achieved through the transformations of Chapter 4 and the projection just described.

As an example we will draw a square in a window of 300×200 pixels and for illustrative purposes use glRotate to turn the square through 30° where $\cos(30) = 0.87$ and $\sin(30) = 0.5$. The square does not appear as a square due to the aspect ratio $\neq 1$. The model view matrix is accessed by means of glGetFloatv(GL_MODELVIEW_MATRIX, array); and note should be made of the column ordering in the matrix. gluOrtho2D () and glOrtho ( ) behave in a similar fashion if the near and far z-coordinates are set to -1 and 1 respectively.

```
GLsizei h   = 200 ;  // initial height of window      matest.cpp
GLsizei w   = 300 ;  // initial width of window

void DisplayMatrixSquare ( void ) {
        float marray[16], parray[16];
```

```
      int r, c;
glClear ( GL_COLOR_BUFFER_BIT );
//Gets 16 values (4x4) of modelview matrix - try it & see!
glRotatef( 30.0, 1.0, 0.0, 0.0);
cout << "30 degree rotation about x Matrix values \n";
glGetFloatv(GL_MODELVIEW_MATRIX, marray);
for(c=0; c<4; c++) {
        for(r=c; r< 16; r= r+4) cout << marray[r] <<"   ";
        cout << "\n";
}
cout << "\n";

glColor3f(0.0f, 0.0f, 1.0f);
  glBegin(GL_POLYGON);
    glVertex2d(-25.0,-25.0);   //Draw square
    glVertex2d(25.0,-25.0);
    glVertex2d(25.0,25.0);
    glVertex2d(-25.0,25.0);
  glEnd();
glFlush();
}


void MyInit ( ) {
float marray[16], parray[16];
int r, c;
glClearColor   ( 1.0, 1.0, 0.0, 0.0 );
glColor3f(0.0, 0.0, 1.0);
glMatrixMode   ( GL_MODELVIEW );
cout<< fixed << setprecision(3);
glGetFloatv(GL_MODELVIEW_MATRIX, marray);
glLoadIdentity ( );
cout << "Model View Matrix - default values\n";
for(c=0; c<4; c++) {
        for(r=c; r< 16; r= r+4) cout << marray[r] <<"   ";
        cout << "\n";
}
cout << "\n";
}


void ChangeSize(int w, int h)
{
GLfloat parray[16], nRange = 100.0;         //view volume
int c, r;
        if(h == 0) h = 1;
        glMatrixMode(GL_PROJECTION);
```

```
        glLoadIdentity();
    if (w <= h)
        glOrtho (-nRange, nRange, -nRange*h/w, nRange*h/w,
        -nRange, nRange);
    else
        glOrtho (-nRange*w/h, nRange*w/h, -nRange, nRange,
        -nRange, nRange);
//Get 16 values (4x4) of projection matrix
        glGetFloatv(GL_PROJECTION_MATRIX, parray);
        cout << "Projection View Matrix - w="<< w <<" h="
        << h <<"\n";
        for(c=0; c<4; c++) {
                for(r=c; r< 16; r= r+4) cout << parray[r] <<" ";
                cout << "\n";
        }
        glMatrixMode(GL_MODELVIEW);
        glLoadIdentity();
}
```

```
Projection View Matrix - w=200 h = 300
0.010 0.000   0.000 0.000
0.000 0.007   0.000 0.000
0.000 0.000 -0.010 0.000
0.000 0.000   0.000 1.000
```

```
Model View Matrix - identity default values
1.00 0.00 0.00 0.00
0.00 1.00 0.00 0.00
0.00 0.00 1.00 0.00
0.00 0.00 0.00 1.00
```

```
30 degree rotation Model View Matrix values
1.00 0.00   0.00 0.00
0.00 0.87 -0.50 0.00
0.00 0.50   0.87 0.00
0.00 0.00   0.00 1.00
```

The first output of modelview matrix values is the expected identity matrix with the leading diagonal set to one. The second matrix contains the values for sin(30) and cos(30) with a rotation about the vector defined by the origin and (1,0,0) – the x-axis. Thus the values of points to be displayed alter in the y-z plane as defined by rows 2 and 3 of the matrix.

The projection matrix contains the values associated with the orthographic projection of the square onto the screen. Using the nomenclature in (5.1) $t = 150$,

$b = -150, r = 100, l = -100, n = -100$ and $f = 100$ for each of there terms we construct the orthographic projection matrix. Multiplying the orthographic matrix by the rotational matrix gives the values in the final model view matrix. Using the above example we perform these matrix operations for the lower left hand point $(-25, -25)$ of the square

$$
\begin{array}{cccc}
\text{Screen} & \text{Projection} & \text{Modelview} & \text{Vertex} \\
\begin{pmatrix} -0.25 \\ -0.152 \\ -0.875 \\ 0.0 \end{pmatrix} =
& \begin{pmatrix} 0.01 & 0.000 & 0.00 & 0.0 \\ 0.00 & 0.007 & 0.00 & 0.0 \\ 0.00 & 0.000 & -0.01 & 0.0 \\ 0.00 & 0.000 & 0.00 & 1.0 \end{pmatrix}
& \begin{pmatrix} 1.0 & 0.00 & 0.00 & 0.0 \\ 0.0 & 0.87 & -0.50 & 0.0 \\ 0.0 & 0.50 & 0.87 & 0.0 \\ 0.0 & 0.00 & 0.00 & 1.0 \end{pmatrix}
& \begin{pmatrix} -25 \\ -25 \\ 0 \\ 0 \end{pmatrix}
\end{array}
$$

The screen values are normalised and as an example $x = -0.25$ is a point a quarter of the distance from the centre of the window (origin) and the left hand edge of the window ($x = -1$). Students may find it instructive to physically measure distances with a ruler (approximately!) on the screen to verify the correctness of the calculation.

5.4.3 Getting to Grips with Where Things Are

One of the most frustrating parts of graphics is not having an image on the screen! The beginner will have read the theory but still nothing appears and for this reason we are going to experiment practically in this section. The orthographic viewing volume in Fig. 5.3 is implemented in OpenGL using the function

```
glOrtho(left, right, bottom, top, near, far);
```

where the bounding coordinates are shown in Fig. 5.1. If either 'near' or 'far' are *negative* then these clipping planes are behind the viewer. We shall draw lines using glVertex(x, y, z) and in our example the two lines are in different z-positions. The program output is displayed in Fig. 5.9 together with a draft program.

```
#include <windows.h>    //lineOrtho.cpp
#include <GL/glut.h>

void lines ( void );
void MyInit    ( );

void lines ( void ) {
glClear( GL_COLOR_BUFFER_BIT);
glLineWidth(5.0);
glBegin(GL_LINES);
  glColor3f(1.0f, 0.0f, 0.0f); //red
```

```
  glVertex3f(0.0, 0.0, 19.0);
  glVertex3f(30.0, 0.0, 19.0);
  glColor3f(0.0f, 0.0f, 1.0f); //blue
  glVertex3i(50, -50, -2);
  glVertex3i(-50, 50, -2);
glEnd();
glFlush();
}

void MyInit ( void ) {
  glClearColor ( 1.0, 1.0, 1.0, 0.0 );
  glMatrixMode    ( GL_PROJECTION );
  glLoadIdentity ( );
  glOrtho( -50.0, 55.0, -60.0, 50.0, 2.0, -20.0 );
}

void main(int argc, char **argv) {
    glutInit            ( &argc, argv );
    glutInitDisplayMode    (
        GLUT_SINGLE | GLUT_RGB );
    glutInitWindowSize ( 200, 200 );
    glutInitWindowPosition ( 50, 50 );
    glutCreateWindow      ( "lines
                orthographically" );
    MyInit ( );
    glutDisplayFunc( lines);
    glutMainLoop ( );
}
```

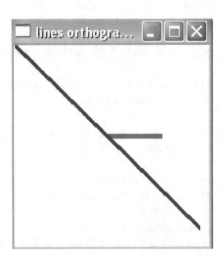

Fig. 5.9 Inside the viewing
volume

The projection volume is specified by glOrtho(−50.0, 55.0, −60.0, 50.0, 1.0, −20.0); while the lines are drawn in the planes $z = 19$ (red) and $z = -2$ (blue). The near and far planes are at $z = 2$ and $z = -20$. Try setting the far plane to −18 and the red line disappears. The far plane is now behind the viewer at $z = 18$ and less than the plane $z = 19$ where the red line was drawn, leaving it outside the viewing box and thus not appearing on the screen. Now try setting the near plane to 1.0 (actually $z = -1$) and all lines will disappear since the blue line is now outside the viewing volume at $z = -2$. Readers should experiment with the orthographic viewing box until they feel comfortable knowing where they are drawing in relation to the view volume! Time spent at this stage on knowing the size of objects and the clipping volume you have allocated will save hours of debugging later on when there appear to be no errors yet nothing appears on the screen.

The lines have been drawn in a 200 × 200 pixel window where the origin (0, 0, 0) is at the centre of the window. It is instructive to draw lines that are partly inside and partly outside the viewing volume to demonstrate the effect of clipping.

5.4.4 Perspective Projection

Perspective projection is the process of drawing an image appear on the screen simulating how it would appear in the real world with parts of the object that are further away appearing smaller – called **foreshortening** of the image. This is achieved by making the viewing volume of the image a truncated pyramid or **frustum** rather than the rectangular box used in parallel orthographic projection. OpenGL provides two ways of doing this using either of the functions gluPerspective() or glFrustum(). The process of performing perspective mapping may be illustrated as follows:

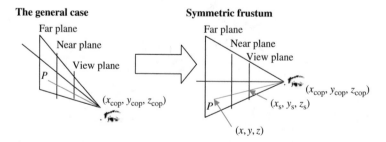

Perspective view is a method whereby we transform a point $P(x, y, z)$ on the object onto the view plane at (x_s, y_s, z_s) such as to give a realistic impression of the object on the screen in terms of size in relation to distance (depth) from the eye at the centre of projection (cop). The first step is to move from the general case and centre the object points about the z-axis with a symmetric bounding frustum using a shearing matrix (see Chapter 4). This is equivalent to a shift operation in the x-z plane of $-(x_{max} + x_{min})/2$ and in the y-z plane of $-(y_{max} + y_{min})/2$ in the near plane, where $(x_{\max}, y_{\max})$ and $(x_{\min}, y_{\min})$ are the bounding points of the frustum volume. In matrix representation this is

$$\begin{pmatrix} 0 \\ 0 \\ z_{near} \\ 1 \end{pmatrix} = \begin{pmatrix} 1 & 0 & sh_{xz} & 0 \\ 0 & 1 & sh_{yz} & 0 \\ 0 & 0 & 1 & 0 \\ 0 & 0 & 0 & 0 \end{pmatrix} \begin{pmatrix} (x_{\max} + x_{\min})/2 \\ (y_{\max} + y_{\min})/2 \\ z_{near} \\ 1 \end{pmatrix} \qquad (5.2)$$

$$\therefore 0 = (x_{\max} + x_{\min})/2 + sh_{xz}\, z_{near}$$
$$\text{and } 0 = (y_{\max} + y_{\min})/2 + sh_{yz}\, z_{near}$$

The shearing matrix elements are

$$sh_{xz} = -(x_{\max} + x_{\min})/2\, z_{near}$$
$$sh_{yz} = -(y_{\max} + y_{\min})/2\, z_{near}$$

Using the same notation as in the orthographic derivation (5.2) may be rewritten as

$$sh_{xz} = -(R + L)/2\, z_{near}$$
$$sh_{yz} = -(T + B)/2\, z_{near}$$

Now consider the line from the point $P(x, y, z)$ to the eye view point at the centre of all the projected rays $(x_{cop}, y_{cop}, z_{cop})$

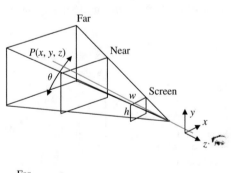

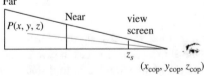

Now for any point (x', y', z') on the line from a vertex point P of the object in the view volume to the centre of projection $(x_{cop}, y_{cop}, z_{cop})$ we can write the ratio of the distances as

$$\frac{x' - x}{x_{cop} - x} = k$$

$$\frac{y' - y}{y_{cop} - y} = k \text{ for } 0 \le k \le 1$$

$$\frac{z' - z}{z_{cop} - z} = k$$

where the line from P to the eye point at the centre of projection passes through the view plane on the screen at (x_s, y_s, z_s). Now in terms of z at the viewing plane

$$k = \frac{z_s - z}{z_{cop} - z}$$

and so substituting for k in the expressions containing x' and y' at (x_s, y_s)

$$x_s = \frac{x(z_{cop} - z_s)}{z_{cop} - z} + \frac{x_{cop}(z_s - z)}{z_{cop} - z} \tag{5.3}$$

and

$$y_s = \frac{y(z_{cop} - z_s)}{z_{cop} - z} + \frac{y_{cop}(z_s - z)}{z_{cop} - z} \tag{5.4}$$

We can construct the rows of our general perspective matrix from (5.3) to (5.4) as

$$\begin{pmatrix} x_s \\ y_s \\ z_s \\ 1 \end{pmatrix} = \begin{pmatrix} \dfrac{z_{cop} - z_s}{z_{cop} - z} & 0 & \dfrac{-x_{cop}}{z_{cop} - z} & \dfrac{x_{cop} z_s}{z_{cop} - z} \\ 0 & \dfrac{z_{cop} - z_s}{z_{cop} - z} & \dfrac{-y_{cop}}{z_{cop} - z} & \dfrac{y_{cop} z_s}{z_{cop} - z} \\ 0 & 0 & S_z & t_z \\ 0 & 0 & -1 & z_{cop} \end{pmatrix} \begin{pmatrix} x \\ y \\ z \\ 1 \end{pmatrix}$$

Equations (5.3) and (5.4) are of the form of a scaling factor (matrix diagonal) associated with x and y in relation to point P on the view plane followed by a translation factor to the view plane. The third and fourth rows of the matrix will be discussed later in this section. The perspective matrix is not practically very usable in this form as it is dependent on each value of z at the object vertices. We overcome this problem by introducing a homogenous-coordinate representation where

$$x_s(z_{cop} - z) = x_h \quad \text{and} \quad y_s(z_{cop} - z) = y_h$$

If we set our centre of projection to be at the origin ($z_{cop} = 0$) and the view plane as the near plane z_s of the frustum then the matrix simplifies to

$$\begin{pmatrix} x_h \\ y_h \\ z_h \\ 1 \end{pmatrix} = \begin{pmatrix} -\text{Near} & 0 & 0 & 0 \\ 0 & -\text{Near} & 0 & 0 \\ 0 & 0 & s_z & t_z \\ 0 & 0 & -1 & 0 \end{pmatrix} \begin{pmatrix} x \\ y \\ z \\ 1 \end{pmatrix} \tag{5.5}$$

To generalise our perspective matrix we must multiply the shear matrix (5.2) by (5.5) to include off-axis situations

$$\begin{pmatrix} -\text{Near} & 0 & 0 & 0 \\ 0 & -\text{Near} & 0 & 0 \\ 0 & 0 & s_z & t_z \\ 0 & 0 & -1 & 0 \end{pmatrix} \begin{pmatrix} 1 & 0 & -(L+R)/(2*\text{Near}) & 0 \\ 0 & 1 & -(T+B)/(2*\text{Near}) & 0 \\ 0 & 0 & 1 & 0 \\ 0 & 0 & 0 & 1 \end{pmatrix} \begin{pmatrix} x \\ y \\ z \\ 1 \end{pmatrix}$$

$$= \begin{pmatrix} -\text{Near} & 0 & (L+R)/2 & 0 \\ 0 & -\text{Near} & (T+B)/2 & 0 \\ 0 & 0 & s_z & t_z \\ 0 & 0 & -1 & 0 \end{pmatrix} \begin{pmatrix} x \\ y \\ z \\ 1 \end{pmatrix}$$

Finally we normalise the perspective matrix for a cube from $(-1, -1, -1)$ to $(1,1,1)$ centred on the origin by scaling in x and y. Thus the projected homogenous coordinates onto the view plane are given by

$$= \begin{pmatrix} s_x & 0 & 0 & 0 \\ 0 & s_y & 0 & 0 \\ 0 & 0 & 1 & 0 \\ 0 & 0 & 0 & 1 \end{pmatrix} \begin{pmatrix} -\text{Near} & 0 & (L+R)/2 & 0 \\ 0 & -\text{Near} & (T+B)/2 & 0 \\ 0 & 0 & s_z & t_z \\ 0 & 0 & -1 & 0 \end{pmatrix} \begin{pmatrix} x \\ y \\ z \\ 1 \end{pmatrix}$$

$$= \begin{pmatrix} -\text{Near}\, s_x & 0 & s_x(L+R)/2 & 0 \\ 0 & -s_y\text{Near} & s_y(T+B)/2 & 0 \\ 0 & 0 & s_z & t_z \\ 0 & 0 & -1 & 0 \end{pmatrix} \begin{pmatrix} x \\ y \\ z \\ 1 \end{pmatrix}$$

$$\therefore \; x_h = -\text{Near}\, x\, s_x + z\, s_x(L+R)/2 = x_s\, h \tag{5.6}$$
$$y_h = -\text{Near}\, y\, s_y + z\, s_y\, (T+B)/2 = y_s\, h \tag{5.7}$$
$$z_h = z\, s_z + t_z = z_s\, h \tag{5.8}$$

Remembering that the centre of projection is at the origin and $h = -z$, the projected point (L, B, Near) corresponds to the homogenised coordinate $(-1, -1, -1)$ and (R, T, Far) to $(1, 1, 1)$, we substitute in (5.6) and (5.7) to obtain the scale factors s_x and s_y

$$s_x = -2/(R - L) \text{ and } s_y = -2/(T - B) \tag{5.9}$$

We now require suitable functions for scaling s_z and translation t_z to complete the matrix. We choose a function that is similar to (5.8) of the form

$$-(s_z\, z + t_z)/z \qquad (5.10)$$

where s_z and t_z are the scaling and translation constants and the function operates for values ± 1 in our normalised cube viewing volume.

$$-(s_o\, z + t_z)/z = 1 \text{ at the Far plane of frustum and}$$
$$-(s_z\, z + t_z)/z = -1 \text{ at the Near (view) plane of the frustum.}$$

Solving (10) for s_z and t_z at z=Far and z=Near we obtain

$$s_z = -(\text{Near} + \text{Far})/(\text{Far} - \text{Near})$$
$$\text{and } t_z = -2\,\text{Far Near}/(\text{Far} - \text{Near}) \qquad (5.11)$$

Our final perspective matrix substituting (9) and (11) is

$$\begin{pmatrix} \dfrac{2\,\text{Near}}{R-L} & 0 & (L+R)/(R-L) & 0 \\ 0 & \dfrac{2\,\text{Near}}{(T-B)} & (T+B)/(T-B) & 0 \\ 0 & 0 & -(\text{Near}+\text{Far})/(\text{Far}-\text{Near}) & -2\,\text{Far Near}/(\text{Far}-\text{Near}) \\ 0 & 0 & -1 & 0 \end{pmatrix}$$

which is the specification for glFrustum().

gluPerspective() creates a frustum symmetric along the line of sight with the field of view angle θ being used to determine the shape of the view volume. The matrix representation of the frustum multiplies the modelview matrix to provide the image.

5.4.5 Understanding the View

With all this theory what can we expect to see, and is it what we expect? There are a number of useful built in functions, which we can use in OpenGL development, which can help with program start up. In the next example we shall use gluCylinder() and gluLookAt() to illustrate how the image changes as we move around in space (Shreiner, 2004). The program works with glOrtho() and glFrustum() (commented out) and readers will benefit from experimenting with both. We are introducing several new features in this program and we give brief overviews of their operation.

    gluLookAt(eyex, eyey, eyez, midx, midy, midz, 0.0, 1.0, 0.0);

This function permits us to look from where we are (eyex, eyey, eyez) to the most appropriate point on object, usually the middle point (midx, midy, midz). By convention we have defined our view volumes by viewing along the z-axis from the origin and it follows that we must define 'above' and 'below' via the positive y-direction (0.0, 1.0, 0.0). Thus by altering the values of the eye coordinates we get a different view of the cylinder object. Rather than manually changing the eye position by typing in new values we are going to generate these by incrementing in x or y via the keyboard to show how the view changes gradually with eye position variation as illustrated in Fig. 5.10.

Each new eye position requires a new model view matrix and if we want to go back to a previous position then we will need to retrieve the matrix for that position. OpenGL provides an area of memory for this purpose called the matrix stack through the functions glPushMatrix() and glPopMatrix().

The OpenGL Utility Toolkit (GLUT) through the glutSpecialFunc (Keys) function provides interaction between OpenGL and the keyboard. In this case we have written a callback function (Keys) where we can use non-ASCII keys to interact with out program (Kilgard, 1996).

In the example we use gluCylinder() to construct a cylinder along the z-axis of length 9 and radius 4. We can use the keyboard arrow keys to move our eye position in both x and y and observe the resulting changing point of view. Readers should experiment with different values for the view volume size using both glOrtho() and glFrustum() to ensure they understand and recognise what they see!

```
static GLfloat eyex = 0.0;              //cylinderlookat.cpp
static GLfloat eyey = 0.0;
static GLfloat midx = 0.0;
static GLfloat midy = 0.0;
static GLfloat midz = 4.5;

void DisplayCylinder ( void );
void MyInit      ( );

void DisplayCylinder( void ) {
GLUquadricObj *cylobj;
glClear( GL_COLOR_BUFFER_BIT);
cylobj = gluNewQuadric();
gluQuadricDrawStyle(cylobj, GLU_FILL);
gluQuadricNormals(cylobj, GLU_FLAT);
glColor3f(0.6, 0.6, 0.6);
glLoadIdentity ();
gluLookAt(eyex, eyey, 0.0, midx, midy, midz, 0.0, 1.0, 0.0);
    glPushMatrix();
      gluCylinder(cylobj, 4.0, 4.0, 9.0, 20, 8);
    glPopMatrix();
glutSwapBuffers();
}
```

```
void MyInit ( void ) {
glClearColor    ( 1.0, 1.0, 1.0, 0.0 );
}


void Keys(int key, int x, int y)
{
        if(key == GLUT_KEY_UP)  eyex = eyex+1.0;
        if(key == GLUT_KEY_DOWN) eyex = eyex-1.0;
        if(key == GLUT_KEY_LEFT) eyey = eyey-1.0;
        if(key == GLUT_KEY_RIGHT) eyey = eyey +1.0;
        glutPostRedisplay();
}


void reshape (int w, int h)
{
   glMatrixMode (GL_PROJECTION);
   glLoadIdentity ();
   glOrtho(-11.0, 11.0, -11.0, 11.0, 11.0, -11.0);
   //glFrustum(-11.0, 11.0, -11.0, 11.0, 1.0, 22.0);
   glMatrixMode(GL_MODELVIEW);
}
```

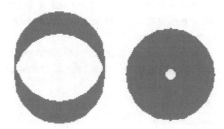

Fig. 5.10 Interactively
changing the point of view

The images shown in Fig. 5.10 are views using orthographic projection on the left and perspective projection on the right of the cylinder.

5.5 Exercises

1. Instead of defining the frustum in terms of left, right, top and bottom we can use a field of view angle θ. Show that the perspective matrix is of the form

$$\begin{pmatrix} \dfrac{\cot(\theta/2)}{\text{aspect}} & 0 & 0 & 0 \\ 0 & \cot(\theta/2) & 0 & 0 \\ 0 & 0 & \dfrac{(\text{Near}+\text{Far})}{(\text{Near}-\text{Far})} & \dfrac{2\,\text{Far}\,\text{Near}}{(\text{Near}-\text{Far})} \\ 0 & 0 & -1 & 0 \end{pmatrix}$$

where 'aspect' is the aspect ratio of the width x to the height y.
Implementation of this matrix form as the gluPerspective function () is part of OpenGL.

2. Modify the program cylinderlookat.cpp, by adding extra key functions to have a variable the view volume and watch the cylinder change in size. Using gluPerspective () allow a key to alter the view angle and output the angle in relation to the size of image. What is the value of θ when the cylinder fills the screen?

5.6 Conclusions

We are now able to move from the actual world in which an object resides and translate this to the two-dimensional screen of a computer monitor. We have explored how the modelview matrix is used to describe the orientation and movement of the object, while the projection matrix specifies a viewing volume and normalises the object dimensions for the purpose of display. The concatenation of the matrix operations leads to a pipeline process. The mathematics behind these functions has been presented to give users confidence and flexibility in the design of the display, rather than using functions in a 'black box' manner. We have explored a hand worked example of the projection matrix moving from the real world to screen world coordinates of the vertices. Experimenting with the last example in Section 5.4.5 will be instructive in helping readers to understand what they see and more importantly what they expected to see, which is often not the same thing in the early stages of a graphics course.

The following chapters will now begin focus on the building of models and applications using the theoretical infrastructure we have developed so far.

Chapter 6
Lighting and Colour

6.1 Introduction

Sight is one of the fundamental human senses and governs our much of our appreciation of the world. In computer graphics, lighting effects give a sense of realism in the form of shadows, highlights and colours. In this Chapter we will study different lighting models and how various forms of illumination contribute to the resultant image.

Light is sometimes described as an electromagnetic radiation with wavelike characteristics and at others times as a particle called a photon. Merging these ideas into a single coherent description occupies many physicists with a reawakened interest in solitary waves. Solitary waves were first observed in the 19th century in water on canals and seem to behave very much like particles. Light shows both a particle like behaviour (pressure moves satellites in orbit) and that of a wave (diffraction around edges). We shall not study the resolution of the wave-particle duality associated with the quantum mechanical descriptions of light, but will still need to understand where colour comes from and how we can mix colours to give realistic representations of artefacts. Colour is the response of the eye and the interpretation of the brain to light of different wavelengths or energies. The eye is composed of two types of cells: cones and rods. The rods do not respond to colour but work at low levels of light and give us the ability to see at night. The cones respond to colour and allow us to see different intensities of colour. Light of one particular wavelength or colour is called monochromatic light and emitted from sources such as Lasers. Light is but one part of the electro magnetic spectrum which includes radio waves, microwaves, x-rays, gamma rays and light itself. We can represent the wave like form of electromagnetic radiation as shown in Fig. 6.1.

6.2 The Electromagnetic Spectrum

The electromagnetic spectrum, which describes all radiation, is made up from components of different wavelengths λ and frequencies f related by the expression

$$c = \lambda f$$

Fig. 6.1 Characteristics of light waves

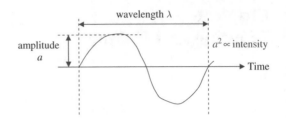

where c is the velocity of light (300,000 km sec^{-1} in vacuum), λ is measured in nanometers (10^{-9} of a metre) and f is measured in cycles (complete wavelengths) per second (Hertz). The time between two points on the wave where the amplitude is the same is called the period T (seconds) of the wave where T = 1/f. The electromagnetic spectrum is summarised in the following Fig. 6.2 moving from short wavelength radiation to longer wavelengths on the right.

The shorter the wavelenght the more penetrating is the radiation with γ rays having a wavelength of $\sim 10^{-3}$ nanometers (nm) and radio waves $\sim 10^{10}$ nm. The visible spectrum lies approximately between 400 nm (blue) and 700 nm (red), a long wavelength being associated with a low frequency of radiation. We shall only be concerned with the visible part of the spectrum in this text.

6.2.1 Colour

The colour of an object is governed by how the atoms from which it is made respond to the light shining on the surface. The different atoms from which we are made absorb X-rays to different degrees as shown in Fig. 3.2 where the Calcium reflects (white) the radiation more strongly than the more water based soft tissue (grey-black). The differential absorption gives rise to colours depending on the composition of an object. On a clear day the sky is blue because the longer wavelengths of sunlight are more strongly absorbed while the shorter wavelength ultra violet and blue is transmitted more easily through the atmosphere and that is the colour we see.

Describing colour in a qualitative manner is usually sufficient for everyday tasks although what two people mean by 'red' may be quite different and depend on quantities such as age, light intensity or material surface. A few years ago we would talk about graphics systems in terms of 4 bit colour and limited resolution. We now expect 24 bit colour systems with 8 bits used for each primary colour (Red, Green, Blue) and a minimal screen resolution of 800×600 pixels. This allows 256 intensity

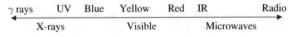

Fig. 6.2 The electromagnetic spectrum

levels for each colour, although most peoples eyes will not resolved changes as small
as this. A level of 0 means no colour (black) and a level of 255 means a maximum
intensity of the colour concerned.

6.2.2 Mixing Colours

We can mix the RGB colours in a colour space by specifying three colour axes with
an origin (0, 0, 0) which is black.

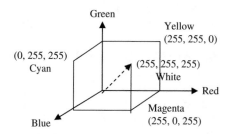

In computer graphics colour is formed additively where by default, the monitor is black and by progressively adding the primary colours the screen changes to
white. Mixing the primary colours by different amounts, gives rise to the millions
of colours that are available in modern 24-bit systems.

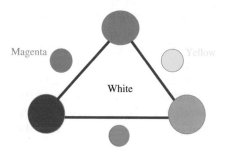

6.2.2.1 Cyan

A plot of a triangle smoothly changing the base colours from each vertex in colour
space is given in Fig. 6.3 followed by the code fragment.

The colour space triangle is grey in the middle as this is on the diagonal to full
white in the top, front, and right hand corner of the colour cube from the colour cube
origin (black).

Fig. 6.3 Mixing red, green, blue (RGB) primary colours

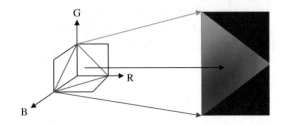

```
void DrawTriangle(void)
{
    glClear(GL_COLOR_BUFFER_BIT);
    glShadeModel(GL_SMOOTH);                    // Smooth shading
    glBegin(GL_TRIANGLES);
    glColor3ub((GLubyte)255,(GLubyte)0,(GLubyte)0);
    glVertex3f(0.0f,200.0f,0.0f);        // Red Apex
    glColor3ub((GLubyte)0,(GLubyte)255,(GLubyte)0);
    glVertex3f(200.0f,-70.0f,0.0f);      // Green
    glColor3ub((GLubyte)0,(GLubyte)0,(GLubyte)255);
    glVertex3f(-200.0f, -70.0f, 0.0f); // Blue
    glEnd();
    glutSwapBuffers();
}
```

By using the three numerical values associated with the RGB components we can define a colour exactly – even if not all displays or printers reproduce in the same way! The colour of an object is the light that is reflected from it and the colour is determined by the dominant light frequency or *hue* that is reflected. Thus we might say the light is 'bluish' if blue is the dominant colour in the spectrum of colours from an object. In the RGB colour model, colours are the result of a linear combination of the three primary colours which each take a value from 0 to 255 as an integer or 0–1.0 in floating point notation. Colour matching is not however straightforward due to the response of the eye not being a simple addition of primary colours. Some colours can be the result of two or more different combinations of colours (Rogers1998).

6.2.3 The Shading Model

In Section 6.2.2 we used glShadeModel(mode); to provide a shading model for mixing the colours in Fig. 6.3. In OpenGl the mode parameter may take the values GL_FLAT or GL_SMOOTH where the former selects the colour from one vertex and applies it to all pixels of a polygon and the latter provides smooth Gouraud shading. Gouraud shading is the process whereby we linearly interpolate the light intensities of the polygon vertices across the surface of the polygon as illustrated in

Fig. 6.4 Linear intensity
interpolation along a scan line

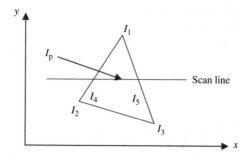

Fig. 6.4. The interpolation removes the discontinuities of light intensity between the junctions of polygons used to construct an object.

Consider the triangular polygon in Fig. 6.4 with colour intensities I_1, I_2, I_3 at the corresponding vertices (x_1, y_1), (x_2, y_2) and (x_3, y_3). A scan line crosses the polygon at points 4 and 5 where the intensity is I_4 and I_5 and we require the intensity at all other points P along the line. We can interpolate the intensity I_4 from the values at I_1 and I_2

$$I_4 = \frac{y_4 - y_2}{y_1 - y_2} I_1 + \frac{y_1 - y_4}{y_1 - y_2} I_2$$

and similarly the intensity I_5 from the values at I_1 and I_3. Using these end point intensities for each scan line we can now calculate the intensity I_p at each point P in the x-direction

$$I_p = \frac{x_5 - x_p}{x_5 - x_4} I_4 + \frac{x_p - x_4}{x_5 - x_4} I_5$$

An alternative to Gouraud shading is to use interpolation of the normal vectors at the vertices to calculate the normal at the points 4 and 5 in Fig. 6.4. Using the same incremental procedure described, we calculate the normals along each scan line. The illumination model is then applied to every pixel along the scan line to obtain the intensity – called Phong shading.

6.3 Lighting and Illumination

We now consider the development of a lighting model, which can be used for computer graphics development. The interaction of colours, shading and light sources leads to the concept of rendering an object onto the screen. There is no complete equation to physically represent this process but rather a number of approximate steps which lead to realistic displays. The general case is shown in Fig. 6.5.

The nature of the object surface, the position of the light source, the colour of both source and object together with observer position all contribute to the total image perception. Object surfaces may be shiny like gloss paint and reflect in well

Fig. 6.5 The contribution of
light, objects and shadows to
image

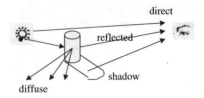

defined directions or rough like cardboard and reflect in a very diffuse manner. There
is a third type of surface where light is both reflected and transmitted through the
material which we refer to as translucence in the case of glass and some plastics.
Within the OpenGL environment, lighting is considered to be the result of three
different components:

Ambient (isotropic) light, which is the uniform background illumination; Diffuse
light is directional and reflected evenly from a surface so that the image is generally
brighter in that direction no matter where we view from; Specular (directional) and
reflected sharply point sources as for instance from a laser.

The three contributions to the overall view of an image have not an exact equivalent in physics but still permit very realistic displays that are computationally
efficient. It must remembered that the reflection of the RGB components will be
different for any given surface and for each of the three forms of illumination. This
will require the programmer to adjust each contribution when setting up the lighting environment. Translucence is another lighting effect although not part of the
illumination model. Translucence occurs when an object both reflects and transmits
light and is simulated by adding a fourth component A, to the RGB model. We will
consider blending later in Chapter 7 of this text.

Diffuse reflection of light is where the light is reflected uniformly in all directions, as may be the case from a rough surface of matt paint, Fig. 6.6. Because the
light is reflected in all directions a simple approximation of a reflection coefficient
is used rather than a strict mathematical relation based on incident and reflected rays
to give a value of how much light is reflected.

Light source

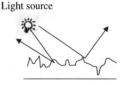

Fig. 6.6 Diffuse reflection
from a rough surface

6.3.1 Setting up the Lighting

In the demonstration we are going to describe, we will bring together a lot of ideas
covered in this and previous chapters by means of the example of a rotating a pyramid with an ambient light background and some diffuse light. We shall rotate the

Fig. 6.7 Initial layout of
pyramid with light source

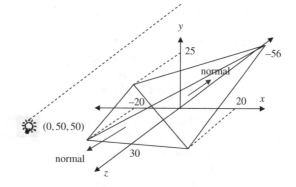

pyramid and see the effect of the reflection of light in a diffuse manner from the
surfaces. We shall keep the ambient and diffuse light components constant while
interactively moving the position of the light source. The pyramid is initialised as
shown in Fig. 6.7 with the light source located in the y-z plane. With this orientation
we shall expect initially to see the smallest face of the pyramid with the highest point
($z = -56$) hidden from view.

Each vertex is stored as an array triple within in a 3×3 array (v) to represent a
single face of the pyramid. In order to represent the reflection of the diffuse component of the light, we shall need to calculate the normal to each face of the pyramid
(see Chapter 4) by extracting two vectors v1 and v2 representing two edges of a face
from the three vertices, normalise and calculate the cross product to give the normal
vector (out). Function glNormal() will be required prior to each drawing of a face
to scale the amount of reflected light depending on the orientation of the face given
by vector *out* to the light source. The pseudo-code for each face is of the form

```
float v[3][3] = {{ first vertex },
                 { second vertex },
                 { third vertex }};
        Normal(v,normal);
        glNormal3fv(normal);
        glVertex3fv(first vertex);
        glVertex3fv(second vertex);
        glVertex3fv(third vertex);
```

We have set up the light source in the DrawIt() function to permit interactive
movement of the light in the $\pm x$-direction as well as rotation of the pyramid using
the keys F7, F8 and the arrow keys respectively. The lighting environment and material properties are initialised in the function Environment().

```
static GLfloat xrot = 0.0, yrot = 0.0;        //lightpyramid.cpp
static GLfloat xpos = 0.0, ypos = 50.0;
```

```
void Normalise(float vector[3])
{
GLfloat length;
      // length of the vector
      length = (float)sqrt((vector[0]*vector[0]) +
               (vector[1]*vector[1]) + (vector[2]*vector[2]));
// avoid divide by zero.
         if(length == 0.0) length = 1.0;
// Divide by the length = unit normal vector.
         vector[0] /= length;
         vector[1] /= length;
         vector[2] /= length;
}

void Normal(float v[3][3], float out[3])
{
float v1[3],v2[3];
static const int x = 0, y = 1, z = 2;

// two vectors from the three points
         v1[x] = v[0][x] - v[1][x];
         v1[y] = v[0][y] - v[1][y];
         v1[z] = v[0][z] - v[1][z];

         v2[x] = v[1][x] - v[2][x];
         v2[y] = v[1][y] - v[2][y];
         v2[z] = v[1][z] - v[2][z];
// cross product to get normal vector in out
         out[x] = v1[y]*v2[z] - v1[z]*v2[y];
         out[y] = v1[z]*v2[x] - v1[x]*v2[z];
         out[z] = v1[x]*v2[y] - v1[y]*v2[x];
         Normalise(out);
}

void DrawIt(void)
{
GLfloat normal[3];
GLfloat  lightPos[] = { xpos, ypos, 50.0, 1.0 };
glClear(GL_COLOR_BUFFER_BIT | GL_DEPTH_BUFFER_BIT);
glLightfv(GL_LIGHT0,GL_POSITION,lightPos);  // position light
// Save the matrix state and do the rotations
glPushMatrix();
         glRotatef(xrot, 1.0, 0.0, 0.0);
         glRotatef(yrot, 0.0, 1.0, 0.0);
// set material grey
```

```
            glColor3ub(128, 128, 128);
            glBegin(GL_TRIANGLES);

float v[3][3] = {{ -20.0,0.0,30.0 },
                 { 0.0, 25.0, 30.0 },
                 { 0.0, 0.0, -56.0 }};
        Normal(v,normal);
                glNormal3fv(normal);
                glVertex3fv(v[0]);
                glVertex3fv(v[1]);
                glVertex3fv(v[2]);

  {
float v[3][3] = {{ 0.0, 0.0, -56.0 },
                 { 0.0, 25.0, 30.0 },
                 { 20.0,0.0,30.0 }};
        Normal(v,normal);
                glNormal3fv(normal);
                glVertex3fv(v[0]);
                glVertex3fv(v[1]);
                glVertex3fv(v[2]);
        }
                glNormal3f(0.0, -1.0, 0.0);
                glVertex3f(20.0,0.0,30.0);
                glVertex3f(-20.0, 0.0, 30.0);
                glVertex3f(0.0, 0.0, -56.0);

        {
float v[3][3] = {{ -20.0, 0.0, 30.0 },
                 { 20.0,0.0,30.0 },
                 { 0.0, 25.0, 30.0 }};
        Normal(v,normal);
                glNormal3fv(normal);
                glVertex3fv(v[0]);
                glVertex3fv(v[1]);
                glVertex3fv(v[2]);
        glEnd();
        }
glPopMatrix();      // Restore matrix state
glutSwapBuffers();  // Display results
}

void Environment()
{
        // Light values and coordinates
```

```
GLfloat   ambientLight[] = { 0.3, 0.3, 0.3, 1.0 };
GLfloat   diffuseLight[] = { 0.9, 0.9, 0.9, 1.0 };

          glEnable(GL_DEPTH_TEST);
          glFrontFace(GL_CCW);
          glEnable(GL_CULL_FACE);

          glEnable(GL_LIGHTING);

// Setup and enable light 0
          glLightfv(GL_LIGHT0,GL_AMBIENT,ambientLight);
          glLightfv(GL_LIGHT0,GL_DIFFUSE,diffuseLight);
          glEnable(GL_LIGHT0);

// Enable colour tracking
          glEnable(GL_COLOR_MATERIAL);

// Set Material properties to follow glColor values
          glColorMaterial(GL_FRONT, GL_AMBIENT_AND_DIFFUSE);

// blue background
          glClearColor(0.0, 0.0, 1.0, 1.0 );
}

void KeyControl(int key, int x, int y)
{
          if(key == GLUT_KEY_F8)          xpos-= 5.0;
          if(key == GLUT_KEY_F7)          xpos+= 5.0;

          if(key == GLUT_KEY_UP)          xrot-= 5.0;
          if(key == GLUT_KEY_DOWN)        xrot += 5.0;
          if(key == GLUT_KEY_LEFT)        yrot -= 5.0;
          if(key == GLUT_KEY_RIGHT)       yrot += 5.0;
          if(xrot > 356.0) xrot = 0.0;
          if(xrot < -1.0)  xrot = 355.0;
          if(yrot > 356.0) yrot = 0.0;
          if(yrot < -1.0)  yrot = 355.0;
          glutPostRedisplay();
}
```

The sample program above produces output as shown in Fig. 6.8 where we see the effect of moving the light source from left to right.

Fig. 6.8 Moving the light
source with ambient and
diffuse lighting

6.3.2 Addition of Specular Light

The surfaces shown in Fig. 6.8 appear three dimensional but rather dull! If we are to
captivate interest in games technology then highlights will add interest and possibly
realism. Ambient and diffuse light provide a good representation to surfaces such as
cloth, cardboard or matt paint but less so in the case of shiny surfaces such as metal
or glass mirrors. Shiny surfaces usually have bright spots and highlights and this
is where we introduce a specular component to the OpenGL lighting model. Specular reflection takes place from a shiny *and* smooth surface to produce highlights
Fig. 6.9, in a well-defined direction.

For a perfectly reflecting surface the angle the angle of incidence θ and the angle
of reflection are equal, although in practice the reflected rays are reflected within an
angular cone φ of light, Fig. 6.9. The Phong model for reflection of specular light
from a source I, is given by the equation

$$r = k_s \, I \, \cos^n(\varphi)$$

where the fraction of the incident light that is reflected k_s is given by ($0 \leq k_s \leq 1$)
and n defines the shininess of the surface. Typically values for n might be: $n \sim 500$
for a mirror, $n \sim 200$ for a shiny surface and $n \sim 1$ for cardboard type surface.

In the next example we observe the effect of the specular component in relation
to highlighting over the more bland effects associated with using only ambient and
diffuse light. We have constructed a cube of sides 40 units long with the origin at
the centre of the cube. Readers should note that the order of the vertices is important
as the cross product for calculating the normal is non commutative with the counter
clockwise normal pointing out towards the viewer, glFrontFace(GL_CCW). If vertices are ordered in a clockwise manner the face will be black and no lighting effects
will be seen. Although each face of the cube is strictly made up from two triangles,

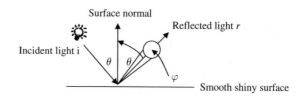

Fig. 6.9 Specular reflection

a single calculation for the normal will suffice since each face is flat and thus we can use glBegin(GL_QUADS) to render the face. It is instructive to move the light source in relation to the cube (keys F3–F8) and observe how the illumination of the image changes. The light source position is printed out for instructional purposes only. The following code can replace the corresponding functions in the previous example to illustrate the effect of specular lighting.

The example of the pyramid was provided in a *hard coded* form where we rendered each face from within the DrawIT() function for purposes of clarity. We now move on to a little more generality in the case of drawing a cube as a precursor to rendering more arbitrary surfaces. We conceive of a cube as made up from six faces or patches, each with four vertices to be used in anticlockwise order, with three coordinates which defines a data structure to represent a cube. The structure or data type would look something like

```
struct patches {
          char type[10];
          char colour;
          float v[4][3];
};
```

For the moment we can ignore the first two components of the structure as they are unnecessary in this example. The third component contains the four vertices for each face in anticlockwise order and the new data type will be of the form

```
patches cubeface[6];
```

as an array of six for the six faces of the cube. Thus all we need to do in the DrawIt() function is to access the data associated with each face or patch, find the normals and render using glVertex3fv(). Instead of hard coding the vertex data we have created a disc file of coordinates (cube.dat) and these are input in the InputData() function.

```
static GLfloat xrot = 0.0, yrot = 0.0;    //lightcubestruct.cpp
static GLfloat xpos = 0.0, ypos = 0.0, zpos = 0.0;
struct patches {
          char type[10];
          char colour;
          float v[4][3];
};
patches cubeface[6];

void InputData()
{        //get cube coordinates from file
int vertex, coord, no_of_faces;
ifstream InPoints("cube.dat", ios::in);
for(no_of_faces=0; no_of_faces<6; no_of_faces++)
```

```
{
        for(vertex = 0; vertex<4; vertex++)
        {
          for(coord=0; coord<3; coord++)
            InPoints >> cubeface[no_of_faces].v[vertex][coord];
        }
}
}

void Normalise(float vector[3])
{
float length;

        length = (float)sqrt((vector[0]*vector[0]) +
                 (vector[1]*vector[1]) + (vector[2]*vector[2]));

        if(length == 0.0) length = 1.0;
        vector[0] /= length;
        vector[1] /= length;
        vector[2] /= length;
}

void Normal(float v[3][3], float out[3])
{
float v1[3],v2[3];
static const int x = 0, y = 1, z = 2;
//find 2 vectors
        v1[x] = v[0][x] - v[1][x];
        v1[y] = v[0][y] - v[1][y];
        v1[z] = v[0][z] - v[1][z];

        v2[x] = v[1][x] - v[2][x];
        v2[y] = v[1][y] - v[2][y];
        v2[z] = v[1][z] - v[2][z];

// cross product in out
        out[x] = v1[y]*v2[z] - v1[z]*v2[y];
        out[y] = v1[z]*v2[x] - v1[x]*v2[z];
        out[z] = v1[x]*v2[y] - v1[y]*v2[x];
        Normalise(out);
}

void DrawIt(void)
{
float normal[3];
```

```
GLfloat  lightPos[3];
int no_of_faces;

lightPos[0] = xpos; lightPos[1] = ypos;
lightPos[2] = zpos; lightPos[3] = 1.0;

glClear(GL_COLOR_BUFFER_BIT | GL_DEPTH_BUFFER_BIT);
        glPushMatrix();
glLightfv(GL_LIGHT0,GL_POSITION,lightPos);

        glPushMatrix();
        glRotatef(xrot, 1.0, 0.0, 0.0);
        glRotatef(yrot, 0.0, 1.0, 0.0);
//grey cube
        glColor3ub(128, 128, 128);
glBegin(GL_QUADS);   //draw cube
for(no_of_faces=0; no_of_faces<6; no_of_faces++)
{
        Normal(cubeface[no_of_faces].v,normal);
        glNormal3fv(normal);
        glVertex3fv(cubeface[no_of_faces].v[0]);
        glVertex3fv(cubeface[no_of_faces].v[1]);
        glVertex3fv(cubeface[no_of_faces].v[2]);
        glVertex3fv(cubeface[no_of_faces].v[3]);
}
glEnd();

        glPopMatrix();
        glutSwapBuffers();
}

void Environment()
{
GLfloat  ambientLight[] = { 0.1, 0.1, 0.1, 1.0 };
GLfloat  diffuseLight[] = { 0.7, 0.7, 0.7, 1.0 };
float specular[] = {1.0, 1.0, 1.0, 1.0};
float emission[] = {0.0, 1.0, 1.0, 1.0};

        glEnable(GL_DEPTH_TEST);
        glFrontFace(GL_CCW);
        glEnable(GL_CULL_FACE);
//set up lighting
glEnable(GL_LIGHTING);
        glLightfv(GL_LIGHT0,GL_AMBIENT,ambientLight);
        glLightfv(GL_LIGHT0,GL_DIFFUSE,diffuseLight);
```

```
        glLightfv(GL_LIGHT0,GL_SPECULAR,specular);

        glEnable(GL_LIGHT0);
//set up material characteristics
        glEnable(GL_COLOR_MATERIAL);
        glColorMaterial(GL_FRONT, GL_AMBIENT_AND_DIFFUSE);
        glMaterialfv(GL_FRONT, GL_SPECULAR, specular);
        glMateriali(GL_FRONT, GL_SHININESS, 128);
        glClearColor(0.0, 0.0, 1.0, 1.0 );
}

void KeyControl(int key, int x, int y)
{       //position of light source
        if(key == GLUT_KEY_F3) xpos-= 5.0;
        if(key == GLUT_KEY_F4) xpos += 5.0;
        if(key == GLUT_KEY_F5) ypos-= 5.0;
        if(key == GLUT_KEY_F6) ypos += 5.0;
        if(key == GLUT_KEY_F7) zpos-= 5.0;
        if(key == GLUT_KEY_F8) zpos += 5.0;
cout << xpos << "  " << ypos << "  " << zpos << "\n";
        //rotate cube about x or y
        if(key == GLUT_KEY_UP)          xrot-= 5.0;
        if(key == GLUT_KEY_DOWN) xrot += 5.0;
        if(key == GLUT_KEY_LEFT)    yrot -= 5.0;
        if(key == GLUT_KEY_RIGHT)  yrot += 5.0;
        if(xrot > 356.0f) xrot = 0.0;
        if(xrot < -1.0f)   xrot = 355.0;
        if(yrot > 356.0f) yrot = 0.0;
        if(yrot < -1.0f)   yrot = 355.0;

        glutPostRedisplay();
}
```

In this example we are allowed to move either the cube by rotation or the light source by position independently of each other using appropriate keys, Fig. 6.10.

Fig. 6.10 An example of the use of specular lighting

6.4 A Synthetic Face

We can now generalise the application of the structure to more non-deterministic surfaces using the triangular patches. There are a number of 3D scanners available, which produce data files of Cartesian coordinates to model a surface (Eyetronics, 2007). For the purpose of this application we shall simplify our surface data on the assumption that such equipment is not always available to students. Further in simplifying the image of a face we shall gain an understanding of the need for much smaller patches for an accurate representation.

6.4.1 Getting the Vertex Coordinates

The simplest way to collect a limited number of coordinates is to overlay the picture with graph paper or superimpose a grid as shown in Fig. 6.11 to capture the $x-y$

Fig. 6.11 Use of grid lines
for data capture

locations while interpolation is required to determine the values of z. For a face the simplest approximation is to consider the head as a sphere and use the distance between the ears as the sphere diameter. The patch data structure is

```
struct patches {
        char type[10];
        char colour;
        float v[3][3];
};
```

for triangular patches. Note that the vertex array is now v[3][3] since there are three vertices rather than the four used for the cube. There are two additions to the vertex coordinates, which readers can use to improve on the current example. The colour of each patch can be specified through a character variable and used to differentiate hair from skin, eyes or lips. The array type[10] was used at the development stage for debugging purposes to indicate which feature was being covered. Clearly the structure can be modified depending on application and is here used to suggest to readers this development. The ordering of vertices is not significant although a row-by-row ordering is convenient. As a first approximation for z we assume $z = 0$ at the ear positions and increases to a maximum at the nose and a minimum at the back of the head. A side view photograph may be used to obtain the approximate values for z. From a photograph we can only approximate the front half of the head. Due to the limits in accuracy and resolution with manual data collection, detailed feature variation is difficult to measure because of the volume of data that is required to capture such features. If we used specular light this is clearly seen as spurious highlights with the varying orientations of patches that in practice cover quite large areas of face. To ameliorate this effect we have used only ambient and diffuse lighting and by orientating the face we can see the size of the patches in Fig. 6.12.

Fig. 6.12 Simulated facial rendering

The software required for the simulated facial rendering is as for the cube, subject to the above variations. A data file of vertex coordinates is supplied for the example in Fig. 6.12 and students are encouraged to use and improve the model from this starter data set.

6.4.2 Moving the Eye and Light Source Together

This form of viewing and illumination is akin to that experienced by a miner where the light source in on the person's helmet. In this situation a variation in the viewing transformation equally affects both the source and viewer since the eye position is the same as that of the light source. In this example we initialise the light source position in the function Environment() at the origin, using glLightfv(GL_LIGHT0,GL_POSITION,lightposition). The DrawIt() rendering function is

```
void DrawIt(void)
{
float normal[3];      // surface normal
GLfloat upx, upy, upz;
int no_of_faces;
glClear(GL_COLOR_BUFFER_BIT | GL_DEPTH_BUFFER_BIT);
    glPushMatrix();
    upx =0; upy = 0; upz =1;
    gluLookAt(xpos, ypos, zpos, 0.0, 0.0, 0.0, upx, upy, upz);

    glColor3ub(128, 128, 128);
glBegin(GL_QUADS);
for(no_of_faces=0; no_of_faces<6; no_of_faces++)
{
        Normal(cubeface[no_of_faces].v,normal);
```

```
        glNormal3fv(normal);
        glVertex3fv(cubeface[no_of_faces].v[0]);
        glVertex3fv(cubeface[no_of_faces].v[1]);
        glVertex3fv(cubeface[no_of_faces].v[2]);
        glVertex3fv(cubeface[no_of_faces].v[3]);
}
glEnd();

    glPopMatrix();
    glutSwapBuffers();
}
```

By varying the position of the light source and viewer using the keys F3–F8, we move around the static cube although this appears as a rotation. In this example only specular light was enabled in the Environment() function, yet the cube is always visible because the eye and light source are operating synchronously using gluLookAt(xpos, ypos, zpos, 0.0, 0.0, 0.0, upx, upy, upz) at (xpos, ypos, zpos).

6.5 Shadows – A Projection

Shadows are not objects, but projections of light falling on an object and subsequently onto a plane. The shadow is where light has been prevented from reaching the plane by the object in front of it and shadows add realism to any image. For simplicity we usually let shadows fall on flat planes like the ground, $y = 0$, where the shadow is referred to as the **shadow polygon** of the illuminated object Fig. 6.13.

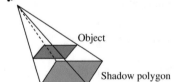

Fig. 6.13 The formation of a shadow

The light source is the centre of projection and thus if we can find the vertices of the shadow polygon which are associated with the corresponding object vertices, then convert them back to world reference frame of reference we can add shadows to our image.

6.5.1 Derivation of the Shadow Outline Using Equation of a Line

Consider the simple case of a line in the $x - y$ plane in Fig. 6.14.

Fig. 6.14 Shadow formation

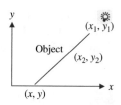

The light source is at (x_1, y_1), the point on the object causing the shadow at (x_2, y_2) and the shadow on the ground $(y = 0)$ at (x, y). Since rays of light travel in straight lines we can use coordinate geometry to find the values of (x, y) as the gradient of the line is constant and given by

$$\frac{y - y_1}{x - x_1} = \frac{y_2 - y_1}{x_2 - x_1}$$

In the general 3D case

$$\frac{x - x_1}{x_2 - x_1} = \frac{y - y_1}{y_2 - y_1} = \frac{z - z_1}{z_2 - z_1}$$

If we consider this line to intersect the $x - z$ plane $(y = 0)$ then we can substitute in the general equation of the line and

$$x = x_2 - y_2 \, {}^* \, \frac{(x_2 - x_1)}{(y_2 - y_1)}$$

$$z = z_2 - y_2 \, {}^* \, \frac{(z_2 - z_1)}{(y_2 - y_1)}$$

are the coordinates of the shadow. We can now write the shadow coordinates in terms of a matrix transform operating on the object coordinates.

$$\begin{pmatrix} x \\ 0 \\ z \\ 1 \end{pmatrix} = \begin{pmatrix} 1 & -(x_2 - x_1)/(y_2 - y_1) & 0 & 0 \\ 0 & 0 & 0 & 0 \\ 0 & -(z_2 - z_1)/(y_2 - y_1) & 1 & 0 \\ 0 & 0 & 0 & 1 \end{pmatrix} \begin{pmatrix} x_2 \\ y_2 \\ z_2 \\ 1 \end{pmatrix}$$

Shadow coordinate = Matrix Transform × Object coordinate

If the light source is a long way away from the object then $y_1 \gg y_2$ and $x_1 \gg x_2$ and the shadow matrix reduces to

$$\begin{pmatrix} 1 & -x_1/y_1 & 0 & 0 \\ 0 & 0 & 0 & 0 \\ 0 & -z_1/y_1 & 1 & 0 \\ 0 & 0 & 0 & 1 \end{pmatrix}$$

Rendering a scene with shadows is really a two-stage process where we draw the object first and then we draw it again after using the matrix transformation. We illustrate this in the next example.

6.5.2 A Polygon Moving Shadow

In this example we will view the shadow cast by a moving light above a red polygon at some arbitrary position above the plane $y = 0$ as shown in Fig. 6.15.

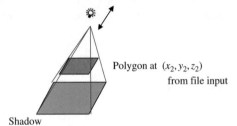

Polygon at (x_2, y_2, z_2)
from file input

Fig. 6.15 Demonstration of shadow formation

Shadow

We shall move the light bulb as a simple harmonic oscillator along the z-axis with the illumination envelope delineated by the blue lines shown in Fig. 6.15. The motion of the light bulb is governed by incrementing the movement during each refresh of the display in the z direction where

$$\text{light}[2] = \text{amplitude} * \sin{(3.142/180.0)}*\text{theta}$$

The amplitude is set to an arbitrary constant suitable for the demonstration. The shadow vertices are calculated from the derivation above for each object vertex as light source oscillates in the z-direction. Using the shadow matrix and the object coordinates at each vertex we calculate the corresponding shadow vertices and render the shadow.

```
float theta=0.0, object[6][4], smcoords[6][4];  //shadmatbook.cpp
float light[3]={0.0, 5.0, 10.0};
int no_of_vertices = 6;

void InData(void) {
ifstream obj("hexagon.txt", ios::in);
int i, vertex;
for(vertex=0; vertex < no_of_vertices; vertex++) { //homog coords
  for(i=0; i<4; i++) obj >> object[vertex][i];
  }
}

void LightDisplay ( void ) {
```

```
  glColor3f(1.0f, 1.0f,0.0f);   // yellow light
  glPointSize(10.0);                // 10 pixels big
  glBegin(GL_POINTS);       //display light
  glVertex3f(light[0], light[1], light[2]);
  glEnd();
}
void MatrixMult(int nvertices, float smatrix[]) {
int row, col, vertex, c1, c2, smrows;
float smsum;
for(vertex = 0; vertex<nvertices; vertex++) {
        c1 = 0; c2 = 4;
        for(smrows = 0; smrows < 4; smrows++) {
                row = 0;
                smsum = 0;
                for(col = c1; col < c2; col++) {
                smsum = smsum + smatrix[col] * object[vertex][row];
                row++;
        }
        c1 = c1 + 4;
        c2 = c1 + 3;
        smcoords[vertex][smrows] = smsum;
    }
}
}


void display(void)
{
float ShadMat[16], x, z;
int i, vertex;
    glMatrixMode (GL_PROJECTION);
    glLoadIdentity ();
    glOrtho(-3.0, 3.0, -6.0, 6.0, -15.0, 15.0);
    glClearColor (1.0, 1.0, 1.0, 0.0);
    glClear(GL_COLOR_BUFFER_BIT|GL_DEPTH_BUFFER_BIT);
    light[2]=2.0*cos((3.142/180.0)*theta); //SHM on z-axis

    gluLookAt(light[0], light[1], 0.0,0.0,0.675,-0.25,0.0,1.0,0.0);
    glEnable(GL_DEPTH_TEST);
    glFrontFace(GL_CCW);
    glEnable(GL_CULL_FACE);

    LightDisplay( );              // shadow illumination
glPushMatrix();
glBegin(GL_POLYGON);
glColor3f(1.0, 0.0, 0.0); // red object for shadow
 for(vertex=0; vertex < no_of_vertices; vertex++) {
```

```
   glVertex3f(object[vertex][0], object[vertex][1], object[vertex][2]);
 }
glEnd();
glPopMatrix();

glPushMatrix();
glColor3f(0.4,0.4,0.4);
glBegin(GL_POLYGON);
 for(i=0;i<15;i++) ShadMat[i]=0.0;
 ShadMat[0]=1.0 ;ShadMat[10]=1.0; ShadMat[15]=1.0;
 for(vertex=0; vertex < no_of_vertices; vertex++) {
   ShadMat[1]= -(object[vertex][0] - light[0]) /(object[vertex][1] - light
   ShadMat[9]= -(object[vertex][2] - light[2]) /(object[vertex][1] - light
   MatrixMult(no_of_vertices, ShadMat);
   x = smcoords[vertex][0];
   z = smcoords[vertex][2];
   glVertex3f(x, 0.0, z); //shadow
     }
glEnd();
glPopMatrix();
glFlush();
glutSwapBuffers();
}

void wait_a_while()
{
   theta = theta + 0.5;
   if(theta>360.0) theta-=360;
   glutPostRedisplay();
}
```

In Fig. 6.16 we have indicated some of the illumination envelope and readers may find it instructive to add this code to the preceding program.

Fig. 6.16 Shadow example

6.6 Exercises

1. In the program shadmatbook.cpp replace use the data file for the pyramid as the object to produce the shadow and modify the display function as appropriate.

2. Familiarise yourself with different light source positions in the program lightcubestruct.cpp and watch the effect on the resultant display. Construct a table of light position in relation to the illumination of different faces of the cube.
3. Develop the data structure used for Fig. 6.12 to increase the resolution and enhance detail to the synthetic face. Further enhancement using skin colour, hair and eye detail should be explored.

6.7 Conclusions

In this chapter we have introduced the effects of ambient, diffuse and specular lighting to enhance the realism of the graphics display. In conjunction with either movement of the object or light source we are able to appreciate movement in relation to the surrounding context. The building of data to represent a complex image such as a face is often not available to most undergraduates and so we have provide a basic data capture system to illustrate the process while referencing commercial capture systems for more advanced courses. A simple introduction to shadow production is provided for planar objects.

Chapter 7
Texture Mapping

7.1 Introduction

Up to now we have drawn single colour shapes with some shading and shadows on simple objects. Texture mapping is the start of introducing realism to an image. Rather than say have just green to represent the grass we might want to paste or texture a picture of grass onto the surface that will be used to represent the ground. Although textures may be one, two or three-dimensional we shall largely be concerned with two-dimensional textures plus an introduction to three-dimensional texturing in this chapter.

The textural impression can be adjusted (modulated) to improve realism by adjusting

- surface colour by means of reflection coefficient
- specular and diffuse reflection (environmental)
- vector normal changes to give dimpled surface (Bump mapping)
- transparency by generating extra surfaces to give new impression (etched glass)

7.2 The Mapping Process

The mapping process involves moving from the texture space to the Cartesian space occupied by the object surfaces. The image to be mapped onto a surface is frequently a picture that has been scanned and stored as a bit map array. Although this array can be thought of as an array of pixels we also refer to it as an array of **texels** since there will not be a one to one correspondence between the photographic image and the surface to which it will be attached.

The bit map is defined in (s, t) texel space and requires a mapping function that pastes texels to the object surface shown in Fig. 7.1. The locations in Cartesian space (x, y) must be some function of s and t for the mapping to be possible. We also see from Fig. 7.1 that there is a problem of where texels go from a rectangular to a triangular image in space and more generally, to any arbitrary shaped on a surface.

The example in Fig. 7.2 shows a mapping from one rectangular shape to another where the main distortion is related to size and thus the mapping is some form

R. Whitrow, *OpenGL Graphics Through Applications,*
© Springer-Verlag London Limited 2008

Fig. 7.1 Mapping between
texel space and image space

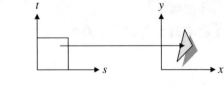

Fig. 7.2 Mapping image to a
picture in a room

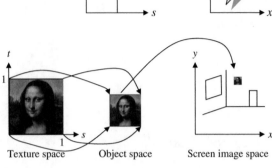

Texture space   Object space   Screen image space

of scaling followed by the projection mapping onto the screen. We can write this
relationship as

$$x = x(s, t)$$
$$y = y(s, t)$$
$$z = z(s, t)$$

For a simple scaling we can associate each texel (s, t) with each image pixel $(x, y,$
$x)$ using the functions

$$\text{glTexCoord2f}(s, t); \qquad \text{glVertex3f}(x, y, z);$$

where $0 \leq s \leq 1$ and $0 \leq t \leq 1$.

The bit map image to be mapped into Cartesian space is read into an array using
the class Read_bmp developed in Chapter 1. Texturing is enabled and disabled using
glEnable() and glDisable() with the symbolic constant GL_TEXTURE_2D.

7.3 Setting up Textures

Setting up a bit map image for texturing purposes requires that we describe the bit
map image in a form that will allow manipulation from the (s, t) texture space to the
(x, y, z) space of an object surface. Some of this manipulation is performed through
linear mapping functions but at the texel to pixel level we need to associate pixels
and texels that correspond in position but may not be of the same size. Texels can be
applied to pixels in a number of ways and the following example is provided to get
you started. Students should consult with the OpenGl reference manual (Shreiner,
2006) to elaborate on the many and complex variations that are available! To provide
a texturing capability we must:

- Have captured a bit map image to an array in memory and specified how each row of pixels in the image are aligned. Each row of pixels should be of a length that is a power of 2.
- Identify each texture object to be used with a unique integer name.
- Specify controls required in moving from image pixel space to the texture space.
- Define the image being used in terms of dimensionality, storage format, size and location in memory.

The following initialisation is given with explanation in C++ type comments after each line.

Image capture

```
//Input BMP image using class Read_bmp developed in chapter 1
//to a 3D array with
//four components for RGBA
glPixelStorei(GL_UNPACK_ALIGNMENT, 1);
//Specify that each row of pixels are byte aligned
```

Texture identifier

```
glGenTextures (1, &texName);
//Generate a one unique integer name for creating texture
//object from bit map image if more than one texture is used,
//texName will be an array and the will be 'n' texture names
glBindTexture(GL_TEXTURE_2D, texName);
//Create texture object with integer name from glGenTextures ()
//for (re)use later in program
//After binding the object to the texture name we now set the
//texture parameters
```

Texture controls

```
glTexParameteri(GL_TEXTURE_2D, GL_TEXTURE_WRAP_S, GL_REPEAT);
//Colour wrapping for 0 ≤ s ≥ 1
//Sets a number of the texture parameters to fill corresponding
//pixels - similar to shrink wrapping an object with polythene
glTexParameteri(GL_TEXTURE_2D, GL_TEXTURE_WRAP_T, GL_REPEAT);
//Colour wrapping for 0 ≤ t ≥ 1
glTexParameteri(GL_TEXTURE_2D, GL_TEXTURE_MAG_FILTER,
GL_NEAREST);
//Colour filtering
// GL_TEXTURE_MAG_FILTER used when pixel maps to a texel of
//smaller area - that is magnify it
//GL_NEAREST value of texel nearest to pixel being textured
glTexParameteri(GL_TEXTURE_2D, GL_TEXTURE_MIN_FILTER,
GL_NEAREST);
```

```
//Colour repeating
//called minifying - when pixel area is > texel area
```

Texture definition
```
glTexImage2D(GL_TEXTURE_2D, 0, GL_RGBA, ww, wh, 0, GL_RGBA,
      GL_UNSIGNED_BYTE, Image);
//Define a 2D image subject to the above conditions
//in terms of texture dimension, level of detail, colour
//storage, image size, border
//size, pixel format, data type and a pointer to where the bit
//map image is stored
```

7.3.1 Drawing the Texture

To display a texture we must first enable using glEnable(GL_TEXTURE_2D); and then associate the texture coordinates (s, t) with the Cartesian coordinates (x, y, z) of the object being textured.

```
glTexCoord2f(s, t); glVertex3f(x, y, z);
```

In the following code three pictures of the Mona Lisa are textured rotated through various angles, Fig. 7.3.

```
#define Width 256      //mona.cpp
#define Height 256

int ww, wh;
static GLubyte Image[Height][Width][4];
static GLuint texName;

#include "Read_bmp.cpp"

void init(void)
{
ip_bmp_file Read_BMP_file;
  Read_BMP_file.header_data();
  glClearColor(0.0, 0.0, 0.0, 0.0);
  glShadeModel(GL_FLAT);
  glEnable(GL_DEPTH_TEST);
  glPixelStorei(GL_UNPACK_ALIGNMENT, 1);
  glGenTextures (1, &texName);
  glBindTexture(GL_TEXTURE_2D, texName);
  glTexParameteri(GL_TEXTURE_2D, GL_TEXTURE_WRAP_S, GL_REPEAT);
  glTexParameteri(GL_TEXTURE_2D, GL_TEXTURE_WRAP_T, GL_REPEAT);
```

```
  glTexParameteri(GL_TEXTURE_2D, GL_TEXTURE_MAG_FILTER,
                  GL_NEAREST);
  glTexParameteri(GL_TEXTURE_2D, GL_TEXTURE_MIN_FILTER,
                  GL_NEAREST);
  glTexImage2D(GL_TEXTURE_2D, 0, GL_RGBA, ww, wh, 0, GL_RGBA,
      GL_UNSIGNED_BYTE, Image);
  glBindTexture(GL_TEXTURE_2D, texName);
}

void display(void)
{
  glClear(GL_COLOR_BUFFER_BIT |  GL_DEPTH_BUFFER_BIT);
  glEnable(GL_TEXTURE_2D);
  glTexEnvf(GL_TEXTURE_ENV, GL_TEXTURE_ENV_MODE, GL_REPLACE);
  glBegin(GL_QUADS);
  glTexCoord2f(0.0, 0.0); glVertex3f(-2.0, -1.0, 0.0);
  glTexCoord2f(0.0, 1.0); glVertex3f(-2.0, 1.0, 0.0);
  glTexCoord2f(1.0, 1.0); glVertex3f(0.0, 1.0, 0.0);
  glTexCoord2f(1.0, 0.0); glVertex3f(0.0, -1.0, 0.0);

  glTexCoord2f(0.0, 0.0); glVertex3f(0.25, -0.25, -0.25);
  glTexCoord2f(0.0, 1.0); glVertex3f(0.0, 1.0, 0.0);
  glTexCoord2f(1.0, 1.0); glVertex3f(1.0, 1.0, -1.0);
  glTexCoord2f(1.0, 0.0); glVertex3f(1.0, -1.0, -1.0);

  glTexCoord2f(0.0, 0.0); glVertex3f(1.41421, -1.0, -1.41421);
  glTexCoord2f(0.0, 1.0); glVertex3f(1.41421, 1.0, -1.41421);
  glTexCoord2f(1.0, 1.0); glVertex3f(2.82842, 1.0, 0.0);
  glTexCoord2f(1.0, 0.0); glVertex3f(2.82841, -1.0, 0.0);
glEnd();
glFlush();
glDisable(GL_TEXTURE_2D);
}

void reshape(int w, int h)
{
  glViewport(0, 0, (GLsizei) w, (GLsizei) h);
  glMatrixMode(GL_PROJECTION);
  glLoadIdentity();
  gluPerspective(60.0, (GLfloat) w/(GLfloat) h, 1.0, 5.0);
  glMatrixMode(GL_MODELVIEW);
  glLoadIdentity();
  glTranslatef(0.0, 0.0, -4.0);
}
```

Fig. 7.3 Texturing a bit map image onto a rectangle

We have attempted to 'lift' one corner of the second image by altering the (x, y, z) values in the function glVertex3f() and while this gives some impression of curvature it is not entirely satisfactory. We shall revisit such ideas later when we address curvature associated with images more generally.

7.4 Mapping onto Curved Surfaces

The previous example was a simple mapping onto a flat surface where texture and Cartesian coordinates are intuitively very similar. To transfer a bit map onto a curved surface we require a function that will convert coordinates in texture space to Cartesian coordinates in object space. To understand this we will first describe surfaces and how they may degenerate into different surfaces.

7.4.1 Mercator Lines of Projection

Consider projection of points on the surface of a sphere through the centre and onto a cylinder surrounding the sphere. Lines of longitude on sphere are parallel vertical lines when projected on the cylinder and the same distance apart.

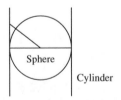

Lines of latitude on the sphere are horizontal lines on the cylinder whose distance apart at the equator is similar on cylinder but get further apart on cylinder as we approach the poles of the sphere.

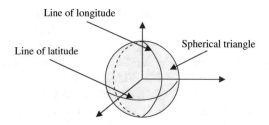

A plane through the centre of a sphere forms what is called a **great circle** and one of these in the case of our earth is the **equator**. The intersection of two planes forms a **Spherical triangle** on the surface of a sphere.

7.4.2 Quadric Surfaces

Quadric surfaces are widely used in graphics and for modelling of objects. The equation representing a general quadric is given by

$$\underbrace{a_1x^2 + a_2y^2 + a_3z^2}_{\text{sphere about origin}} + a_4xy + a_5yz + a_6xz + \underbrace{a_7x + a_8y + a_9z + a_{10}}_{\text{plane}} = 0$$

If the coefficients $a_1 \to a_6 = 0$, then the quadric degenerates to the equation of a plane. Spheres, cones, cylinders are examples of what we call quadrics and the GLUT library provides extensions for drawing quadrics while the basic OpenGL library only supports points, lines and polygons. The following routines are used for drawing a quadric:

```
gluNewQuadric() - create quadric object & return pointer to
object
gluQuadricDrawStyle() - render quadric as points / lines /
filled polygons
gluQuadricNormals() - for illuminated objects - one normal
                    per vertex / one normal per face / no normals
gluQuadricTexture() - if texturing required
gluSphere() - sphere-rendering routine at origin
gluDeleteQuadric (object pointer) - finish with object

A quadric surface is identified as follows
GLUquadricOBJ *obptr;
objptr = gluNewQuadric();   //creates state variable for the
//drawing
gluQuadricDrawStyle(objptr, GLU_FILL //render with polygons
                                 //counter clockwise
                    GLU_LINE //render with lines
```

```
                              GLU_SILHOUETTE // render with lines
                                            //[not edges]
                              GLU_POINT //render with points);
gluQuadricNormals(objptr,     GLU_NONE //no Normal generation
                              GLU_FLAT //one Normal per facet
                              GLU_SMOOTH //one Normal per vertex);
gluQuadricTexture(objptr, GL_TRUE // generate texture);

and if a sphere is the required surface
gluSphere(objptr, radius, slices around z axis, stacks along
z axis / up y axis);
```

7.4.3 Mapping onto a Spherical Surface

Adding texture to a solid surface requires a mapping operation from texture to object space (Rogers, 1998). We map from texture co-ordinates (s, t) to image co-ordinates (x, y, z) via intermediate polar co-ordinates (r, θ, φ), which can be used to describe a spherical object.

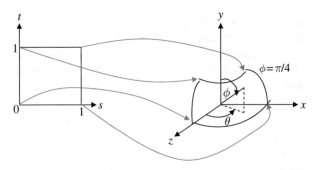

Fig. 7.4 Relationship between texture (s, t) and Cartesian coordinates (x, y, z)

If we assume a linear mapping relationship between (s, t) and (θ, ϕ) of the form

$$\theta = As + B \quad \text{and} \quad \phi = Ct + D$$

where the relation between the Cartesian coordinates (x, y, z) and the polar angles is

$$x = \sin(\theta) \sin(\phi) \quad \text{and} \quad y = \cos(\phi) \quad \text{and} \quad z = \cos(\theta) \sin(\phi)$$

from Fig. 7.4. In our first example we will map the whole bit map onto the part of a sphere defined by θ from $-\pi/2$ to $\pi/2$ with φ taking values between $\pi/4 < \varphi < \pi/2$.

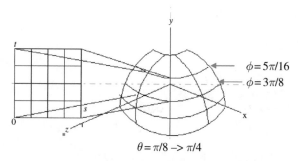

Fig. 7.5 Mapping - example 1

We now calculate the object co-ordinates (x, y, z) of one patch, Fig. 7.5 on a quadrant of the sphere and map the corresponding texture co-ordinates (s, t). We use the intermediate mapping $s \leftrightarrow \theta$ and $t \leftrightarrow \varphi$ to find x, y, z

$$\theta = As + B \qquad \varphi = Ct + D$$

When $s = 0, \theta = \pi/8$ and when $s = 1, \theta = \pi/4$. Substituting we solve for B and A

$$\pi/8 = B \quad \text{and} \quad \pi/4 = A + B$$
$$\therefore A = \pi/8$$

Similarly when $t = 1, \varphi = 5\pi/16$ and when $t = 0, \varphi = 3\pi/8$

$$3\pi/8 = D \quad \text{and} \quad 5\pi/16 = C + 3\pi/8$$
$$\therefore C = -\pi/16$$

Thus rewriting our mapping function with the values for A, B, C and D

$$\theta = (s + 1)^*\pi/8$$
$$\varphi = \pi/16(6 - t)$$

The mapping will be performed in procedure display() in the following example, Fig. 7.6.

The consistent ordering of points is important i.e. $0,0 - 0,1 - 1,1 - 1,0$ and the corresponding x, y, z points in Cartesian space for correct images. The image file (phantom.bmp) is included with the accompanying web site as a 256×256 bit map file.

```
#define Width 256 //spherem.cpp
#define Height 256

int ww, wh;
static GLubyte Image[Height][Width][4];
static GLuint texName;
```

```
#include "Read_bmp.cpp"

void init(void)
{
ip_bmp_file Read_BMP_file;
  Read_BMP_file.header_data();
  glClearColor(1.0, 0.0, 0.0, 0.0);
  glShadeModel(GL_FLAT);
  glEnable(GL_DEPTH_TEST);
  glPixelStorei(GL_UNPACK_ALIGNMENT, 1);
  glGenTextures (1, &texName) ;
  glBindTexture(GL_TEXTURE_2D, texName);
  glTexParameteri(GL_TEXTURE_2D, GL_TEXTURE_WRAP_S, GL_REPEAT);
  glTexParameteri(GL_TEXTURE_2D, GL_TEXTURE_WRAP_T, GL_REPEAT);
  glTexParameteri(GL_TEXTURE_2D, GL_TEXTURE_MAG_FILTER,
                  GL_NEAREST);
  glTexParameteri(GL_TEXTURE_2D, GL_TEXTURE_MIN_FILTER,
                  GL_NEAREST);
  glTexImage2D(GL_TEXTURE_2D, 0, GL_RGBA, ww, wh, 0, GL_RGBA,
               GL_UNSIGNED_BYTE, Image);
  }
  void display(void)
  {
  float theta, phi, x, y, z;
  float theta1, theta2, phi1, phi2;
  glClear(GL_COLOR_BUFFER_BIT | GL_DEPTH_BUFFER_BIT);
  glEnable(GL_TEXTURE_2D);
  glTexEnvf(GL_TEXTURE_ENV, GL_TEXTURE_ENV_MODE, GL_REPLACE);
  glBindTexture(GL_TEXTURE_2D, texName);
  glBegin(GL_QUADS);
//Not very tidy code! - Used to illustrate clearly?
  phi1 = 3.142/2.0; phi2 = 6.0*3.142/16.0;
do {
    theta1 = -3.142/2.0; theta2 = -3.0*3.142/8.0;
  do {
   theta = theta1;
   phi = phi1;
   x = 2*sin(theta)*sin(phi);
   y = 2*cos(phi);
   z = 2*cos(theta)*sin(phi);
        glTexCoord2f(0, 0); glVertex3f(x, y, z);
   theta = theta2;
   x = 2*sin(theta)*sin(phi);
   y = 2*cos(phi);
   z = 2*cos(theta)*sin(phi);
```

```
 glTexCoord2f(0, 1); glVertex3f(x, y, z);
 phi = phi2;
 x = 2*sin(theta)*sin(phi);
 y = 2*cos(phi);
 z = 2*cos(theta)*sin(phi);
 glTexCoord2f(1, 1); glVertex3f(x, y, z);
 theta = theta1;
 x = 2*sin(theta)*sin(phi);
 y = 2*cos(phi);
 z = 2*cos(theta)*sin(phi);
 glTexCoord2f(1, 0); glVertex3f(x, y, z);

 theta1 = theta2;
 theta2 = theta2+ 3.142/8.0;
 } while(theta2<=3.142/2.0);
 phi1 = phi2;
 phi2 = phi2 - 3.142/16.0;
} while (phi2>=3.142/4.0);
glEnd();
glFlush();
glDisable(GL_TEXTURE_2D);
}

void reshape(int w, int h)
{
 glViewport(0, 0, (GLsizei) w, (GLsizei) h);
 glMatrixMode(GL_PROJECTION);
 glLoadIdentity();
 gluPerspective(60.0, (GLfloat) w/(GLfloat) h, 1.0, 30.0);
 glMatrixMode(GL_MODELVIEW);
 glLoadIdentity();
 glTranslatef(0.0, 0.0, -3.6);
}
```

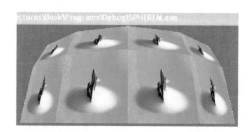

Fig. 7.6 Patching a bit map
image onto part of a sphere

7.4.4 Mapping one Image to Sphere

In previous example we mapped each bit map image to each patch on sphere and obtained a patchwork of the texture image. We now map a single image onto the whole part of the sphere concerned, Fig. 7.7. In this situation we need to map corresponding positions in (s, t) space to whole of the (x, y, z) space.

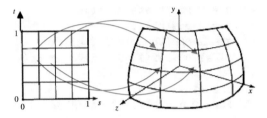

Fig. 7.7 Mapping texture to total object surface

With this form of mapping corresponding areas of the texture image are mapped to related regions of the object surface. We shall again use the intermediate mapping $s \leftrightarrow \theta$ and $t \leftrightarrow \varphi$ to find corresponding values for (x, y, z) where

$$\theta = As + B \qquad \varphi = Ct + D$$

If we consider the part of a sphere in the first octant then

$$\begin{aligned} s &= 0, \quad \theta = 0 \\ s &= 1, \quad \theta = \pi/2 \end{aligned}$$

Substituting in the function for θ

$$\begin{aligned} 0 &= B \quad \text{and} \quad \pi/2 = A + B \\ &\therefore A = \pi/2 \end{aligned}$$

Similarly when $t = 1$, $\varphi = \pi/4$ and when $t = 0$, $\varphi = \pi/2$

$$\begin{aligned} \pi/4 &= C + D \quad \text{and} \quad \pi/2 = D \\ &\therefore C = -\pi/4 \end{aligned}$$

The linear transforms for this mapping are

$$\theta \quad = s * \pi/2$$

and

$$\varphi = \pi/2 * (1.0 - t/2.0)$$

The linear mappings are implemented in the display function following which can replace the corresponding function in the previous program. The texture image is divided into patches of size 'resolution' and (s, t) is incremented from 0 to 1 by this value. Using the linear transforms we may calculate (θ, φ) and thus the corresponding values of (x, y, z).

```
void display(void)
{
  float theta, phi, x, y, z, s, t, sstart, sinc, send, tstart,
  tinc, tend;
  float resolution;
  glClear(GL_COLOR_BUFFER_BIT | GL_DEPTH_BUFFER_BIT);
  glEnable(GL_TEXTURE_2D);
  glTexEnvf(GL_TEXTURE_ENV, GL_TEXTURE_ENV_MODE, GL_REPLACE);
  glBindTexture(GL_TEXTURE_2D, texName);
  glBegin(GL_QUADS);
  //resolution = 0.125;
  resolution = 1.0;
  tstart = 0.0; tend = resolution;
  tinc = resolution;
do {
  sstart = 0.0; send = resolution;
  sinc = resolution;
  do {
  t=tstart;
  for(s=sstart; s<=send; s=s+sinc) {
      theta = 3.142 * s / 2.0;
      phi = (1.0 - t/2.0) * 3.142 / 2.0;
      x = 2.0*sin(theta)*sin(phi);
      y = 2.0*cos(phi);
      z = 2.0*cos(theta)*sin(phi);
              glTexCoord2f(s, t); glVertex3f(x, y, z);
      }
    t=tend;
  for(s=send; s>=sstart; s=s-sinc) {
      theta = 3.142 * s / 2.0;
      phi = (1.0 - t/2.0) * 3.142 / 2.0;
      x = 2.0*sin(theta)*sin(phi);
      y = 2.0*cos(phi);
      z = 2.0*cos(theta)*sin(phi);
              glTexCoord2f(s, t); glVertex3f(x, y, z);

      }
  sstart = send; //next col
  send = sstart + sinc;
```

```
  } while(send < 1.0);
  tstart = tend;
  tend = tstart + tinc;
} while(tend < 1.0);
glEnd();
glFlush();
glDisable(GL_TEXTURE_2D);
}
```

Fig. 7.8 Texturing showing
the effect of patch size

The increments in the texture coordinates (s, t) used to calculate (x, y, z) govern the smoothness of the textured surface produced, Fig. 7.8.

7.4.5 Cylinder Texturing Mapping

To map an image onto a cylinder we again use the linear relations

$$\theta = As + B \quad \text{and} \quad \varphi = Ct + D$$

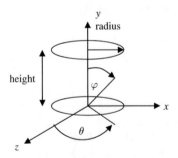

Now when $s = 0$, $\theta = 0$ and when $\theta = 2\pi$, $s = 1$

$$\therefore \theta = 2 \pi u$$

Similarly when $t = 0$, $\varphi = \pi/2$ and when $t = 1$ then $\varphi = \tan^{-1}(\text{radius/height})$

$$\therefore \varphi = [\tan^{-1}(\text{radius/height}) - \pi/2]t + \pi/2$$

The Cartesian coordinates (x, y, z) may also be written in cylindrical coordinates as

$$x = \text{radius}^* \sin(\theta)$$
$$y = \text{radius}/\tan(\varphi)$$
$$z = \text{radius}^* \cos(\theta) \quad \text{for } 0 \le \theta \le 2\pi$$
$$\text{and } \tan^{-1}(\text{radius/height}) < \varphi < \pi/2$$

If the (radius/height) term is large, errors will occur in calculating the value of φ and thus users should test for these when the height is tending to zero. Readers should note that depending on the position of the viewer and the relative height of the cylinder the perspective projection may produce a different view of the top and bottom faces of the cylinder, Fig. 7.9.

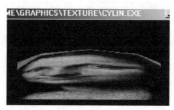

Fig. 7.9 Texture mapping onto a cylinder

7.4.6 Mapping to a Circle

For the mapping to a circle an alternative approach is described where the image is cut into slices that correspond to slices of the circle.

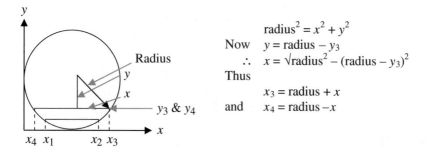

$$\text{radius}^2 = x^2 + y^2$$

Now $y = \text{radius} - y_3$

$\therefore \quad x = \sqrt{\text{radius}^2 - (\text{radius} - y_3)^2}$

Thus

$$x_3 = \text{radius} + x$$

and $\quad x_4 = \text{radius} - x$

Using the same reasoning in the $(s - t)$ plane we can determine to corresponding values of s and t for (x_1, y_1) to (x_4, y_4) by proportionality of the radii in each plane.

$$s_3 = x_3 * 0.5/\text{radius}$$
$$s_4 = x_4 * 0.5/\text{radius}$$
$$t_3 = t_3 + \text{yinc} * 0.5/\text{radius}$$
$$t_4 = t_3$$

and $\text{yinc} = y_3 - y_2$. The incremental value for y is dependent on the user.

7.4.7 Mapping to a Cone

The mapping process is illustrated in Fig. 7.10 and Fig. 7.11.

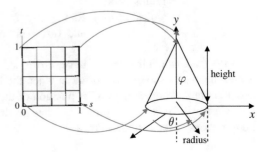

Fig. 7.10 Texture mapping of a cone

We will assume the linear mapping function

$$s = A^*\theta + B$$

variation in s where

$$s = 0, \ \theta = -\pi/2$$

and

$$s = 1, \ \theta = \pi/2$$

then substituting

$$0 = -\pi/2 \ ^* A + B$$

and

$$1 = A \ ^* \ \pi/2 + B$$
$$2 \ ^* B = 1$$
$$\therefore B = 0.5$$

Similarly

$$1 = A \ ^* \ \pi/2 + 0.5$$
$$\therefore \quad A = 1/\pi$$

Thus

$$\theta = (s - B)/A$$
$$= \pi \ ^* (s - 0.5)$$

This mapping function will work by patching around the surface of the cone for any given radius. We can vary the size of the patches by moving up from the base of the cone and using a new radius for each strip or layer of patches where the radius can be found from the relationship

$$\tan(\varphi) = \text{radius/yheight}$$

At the base of the cone the lowest row of patches the Cartesian coordinates are

$$x = \text{radius\_next}^* \sin(\theta)$$
$$y = \text{ystart}$$
$$z = \text{radius\_next}^* \cos(\theta)$$

where radius_next is initialised to the radius of the cone base and s is increasing from 0 to 1. On the top edge of the patch the radius has decreased as we move up the cone and s decreases.

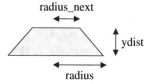

Fig. 7.11 The effect of moving up the sides of the cone

If we let 'ydist' be the width of the patch, then

$$\text{radius\_next} = (\text{height} - \text{ydist}) * \tan(\varphi)$$
$$y = y + \text{ydist}$$
$$x = \text{radius\_next} * \sin(\text{theta});$$
$$z = \text{radius\_next} * \cos(\text{theta});$$

Finally we move up to the next layer of patches by resetting the variables for this layer

$$\text{yheight} = \text{yheight} - \text{ydist}$$
$$\text{ystart} = y$$
$$\text{radius} = \text{radius\_next}$$

The display function for a cone where $-\pi/2 \le \theta \le \pi/2$ is

```
void display(void)
{
  float theta, x, y, z, s, t, sstart, sinc, send, tstart, tinc, tend;
  float resolution, radius, radtmp, yheight, ydist, ystart, tanphi;
  glClear(GL_COLOR_BUFFER_BIT |  GL_DEPTH_BUFFER_BIT);
  glEnable(GL_TEXTURE_2D);
  glTexEnvf(GL_TEXTURE_ENV, GL_TEXTURE_ENV_MODE, GL_REPLACE);
  glBindTexture(GL_TEXTURE_2D, texName);
```

```
  glBegin(GL_QUADS);
  yheight = 2.0;
  ystart = 0.0;
  resolution = 0.25;
  ydist = yheight * resolution;
   tstart = 0.0; tend = 0.25;
   tinc = resolution;
   radius = 1.5;
   tanphi = radius/yheight;
  do {
   sstart = 0.0; send = resolution;
   sinc = resolution;
do {
   t = tstart;
   radtmp = radius;
   for(s=sstart; s<=send; s=s+sinc) {
     theta = 3.142 * (s - 0.5);
     x = radtmp*sin(theta);
     y = ystart; //vstart;
         z = radtmp*cos(theta);
     glTexCoord2f(s, t); glVertex3f(x, y, z);
     }
     t = tend;
     radtmp = (yheight - ydist) * tanphi;
     y = y + ydist;
   for(s=send; s>=sstart; s=s-sinc) {
     theta = 3.142 * (s - 0.5);
     x = radtmp*sin(theta);
     z = radtmp*cos(theta); //2.0
     glTexCoord2f(s, t); glVertex3f(x, y, z);
     }
   sstart = send; //next col
   send = sstart + sinc;
   } while(send <=1.0);
  yheight = yheight - ydist;
  ystart = y;
  radius = radtmp;
  tstart = tend;
  tend = tstart + tinc;
  } while(tend <=1.0);
glEnd();
glFlush();
glDisable(GL_TEXTURE_2D);
}
```

Results are displayed in Fig. 7.12.

Fig. 7.12 Texturing a cone

7.4.8 Mapping onto a General Surface

Up to this point we have covered surfaces where there has been an analytic relationship between the surface and the image to be used for texturing. For surfaces where no such geometric relation exists we use an approximation of computing the corresponding positions of texel and Cartesian coordinate in each space. Formally this may be written as follows

```
for each y line {
    for each x position on line{
        read texture s(x,y) and t(x,y)
        copy texture (s, t) value to image space location (x, y)
    }
}
```

To illustrate we create a sinusoidal surface $\sin(x, y)$ and paste our image where the sinusoid x takes values $0 \rightarrow 2\pi$ in Fig. 7.13.

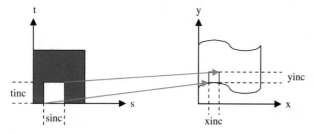

Fig. 7.13 Texturing for general objects

The resolution or size of each patch governs the quality of replication on the object with the limit being the individual texels. We represent the sinusoidal shape as

$$z = \sin(2 \pi x)$$

and increment x from 0 to 1. An example of code to perform the more general surface patching follows.

```
void display(void)
{
float x, y, z, s, t, sstart, sinc, send, tstart, tinc, tend;
float resolution, xstart, ystart, xinc, yinc, xorigin;
  glClear(GL_COLOR_BUFFER_BIT |   GL_DEPTH_BUFFER_BIT);
  glEnable(GL_TEXTURE_2D);
  glTexEnvf(GL_TEXTURE_ENV, GL_TEXTURE_ENV_MODE, GL_REPLACE);
  glBindTexture(GL_TEXTURE_2D, texName);
glBegin(GL_QUADS);
  resolution = 0.0625;
  xstart=0.0; ystart=0.0;
  xorigin = 0.0;
  xinc=0.0625; yinc=0.0625;
  tstart = 0.0;
  tinc = resolution;
  sinc = resolution;
  sstart = -sinc;
do {
  sstart = sstart+sinc; send = resolution;
  sinc = resolution;
   do {
    s=sstart; x=xstart;
    t=tstart; y=ystart;
    z=sin(6.284*x);
      glTexCoord2f(s, t); glVertex3f(x*2.0, y, z);
    s=sstart+sinc; x=xstart+xinc;
    z=sin(6.284*x);
      glTexCoord2f(s, t); glVertex3f(x*2.0, y, z);
      t=tstart+tinc; y=ystart+yinc;
      glTexCoord2f(s, t); glVertex3f(x*2.0, y, z);
    s=sstart; x=xstart;
    z=sin(6.284*x);
      glTexCoord2f(s, t); glVertex3f(x*2.0, y, z);
    send = sstart + sinc;
    sstart = sstart+ sinc; xstart = xstart + xinc;
   } while(send <1.0);
  tstart = tstart+ tinc;
  sstart = -sinc;
  tend = tstart +tinc;
  xstart = xorigin;
  ystart = ystart+ yinc;
} while(tend <=1.0);
glEnd();
glFlush();
glDisable(GL_TEXTURE_2D);
}
```

An example of generalised mapping is displayed in Fig. 7.14.

Fig. 7.14 An example of
general surface patching

7.4.9 *Mapping onto a Contour Surface*

In Chapter 9 we develop a means of creating a 3D surface from a number of contours
that might represent terrain height as seen by the microwave reflection times from
an aircraft or satellite. We have simplified the data collection to using just graph
paper since resources for most of us are limited! The contours are linked to create a
series of quadrilateral patches that make up the surface in Fig. 9.9. The size of the
quadrilaterals in practice would be variable depending on the level of detail required
at any point on the terrain map, although for our purposes we have kept it fixed to
simplify data capture. Each patch in Cartesian space receives a corresponding part of
the bit map used to texture the total surface. The mapping is illustrated in Fig. 7.13
except that we replace the Cartesian sinusoid with the surface generated by contour
profiles of terrain - in this example Mount Fuji in Japan. The terrain is for illustrative
purposes only in Fig. 7.15.

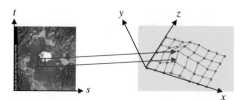

Fig. 7.15 Mapping onto a
general terrain

To perform the mapping we need the maximum size of the region in the $x - z$
plane to scale each point on the terrain and move to the appropriate positions for s,
t in the texture plane. This may be written as

$$\frac{x_i}{x_{\max}} = s_i \quad \text{and} \quad \frac{z_j}{z_{\max}} = t_j$$

```
void display ()
{
int i, istart, iend;
float s, t;
glClear(GL_COLOR_BUFFER_BIT | GL_DEPTH_BUFFER_BIT);
        glColor3f(0.0f, 0.0f,1.0f);
        glRotatef(rot[0], 1.0f, 0.0f, 0.0f);
        glRotatef(rot[1], 0.0f, 1.0f, 0.0f);
```

```
glPointSize(3.0);
glBegin(GL_POINTS);
        for(i=0; i < no_of_pts; i++) glVertex3f(xdata[i],
        ydata[i], zdata[i]);
glEnd();

glColor3f(1.0f, 0.0f,0.0f);
istart = 0;
iend = 6;
        do {
        glBegin(GL_LINE_STRIP);
        for(i=istart; i <= iend; i=i++) {
                glVertex3f(xdata[i], ydata[i], zdata[i]);
                glVertex3f(xdata[i+1], ydata[i+1], zdata[i+1]);
                glVertex3f(xdata[i+9], ydata[i+9], zdata[i+9]);
                glVertex3f(xdata[i+8], ydata[i+8], zdata[i+8]);
                glVertex3f(xdata[i], ydata[i], zdata[i]);
        }
        glEnd();
        istart = istart + 8;
        iend = istart + 6;
        } while(iend < no_of_pts-7);

   glEnable(GL_TEXTURE_2D);
   glTexEnvf(GL_TEXTURE_ENV, GL_TEXTURE_ENV_MODE, GL_REPLACE);
   glBindTexture(GL_TEXTURE_2D, texName);
//a patch structure access
istart = 0;
iend = 6;
        do {
        glBegin(GL_QUADS);
        for(i=istart; i <= iend; i=i++) {
                s = xdata[i] / xmax; t = zdata[i] / zmax;
                glTexCoord2f(s, t); glVertex3f(xdata[i],
                ydata[i], zdata[i]);
                s = xdata[i+1] / xmax; t = zdata[i+1] / zmax;
                glTexCoord2f(s, t); glVertex3f(xdata[i+1],
                ydata[i+1], zdata[i+1]);
                s = xdata[i+9] / xmax; t = zdata[i+9] / zmax;
                glTexCoord2f(s, t); glVertex3f(xdata[i+9],
                ydata[i+9], zdata[i+9]);
                s = xdata[i+8] / xmax; t = zdata[i+8] / zmax;
                glTexCoord2f(s, t); glVertex3f(xdata[i+8],
                ydata[i+8], zdata[i+8]);
        }
```

```
        glEnd();
        istart = istart + 8;
        iend = istart + 6;
        } while(iend < no_of_pts-7);
glDisable(GL_TEXTURE_2D);
glFlush();
}
```

Fig. 7.16 Different views of
the terrain

Using this method we are able to look 'around' the mountain and gain an impression of what is on the other side in Fig. 7.16. A combination of more accurate contour data capture and where necessary, curve smoothing (Chapter 9) enables the user to gain improved understanding on images.

7.5 Adding Some Movement – A Rotating Hemisphere

We introduced some movement in Chapter 4 when we looked at transformations and now we will generalise this motion with motion controlled both by the keyboard and mouse for a number of examples of textured objects. The readers should change from single to double buffering and use glutSwapBuffers() in place of glFlush() and observe the smoother operation of software where real time movement is required.

In this example we shall texture one half of a sphere where in Fig. 7.4 $0 \leq \varphi \leq \pi$ and $-\pi/2 \leq \theta \leq \pi/2$ and provide motion via the arrow keys about the x and y-axes. Solving the linear mapping for these conditions

$$\theta = \pi * (s - 0.5)$$
$$\varphi = (1.0 - t) * \pi$$

Keyboard control of our program is provided by the utility library function glutSpecialFunc(), which behaves similarly to glutKeyboardFunc() except that we can access non-ASCII keys. The function requires the address as argument of the function that defines the use of non-ASCII keys which in this case are the increments/decrements in the angles of rotation of the hemisphere.

```
#define Width 256              //spmove.cpp
#define Height 256

static GLfloat xRot = 0.0f;
static GLfloat yRot = 0.0f;
```

```
int ww, wh;
static GLubyte Image[Height][Width][4];
static GLuint texName;

#include "Read_bmp.cpp"

void start ( void )
{
ip_bmp_file Read_BMP_file;
   Read_BMP_file.header_data();

   glPixelStorei(GL_UNPACK_ALIGNMENT, 1);
   glGenTextures (1, &texName) ;
   glBindTexture(GL_TEXTURE_2D, texName);
   glTexParameteri(GL_TEXTURE_2D, GL_TEXTURE_WRAP_S, GL_REPEAT);
   glTexParameteri(GL_TEXTURE_2D, GL_TEXTURE_WRAP_T, GL_REPEAT);
   glTexParameteri(GL_TEXTURE_2D, GL_TEXTURE_MAG_FILTER,
   GL_NEAREST);
   glTexParameteri(GL_TEXTURE_2D, GL_TEXTURE_MIN_FILTER,
   GL_NEAREST);
   glTexImage2D(GL_TEXTURE_2D, 0, GL_RGBA, ww, wh, 0, GL_RGBA,
        GL_UNSIGNED_BYTE, Image);
   glEnable ( GL_CULL_FACE );
   glEnable ( GL_BLEND );
   glBlendFunc ( GL_ONE, GL_ONE );
   glClearColor ( 0.0, 0.0, 0.0, 0.0 );
}


void display(void)
{
float theta, phi, x, y, z, s, t, sstart, sinc, send, tstart,
tinc, tend;
float resolution;

   glClear(GL_COLOR_BUFFER_BIT | GL_DEPTH_BUFFER_BIT);
   glEnable(GL_TEXTURE_2D);
   glTexEnvf(GL_TEXTURE_ENV, GL_TEXTURE_ENV_MODE, GL_REPLACE);
   glBindTexture(GL_TEXTURE_2D, texName);

   glPushMatrix();
    glRotatef(xRot, 1.0f, 0.0f, 0.0f);
    glRotatef(yRot, 0.0f, 1.0f, 0.0f);

   glBegin(GL_QUADS);
    resolution = 0.125;
```

```
    tstart = 0.0; tend = resolution;
    tinc = resolution;
    do {
     sstart = 0.0; send = resolution;
     sinc = resolution;
     do {
      t=tstart;
      for(s=sstart; s<=send; s=s+sinc) {
          theta = 3.142 * (s - 0.5); //-pi/2 -> pi/2
          phi = (1.0 - t) * 3.142; //0 -> pi
          x = 2.0*sin(theta)*sin(phi);
          y = 2.0*cos(phi);
          z = 2.0*cos(theta)*sin(phi);
          glTexCoord2f(s, t); glVertex3f(x, y, z);
      }
      t=tend;
      for(s=send; s>=sstart; s=s-sinc) {
          theta = 3.142 * (s - 0.5); //-pi/2 -> pi/2
          phi = (1.0 - t) * 3.142; //0 -> pi
          x = 2.0*sin(theta)*sin(phi);
          y = 2.0*cos(phi);
          z = 2.0*cos(theta)*sin(phi);
          glTexCoord2f(s, t); glVertex3f(x, y, z);
      }
      sstart = send; //next col
      send = sstart + sinc;
     } while(send <=1.0);
   tstart = tend; //next row
   tend = tstart + tinc;
   } while(tend <= 1.0);
glEnd();
glFlush();
glDisable(GL_TEXTURE_2D);
glPopMatrix();
}
void reshape(int w, int h)
{
   glViewport(0, 0, (GLsizei) w, (GLsizei) h);
   glMatrixMode(GL_PROJECTION);
   glLoadIdentity();
   gluPerspective(70.0, (GLfloat) w/(GLfloat) h, 1.0, 30.0);
   glMatrixMode(GL_MODELVIEW);
   glLoadIdentity();
   glTranslatef(0.0, 0.0, -3.6);
}
```

```
void ArrowKeys(int key, int x, int y)
{
        if(key == GLUT_KEY_UP) xRot-= 5.0f;
        if(key == GLUT_KEY_DOWN) xRot += 5.0f;
        if(key == GLUT_KEY_LEFT) yRot -= 5.0f;
        if(key == GLUT_KEY_RIGHT) yRot += 5.0f;
        if(xRot > 356.0f) xRot = 0.0f;
        if(xRot < -1.0f) xRot = 355.0f;
        if(yRot > 356.0f) yRot = 0.0f;
        if(yRot < -1.0f) yRot = 355.0f;
        glutPostRedisplay();
}
```

Fig. 7.17 Rotating a
hemisphere using arrow keys

7.5.1 Movement via the Mouse

We have seen image movement resulting from using the keyboard. The glut library
also provides an animation support capability through the operation of the mouse
(glutMouseFunc and glutMotionFunc).

GlutMouseFunc permits interaction with the program whenever the mouse
moves with one of the buttons pressed at location (x, y) in the window. glutMotionFunc takes an argument which is a function containing the x, y position of the
mouse and is called when the mouse moves.

Movement about the y-axis is simulated by moving the mouse in the $\pm x$ direction
and similarly in the $\pm y$ direction for rotation about the x-axis with in the case of our
code, the left hand mouse button depressed. The mouse obviously cannot move in
an angular fashion as it's on a flat table! Thus the rotation about corresponding axes
is defined by linear changes in mouse position to simulate rotation. A zoom facility
(in the z direction) is provided by depressing the right mouse button and moving the
mouse in the x direction.

The function glutMouseFunc() uses a user written function mouse(), which
returns the position of the mouse cursor as it moves across the window and this
position is passed to glutMotionFunc() through global variables (mouseX, mouseY)
via the function motion() where zoom and rotation are simulated from the linear

motion of the mouse, Fig. 7.17. Readers are encouraged to modify the following program to provide rotation about the z-axis.

```cpp
//Realtime Animation via Mouse
int width = 300; //FlagRot.cpp
int height = 300;
int ww,wh;
const char *Win_Title = "Movement with mouse";

GLfloat xrot=0.0, yrot=0.0; //rotate using mouse
GLfloat zvalue = 50.0f; //Translate distance for camera

int mouseX = 0;
int mouseY = 0;
int mouseState = 0;
int mouseButton = 0;

static GLubyte Image[256][256][4];
static GLuint texName;

#include "Read_bmp.cpp"

void start ( void )
{
ip_bmp_file Read_BMP_file;
  Read_BMP_file.header_data();
  glPixelStorei(GL_UNPACK_ALIGNMENT, 1);
  glGenTextures (1, &texName) ;
  glBindTexture(GL_TEXTURE_2D, texName);
  glTexParameteri(GL_TEXTURE_2D, GL_TEXTURE_WRAP_S, GL_REPEAT);
  glTexParameteri(GL_TEXTURE_2D, GL_TEXTURE_WRAP_T, GL_REPEAT);
  glTexParameteri(GL_TEXTURE_2D, GL_TEXTURE_MAG_FILTER, GL_NEAREST);
  glTexParameteri(GL_TEXTURE_2D, GL_TEXTURE_MIN_FILTER, GL_NEAREST);
  glTexImage2D(GL_TEXTURE_2D, 0, GL_RGBA, ww, wh, 0, GL_RGBA,
        GL_UNSIGNED_BYTE, Image);
  glEnable ( GL_CULL_FACE );
  glEnable ( GL_BLEND );
  glBlendFunc ( GL_ONE, GL_ONE );
  glClearColor ( 0.0, 0.0, 0.0, 0.0 );
}

void display(void)
{
  float x, y, z, s, t, sstart, sinc, send, tstart, tinc, tend;
  float resolution, xstart, ystart, xinc, yinc, xorigin;
  glClear(GL_COLOR_BUFFER_BIT |  GL_DEPTH_BUFFER_BIT);
```

```
  glEnable(GL_TEXTURE_2D);
  glTexEnvf(GL_TEXTURE_ENV, GL_TEXTURE_ENV_MODE, GL_REPLACE);
  glBindTexture(GL_TEXTURE_2D, texName);

glMatrixMode(GL_MODELVIEW);
        glLoadIdentity();
        glTranslatef(0.0f, 0.0f, -zvalue);
        glRotatef(xrot, 1.0f, 0.0f, 0.0f);
        glRotatef(yrot, 0.0f, 1.0f, 0.0f);
        glTranslatef(-1.0, -0.5, 0.0);

glBegin(GL_QUADS);
  resolution = 0.0625;
  xstart=0.0; ystart=0.0;
  xorigin = 0.0;
  xinc=0.0625; yinc=0.0625;
  tstart = 0.0;
  tinc = resolution;
  sinc = resolution; sstart = -sinc;
do {
  sstart = sstart + sinc; send = resolution;
  sinc = resolution;
   do {
    s = sstart; x=xstart;
    t = tstart; y=ystart;
    z=sin(6.284*x);
      glTexCoord2f(s, t); glVertex3f(x*2.0, y, z);
    s = sstart + sinc; x=xstart+xinc;
    z=sin(6.284*x);
      glTexCoord2f(s, t); glVertex3f(x*2.0, y, z);
    t= tstart + tinc; y=ystart+yinc;
      glTexCoord2f(s, t); glVertex3f(x*2.0, y, z);
    s = sstart; x=xstart;
    z=sin(6.284*x);
      glTexCoord2f(s, t); glVertex3f(x*2.0, y, z);
    send = sstart + sinc;
    sstart = sstart + sinc; xstart = xstart + xinc; //next col
    } while(send <1.0);
  tstart = tstart + tinc; //next row
  sstart = -sinc;
  tend = tstart + tinc;
  xstart = xorigin;
  ystart = ystart+ yinc;
} while(tend <= 1.0);
glEnd();
glFlush();
```

```
glDisable(GL_TEXTURE_2D);
glutSwapBuffers();
}

void resize(int w, int h)
{
        if (!h) return;
        width = w;
        height = h;
        glMatrixMode(GL_PROJECTION);
        glLoadIdentity();
        gluPerspective(60, (double) width / height, 1, 1000);
        glutPostRedisplay();
}

void motion(int x, int y)
{
if (mouseState == GLUT_DOWN){
        if (mouseButton == GLUT_LEFT_BUTTON){
                xrot -= (mouseX - x); //rot about y-axis
                yrot -= (mouseY - y); //rot about x-axis
        }else{
                if (mouseButton == GLUT_RIGHT_BUTTON){
                        zvalue += (mouseX - x)*0.1; //zoom z
                        if (zvalue>200) zvalue=200.0;
                        if (zvalue<5) zvalue=5.0;
                }
        }
}
        mouseX = x;
        mouseY = y;
        glutPostRedisplay();
}

void mouse(int btn, int state, int x, int y)
{
        if (state == GLUT_DOWN){
                mouseState = state;
                mouseButton = btn;
                mouseX = x;
                mouseY = y;
        }else{
    mouseState = 0;
        }
}
```

```
void instructions (void)
{
        glClearColor(0.0f, 0.2f, 0.3f, 0.0f);
        glEnable(GL_DEPTH_TEST);
        cout << "Press Left Mouse Button to Rotate \n";
        cout << "Press Right Mouse Button to Zoom In and Out\n";
        cout << "by moving left to right\n";
}

void main (void)
{
        instructions();
        glutInitDisplayMode(GLUT_RGB | GLUT_DOUBLE | GLUT_DEPTH);
        glutInitWindowSize(width, height);
        glutCreateWindow(Win_Title);
        start();
        glutMouseFunc(mouse);
        glutMotionFunc(motion);
        glutDisplayFunc(display);
        glutReshapeFunc(resize);
        glutMainLoop();
}
```

Readers may have noticed that for some rotations the image disappears – why?

7.6 Using Bit Maps to Provide Context

In this section we shall provide movement in relation to several images that may be used to make up the environmental context of the motion. In the first example we build a wall with a window and view the scene outside the window. As we move around one side of the wall the view through the window will change depending on the position of the viewer.

The problem is illustrated as follows with an image to represent the scene through the window and further plain red image to represent the wall. The viewer can be thought of as inside a room walking around while looking out of the window.

As the viewer moves in the room, the view observed through the window will change. Clearly we shall need two images; the red brick wall and a picture of the outside world, which in this case is a Tiger Moth aircraft, Fig. 7.18. It is noted that increasing the number of images will require a computer with more memory and this can be a significant factor when we consider three-dimensional texturing.

The class used for reading a bit map file (Read_bmp.cpp) has been sufficient where only one image is required, but we now further generalise this class to permit the use of multiple images for texturing. The function WidthHeight is the same as we have used already and the output is a one-dimensional array of unsigned bytes

Fig. 7.18 Providing an
environment with several
images

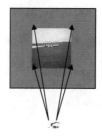
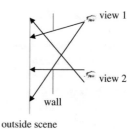

for each of the RGB components. The size of the memory location required to store
a bit map file is given by

$$\text{Size of array} = \text{Image Height} \times \text{Image Width} \times 3$$

A pointer to a memory space array is returned which is then converted to the 3D
array as required by OpenGl. The multiple file reader class listing follows and is
suitable for reading any bit map file with the only input required being the name of
the file.

```
//general file reader
GLubyte* makeImage(void);

class ip_bmp_file
{
public:

long int WidthHeight(int pix1, int pix2) {
long int num, n ,rem;
n = 8;
num = 0;
do { //high byte only
  rem = pix2 % 2;
  num = num + rem * pow(2, n);
  pix2 = pix2 /2;
  n++;
} while(n <= 16);
num = num + pix1;
return(num);
}

GLubyte* makeImage(void)
{
unsigned char pixel;
char filename[25];
int i, pixlow, pixhigh, pix3, pix4, image_size;
```

```
//GLubyte* image_ptr = new GLubyte[image_size];

cout << "Input image file name ";
cin >> filename;
ifstream inpaint( filename, ios::binary);
if(!inpaint) {
            cout << "File not opened\n";
    exit(1);
}
for(i=1; i<=54; i++) {
            inpaint >> pixel; //go to start of data after header stuff
   if(i == 19) pixlow = pixel; //low
            if(i == 20) pixhigh = pixel; //high
            if(i == 23) pix3 = pixel; //low
            if(i == 24) pix4 = pixel; //high
    }
ww = WidthHeight( pixlow, pixhigh);
wh = WidthHeight( pix3, pix4);
cout << "\nx width = " << ww << "y height = " << wh << endl;
image_size = ww * wh * 3;
GLubyte* image_ptr = new GLubyte[image_size];
for (i = 0; i < image_size; i=i+3) {
  pixel = inpaint.get();
  image_ptr[i] = pixel;
  pixel = inpaint.get();
  image_ptr[i+1] = pixel;
  pixel = inpaint.get( );
  image_ptr[i+2] = pixel;
  }
return(image_ptr);
}
};
```

In the example we could construct the wall with a number of flat coloured planes with a gap for the window. An easier way however is to use a single flat plane image of say bricks with a hole to represent a window in the middle. To achieve this we now make use of the alpha value about which, we have remained silent until now through the process of blending.

7.6.1 Blending

We are well versed with the RGB values that combine to make up the colour intensity of individual pixels. The alpha (A) component of RGBA permits users to combine the value of the colour of a pixel currently being processed with that of other pixels already in the frame buffer if they are in the same region of interest and the blending facility is enabled. The smaller the value of *A* the more transparent a surface becomes and it is this capability that will allow us to create a window in a wall. The colours of one image may be combined with other colours of a pixel already stored in the frame buffer using the function glBlendFunc(source, destination). The parameters 'source' and 'destination' take values between 0 and 1 for the corresponding blending factors where 0 is complete transparency.

When creating a display it is important to remember which images are in the background and which are in the foreground else blending will operate between planes, which you might not intend! In this example the scene outside the window is stored in the array Image and the file tigermoth.bmp is supplied for this. The file bricks.bmp is an image of a wall. Since we have two textures, two integer names are created in texName[0] and texName[1]. Once the file used to represent the wall has been read, some of the alpha channel values are set to zero to facilitate transparency to pixels already stored in the frame buffer (in this case the external background scene of the aircraft). Blending is then enabled using

```
glEnable ( GL_BLEND );
glBlendFunc ( GL_SRC_ALPHA, GL_ONE_MINUS_SRC_ALPHA );
```

After each movement induced by 'x / X' keyboard input the display must be recalculated in the keyboard call back function keys due to the repositioning of the viewer, before using glutDisplayFunc(display).

```
#define Width 256          //WallViewclass.cpp
#define Height 256

int ww, wh;
static GLubyte Image[Height][Width][4], Wall[Height][Width][4];
static GLuint texName[2];

#include "cRead_Gen_bmp.cpp"

void LooksLike()
{
GLubyte* image_store;
int r, c, i;
ip_bmp_file Read_a_BMP_file;

image_store = Read_a_BMP_file.makeImage();
i = 0;
for (r = 0; r < wh; r++) {
  for (c = 0; c < ww; c++) {
  Image[r][c][2] = image_store[i];
  i++;
  Image[r][c][1] = image_store[i];
```

```
    i++;
    Image[r][c][0] = image_store[i];
    i++;
    Image[r][c][3] = (GLubyte) 255;
    }
}
  glClearColor(0.0, 0.0, 0.0, 0.0);
  glShadeModel(GL_FLAT);
  glEnable(GL_DEPTH_TEST);
  glPixelStorei(GL_UNPACK_ALIGNMENT, 1);
  glGenTextures (2, texName) ;
  glBindTexture(GL_TEXTURE_2D, texName[0]);
  glTexParameteri(GL_TEXTURE_2D, GL_TEXTURE_WRAP_S, GL_CLAMP);
  glTexParameteri(GL_TEXTURE_2D, GL_TEXTURE_WRAP_T, GL_CLAMP);
  glTexParameteri(GL_TEXTURE_2D, GL_TEXTURE_MAG_FILTER, GL_NEAREST);
  glTexParameteri(GL_TEXTURE_2D, GL_TEXTURE_MIN_FILTER, GL_NEAREST);
  glTexImage2D(GL_TEXTURE_2D, 0, GL_RGBA, ww, wh, 0, GL_RGBA,
        GL_UNSIGNED_BYTE, Image);
// now wall input
image_store = Read_a_BMP_file.makeImage();
i = 0;
for (r = 0; r < wh; r++) {
  for (c = 0; c < ww; c++) {
  Wall[r][c][2] = image_store[i];
  i++;
  Wall[r][c][1] = image_store[i];
  i++;
  Wall[r][c][0] = image_store[i];
  i++;
  Wall[r][c][3] = (GLubyte) 255;
  if(r > 70 && r < 185) {
  if (c > 70 && c < 185) Wall[r][c][3] = (GLubyte) 0;
  }
  }
}
glEnable ( GL_BLEND );
glBlendFunc ( GL_SRC_ALPHA, GL_ONE_MINUS_SRC_ALPHA );
  glBindTexture(GL_TEXTURE_2D, texName[1]);
  glTexParameteri(GL_TEXTURE_2D, GL_TEXTURE_WRAP_S, GL_CLAMP);
  glTexParameteri(GL_TEXTURE_2D, GL_TEXTURE_WRAP_T, GL_CLAMP);
  glTexParameteri(GL_TEXTURE_2D, GL_TEXTURE_MAG_FILTER, GL_NEAREST);
  glTexParameteri(GL_TEXTURE_2D, GL_TEXTURE_MIN_FILTER, GL_NEAREST);
  glTexEnvf(GL_TEXTURE_ENV, GL_TEXTURE_ENV_MODE, GL_REPLACE);
  glTexImage2D(GL_TEXTURE_2D, 0, GL_RGBA, ww, wh, 0, GL_RGBA,
        GL_UNSIGNED_BYTE, Wall);
  glEnable(GL_DEPTH_TEST);
```

```
  glFrontFace(GL_CCW);
  glEnable(GL_CULL_FACE);
  glEnable(GL_COLOR_MATERIAL);
  glClearColor(0.0f, 0.0f, 1.0f, 1.0f);
  glEnable(GL_TEXTURE_2D);
}

static GLdouble viewer[]= {0.0, 0.0, 5.0};
// initial viewer location

void display()
{
float zd, xy;
glClear(GL_COLOR_BUFFER_BIT | GL_DEPTH_BUFFER_BIT);

glPushMatrix();
// set up background scene from window
glBindTexture(GL_TEXTURE_2D, texName[0]);
zd = -5.5; //more -ve further into screen
xy = 3.0;
gluLookAt(viewer[0],viewer[1],viewer[2], 0.0, 0.0, 1.5,
                                 0.0, 1.0, 0.0);
  glBegin(GL_QUADS);
    glTexCoord2f(0.0, 0.0); glVertex3f(-xy, -xy, zd);
    glTexCoord2f(1.0, 0.0); glVertex3f(xy, -xy, zd);
    glTexCoord2f(1.0, 1.0); glVertex3f(xy, xy, zd);
    glTexCoord2f(0.0, 1.0); glVertex3f(-xy, xy, zd);
  glEnd();

glFlush();
glPopMatrix();
// set up wall in front with window
glBindTexture(GL_TEXTURE_2D, texName[1]);
zd = -4.5;
xy = 1.2;
  glBegin(GL_QUADS);
                 glTexCoord2f(0.0, 0.0); glVertex3f(-xy, -xy, zd);
      glTexCoord2f(1.0, 0.0); glVertex3f( xy, -xy, zd);
      glTexCoord2f(1.0, 1.0); glVertex3f( xy, xy, zd);
      glTexCoord2f(0.0, 1.0); glVertex3f(-xy, xy, zd);
    glEnd();
glutSwapBuffers();
}

void keys(unsigned char key, int x, int z)
{
```

```
if(key =='x' ) viewer[0]-= 0.1;
if(key =='X') viewer[0]+= 0.1;
display();
}
void myReshape(int w, int h)
{
glMatrixMode(GL_PROJECTION);
glLoadIdentity();
gluPerspective(45.0, w/h, 2.0, 20.0);
glMatrixMode(GL_MODELVIEW);
}
```

Fig. 7.19 Moving the viewer position to simulate a different scene from window

In Fig. 7.19 we see the effect of using the character 'x' as keyboard input to move the viewer position using gluLookAt() with respect to the external world of the airfield.

7.6.2 Manipulating Pixels

Magnifying glasses and telescopes are common instruments for enhancing images and OpenGL provides facilities to simulate such operations. Pixels can be read from the display buffer and written to image memory using glReadPixels and glDrawPixels functions. We can read a rectangular block of pixels starting at the bottom left hand corner (x, y) and specifying the width and height of the block. The block of pixels can then be repositioned using glRasterPos3i to some other point on the display and the zoom function glPixelZoom used to effect a magnification.

It should be remembered that the display origin (0, 0) is the top left hand corner of the screen. In delineation of the area of image to be magnified we have used the left mouse button to specify the corners of the pixel block and the right button to exit the mouse interaction and stored the points in a file coords.txt. There is some simple data error correction in the function DrawSquare() due to the writer experiencing

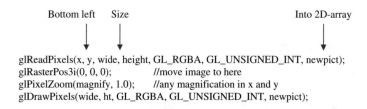

```
glReadPixels(x, y, wide, height, GL_RGBA, GL_UNSIGNED_INT, newpict);
glRasterPos3i(0, 0, 0);          //move image to here
glPixelZoom(magnify, 1.0);       //any magnification in x and y
glDrawPixels(wide, ht, GL_RGBA, GL_UNSIGNED_INT, newpict);
```

multiple data points when clicking the mouse. I have experienced similar effects
when using a pen and tablet connected in place of the mouse (see Section 3.5).
The points are highlighted in random colours for clarity, ordered from bottom left
in an anticlockwise direction and lines are drawn from the delimited to magnified
region. In the following example, Fig. 7.20 we have magnified by a factor of 2 in
the x-direction.

```cpp
#include <iostream>              //Magnify1.cpp
#include <math.h>
#include <windows.h>
#include <GL/glut.h>
using std::cout;
using std::cin;
using std::endl;
using std::ios;

#include <fstream>
using std::ifstream;
using std::ofstream;

#define Width 256
#define Height 256

static GLfloat xRot = 0.0f;
static GLfloat yRot = 0.0f;
GLfloat size = 3.0 ; // half side of square
int ww, wh;
static GLubyte Image[Height][Width][4];
GLubyte newpict[200][200][4];
static GLuint texName;
int xprev = -1, yprev = -1;
#include "cRead_Gen_bmp.cpp"

ofstream xyfile("coords.txt");

void DrawSquare ( int x, int y ) ;
void Mouse ( int btn, int state, int x, int y ) ;
void ImageRead( );
void drawPict(int x, int y, int wide, int ht);
```

```
void start ( void )
{
GLubyte* image_store;
int r, c, i;
ip_bmp_file Read_a_BMP_file;

image_store = Read_a_BMP_file.makeImage ();
i = 0;
for (r = 0; r < wh; r++) {
  for (c = 0; c < ww; c++) {
  Image[r][c][2] = image_store[i];
  i++;
  Image[r][c][1] = image_store[i];
  i++;
  Image[r][c][0] = image_store[i];
  i++;
  Image[r][c][3] = (GLubyte) 255;
  }
}

glPixelStorei(GL_UNPACK_ALIGNMENT, 1);
  glGenTextures (1, &texName) ;
  glBindTexture(GL_TEXTURE_2D, texName);
  glTexParameteri(GL_TEXTURE_2D, GL_TEXTURE_WRAP_S, GL_REPEAT);
  glTexParameteri(GL_TEXTURE_2D, GL_TEXTURE_WRAP_T, GL_REPEAT);
  glTexParameteri(GL_TEXTURE_2D, GL_TEXTURE_MAG_FILTER, GL_NEAREST);
  glTexParameteri(GL_TEXTURE_2D, GL_TEXTURE_MIN_FILTER, GL_NEAREST);
  glTexImage2D(GL_TEXTURE_2D, 0, GL_RGBA, ww, wh, 0, GL_RGBA,
                 GL_UNSIGNED_BYTE, Image);
  glEnable ( GL_CULL_FACE );
  glEnable ( GL_BLEND );
  glBlendFunc ( GL_ONE, GL_ONE );
  glClearColor ( 0.0, 0.0, 0.0, 0.0 );
}
void Mouse ( int btn, int state, int x, int y ) {
        if ( GLUT_LEFT_BUTTON == btn && GLUT_DOWN == state )
        DrawSquare ( x, y ) ;
        cout << x << " " << y << "\n";
    if ( GLUT_RIGHT_BUTTON == btn && GLUT_DOWN == state ) {
                 xyfile << "End of data";
        xyfile.close( );
      ImageRead();
         }
}

void DrawSquare ( int x, int y ) {
```

```
              //convert x,y,z from Windows convention to OpenGL
float xx, yy, xp, yp, xm, ym, z, scalex, scaley, sc;
   xx = x-175; yy = y-125; z = 6.0/ 4.5;
   z = 1.5;
   scalex = 7.0 / 350.0; scaley = -5.0 / 250.0;
   sc = 0.01;
          xp= xx* scalex + size* sc ; yp= yy*scaley + size * sc ;
   xm= xx * scalex - size * sc ; ym= yy*scaley - size * sc ;
          //set up random colour
   glColor3ub ( (GLubyte)rand( ) % 256,
                                    (GLubyte)rand( ) % 256,
             (GLubyte)rand( ) % 256 ) ;
        if( x == xprev && y == yprev) { //clean up? data
                    cout <<"Duplicate noise x-y data\n";
        }
          else {
                    xyfile << x << " " << y << endl;
                    xprev = x; yprev = y;
        }
   glBegin ( GL_POLYGON ) ;
      glVertex3f ( xp, yp, z ) ;
      glVertex3f ( xm, yp, z ) ;
      glVertex3f ( xm, ym, z ) ;
      glVertex3f ( xp, ym, z ) ;
    glEnd ( ) ;
    glFlush ( ) ;
}

void display(void)
{
    float theta, phi, x, y, z, u, v;
    float resolution, ustart, uinc, uend, vstart, vinc, vend;
    glClear(GL_COLOR_BUFFER_BIT | GL_DEPTH_BUFFER_BIT);
    glEnable(GL_TEXTURE_2D);
    glTexEnvf(GL_TEXTURE_ENV, GL_TEXTURE_ENV_MODE, GL_REPLACE);
    glBindTexture(GL_TEXTURE_2D, texName);
    glPushMatrix();
          glTranslatef(-2.0, 0.0, 0.0);

glBegin(GL_QUADS);
    resolution = 0.125;
      vstart = 0.0; vend = resolution;
      vinc = resolution;
    do {
      ustart = 0.0; uend = resolution;
      uinc = resolution;
```

```
   do {
    v=vstart;
    for(u=ustart; u<=uend; u=u+uinc) {
         theta = 3.142 * (u - 0.5);
       phi = (1.0 - v) * 3.142;
         x = 2.0*sin(theta)*sin(phi);
         y = 2.0*cos(phi);
         z = 2.0*cos(theta)*sin(phi);
                   glTexCoord2f(u, v); glVertex3f(x, y, z);
       }
       v=vend;
    for(u=uend; u>=ustart; u=u-uinc) {
       theta = 3.142 * (u - 0.5);
       phi = (1.0 - v) * 3.142;
                   x = 2.0*sin(theta)*sin(phi);
             y = 2.0*cos(phi);
             z = 2.0*cos(theta)*sin(phi);
                     glTexCoord2f(u, v); glVertex3f(x, y, z);
        }
    ustart = uend;
    uend = ustart +uinc;
    } while(uend <=1.0);
    vstart = vend;
    vend = vstart +vinc;
} while(vend <=1.0);
glEnd();
glFlush();
glDisable(GL_TEXTURE_2D);
glPopMatrix();
glutSwapBuffers();
}
void reshape(int w, int h)
{
  glMatrixMode(GL_PROJECTION);
   glLoadIdentity();
   gluPerspective(100.0, (GLfloat) w/(GLfloat) h, 1.5, -0.1);
   glMatrixMode(GL_MODELVIEW);
   glLoadIdentity();
   glTranslatef(0.0, 0.0, -3.6);
  }

void ImageRead()
{
int x1, y1, x2, y2, x3, y3, x4, y4, wide, ht, xx, my, z, xpos;
float xmagnify;
ifstream xyfile("coords.txt");
```

```
xyfile >>x1 >>y1;
xyfile >>x2 >>y2;
xyfile >>x3 >>y3;
xyfile >>x4 >>y4;
cout << "Region delimited " << x1 << " " << y1 <<"\n";
cout << "\t\t" << x4 << " " << y4 <<" to be magnified\n";
ht = abs(y1-y4);
wide = abs(x1-x2);
xpos =10;
xmagnify = 2.0; z = -100;
xx = x1-175; my = 250 - y1;
glRasterPos3i(xpos, 0, z);
glPixelZoom(xmagnify, 1.0);
glReadPixels(x1, my, wide, ht, GL_RGBA, GL_UNSIGNED_INT, newpict);
glDrawPixels(wide, ht, GL_RGBA, GL_UNSIGNED_INT, newpict);
glColor3f(1.0, 0.0, 0.0);
glBegin ( GL_LINES ); //show region
   glVertex3i ( xx, 125-y1, z );
   glVertex3i ( xpos, 0, z );
   glVertex3i ( xx +wide, 125-y1, z );
   glVertex3i ( xmagnify*wide+xpos, 0, z );
   glVertex3i ( xx, 125-y1+ht, z );
   glVertex3i ( xpos, ht, z );
   glVertex3i ( xx+wide, 125-y1+ht, z ) ;
   glVertex3i ( xmagnify*wide+xpos, ht, z );
   glEnd ( );
   glFlush();
}
```

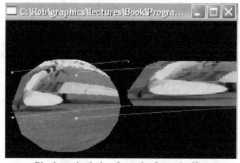

Fig. 7.20 Pixel manipulation
from the frame buffer

Pixel manipulation from the frame buffer

7.7 Three-dimensional Texturing

The texturing used up to this point can be thought of as akin to wrapping polythene around a parcel. A number of applications now produce data in a solid 3D form and contain information 'inside' the solid, which is not seen, on the surface. This occurs in medical images from magnetic resonance imaging (MRI) and computer tomography (CT) scanners where detail inside of organs is needed. Similarly in geophysics one is interested in what is underground and hidden, particularly in the oil and gas industry. The operator of these systems requires that one can 'cut' though the solid in any plane and see the internal detail.

The OpenGl implementation used for this section is Mesa 1.5 and readers should check their version as 3D texturing is not shipped with all systems at this time (2007). A 3D texture can be thought of as a series of cubes or voxels and when we cut through the 3D texture space, we expose a 2D plane of texels. The scanners build up a series of images at some distance apart and these are stored as pixel planes. Putting the planes together and joining them provides information that cannot be extracted from a single plane or easily integrated together by looking at individual planes. The first example is a slight modification from Shreiner 2005 with simulated image data of a red cube hidden inside a white cube. The cubic texture is $16 \times 16 \times 16$ cubes in the (r, s, t) directions in texture space and initialise to white. For purposes of illustration we have set up a red voxel cube of $4 \times 4 \times 4$ where the start location is at $(8, 6, 6)$ in texture space inside the white cube with two more coloured objects at different positions. The display plane in texture space is defined by the y-axis and we move a plane about this axis as shown in Fig. 7.21 which will provide different views of the red object internal to the surrounding white cube.

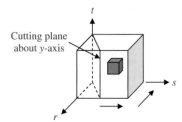

Fig. 7.21 Extracting information from a 3D texture

The cutting plane is initially located in the r–t texture plane and we increase the value of s using the right arrow key until $s = 1$. Continued use of the right arrow key decreases r until the plane lies in the s–t plane and this movement allows us to view internal detail (the red cube) in the texture. In the following example the coordinates defining the plane are output with each keystroke and readers should check the view in relation to the position of the internal cube.

```
void display(void)
{
glClear(GL_COLOR_BUFFER_BIT | GL_DEPTH_BUFFER_BIT);
glPushMatrix();
```

```
cout << xinc <<" 1/0 " << zinc<< "\n";
glBegin(GL_QUADS);
   glTexCoord3f(0.0, 0.0, 0.0); glVertex3f(-1.0, -0.5, 0.0);
   glTexCoord3f(0.0, 1.0, 0.0); glVertex3f(-1.0, 1.5, 0.0);
   glTexCoord3f(xinc, 1.0, zinc); glVertex3f(1.0, 1.5, 0.0);
   glTexCoord3f(xinc, 0.0, zinc); glVertex3f(1.0, -0.5, 0.0);
glEnd();
glFlush();
glPopMatrix();
}
void ArrowKeys(int key, int x, int y)
{
        if(key == GLUT_KEY_RIGHT) xinc += 0.1;
        if(xinc >1.0) {
                xinc = 1.0;
                zinc -= 0.1;
        }
        glutPostRedisplay();
}
```

The complete program together with a starter data file is provided on the Web site.

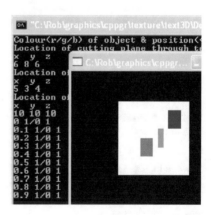

Fig. 7.22 Different views of internal objects

7.7.1 Simulation of a Spherical Object

The next example simulates the creation from a number of 2D scans or slices through a sphere of a solid model. The sphere should be described rather more accurately as an 'egg' shape to permit a clearer explanation with no loss of generality. The scans are of a circular shape with each RGB value set at 128 if the scan point is not black (or nearly so). Each slice is of a height (t) and width (s) of 16×16 pixels with a depth (r) of 16 as shown in Fig. 7.23. In real situations these values would be larger to represent detail but on a typical PC this is acceptable for speed of processing image movement and interaction.

Fig. 7.23 Simulation of a
number of 2D image slices

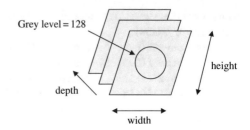

The scanned image file is 24 bit pixels stored as unsigned bytes giving an image size
of $3 \times 16 \times 16$ (768) bytes for each plane in r and a sample data file (sphere.txt) is
provided on the Web site. In the previous example we moved through texture space and
observed the corresponding image cut in Cartesian space, Fig. 7.22. We now consider
representation by filling in the space between each depth plane with 16×16 cubes of a
colour representing the objects in seen in each 2D slice. In the limit these cubes would
reduce to the size of individual pixels with a z-depth when they would be termed voxels.
In Chapter 6 we developed a data structure for representing a cube, which we will now
use to facilitate our model and in the first case give a different colour to each slice
between the planes to provide visual clarity. We scan each y-line of the file sphere.txt,
to find the end points (x) of the circle, which correspond to the beginning and end of the
grey level for that y-line in each 2D image. The locations between the two points define
the number of cubes to be rendered as shown in Fig. 7.24.

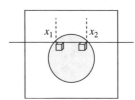

Fig. 7.24 Rendering each
disc with cubes

```
#include <stdlib.h>          //sphereofcubesrot.cpp
#include <iostream>          //sphere.txt & cube.dat
using std::cout;
using std::cin;
using std::endl;
using std::ios;

#include <fstream>
using std::ifstream;
using std::ofstream;
#include <math.h>
#include <windows.h>
#include <GL/glut.h>
#define Width 16
#define Height 16
```

```
#define Depth 16

static GLubyte image[Depth][Height][Width][3];
static GLuint texName[2];
static GLfloat inc = 0.0;
GLfloat rot[]={0.0, 0.0, 0.0};
int r, t, s, rgb, xstart, ystart, zstart, xend, flag;
int mouseX = 0;
int mouseY = 0;
int mouseState = 0;
int mouseButton = 0;
struct patches {
        char type[10];
        char colour;
        float v[4][3];
};
patches cubeface[6];

void makeImage(void)
{
char filename[25];
int blue, green, red;
cout << "Colour(r/g/b) sphere file: ";
cin >> filename;
   ifstream inpos(filename, ios ::in);
   if(!inpos) { cout << "File would not open\n";
                                exit(1);
                        }
for (r = 0; r < Depth; r++) {
        for (t = 0; t < Height; t++) {
                for (s = 0; s < Width; s++) {
                        inpos >> red;
                        image[r][t][s][0] = (GLubyte) red;
                        inpos >> green;
                        image[r][t][s][1] = green;
                        inpos >> blue;
                        image[r][t][s][2] = blue;

                }
        }
}
}

void InputData()
{
int vertex, coord, no_of_faces;
```

```
float scale=0.5;
makeImage();
ifstream InPoints("cube.dat", ios::in);
for(no_of_faces=0; no_of_faces<6; no_of_faces++)
{
for(vertex = 0; vertex<4; vertex++)
{
        for(coord=0; coord<3; coord++)
        {
            InPoints >> cubeface[no_of_faces].v[vertex][coord];
                    cubeface[no_of_faces].v[vertex][coord]
        =cubeface[no_of_faces].v[vertex][coord]*scale;
        }
}
}
}

void cube_draw(int x1, int x2, int y, int z) {
int i, no_of_faces, no_of_cubes;
no_of_cubes = x2 - x1;

for(i = 0; i<no_of_cubes; i++) {
        glPushMatrix();
        glTranslatef( -Width/2 +(float) x1, -Height/2 + (float) y,
        -Depth/2 + (float) z);
        glBegin(GL_QUADS);
                for(no_of_faces=0; no_of_faces<6; no_of_faces++) {
                            glVertex3fv(cubeface[no_of_faces].v[0]);
                            glVertex3fv(cubeface[no_of_faces].v[1]);
                            glVertex3fv(cubeface[no_of_faces].v[2]);
                            glVertex3fv(cubeface[no_of_faces].v[3]);
                }
        glEnd();
        x1++;
        glPopMatrix();
}
}
void display(void)
{
int r, s, t, rgb, flag, xstart, ystart, zstart;
float slicecolour[Depth][3] = {
        {1.0, 0.0, 0.0}, {0.0, 1.0, 0.0}, {0.0, 0.0, 0.0},
        {0.0, 1.0, 1.0}, {1.0, 1.0, 0.0}, {1.0, 1.0, 1.0},
        {1.0, 0.0, 1.0}, {0.5, 0.5, 0.0}, {0.5, 0.5, 0.5},
        {0.5, 0.0, 0.0}, {0.0, 0.5, 0.0}, {0.0, 0.0, 0.5},
```

```
                {0.5, 0.0, 0.5}, {0.0, 0.5, 0.5}, {1.0, 1.0, 1.0},
                {1.0, 0.0, 0.0}
};
glClear(GL_COLOR_BUFFER_BIT | GL_DEPTH_BUFFER_BIT);

glMatrixMode(GL_MODELVIEW);
        glLoadIdentity();
        glRotatef(rot[0], 1.0f, 0.0f, 0.0f);
        glRotatef(rot[1], 0.0f, 1.0f, 0.0f);

for(r=0; r<Depth; r++) {
        glColor3f(slicecolour[r][0], slicecolour[r][1],
        slicecolour[r][2]);
        for(t=0; t<Height; t++) {
                flag = 0;
                xstart = 0; xend = 0;
                for(s=0; s<Width; s++) {
                        rgb = 0;
                        if( (int) image[r][t][s][rgb] == 0)
                        { //mono only
                                if(flag == 1) cube_draw(xstart,
                                xend, ystart, zstart);
                                flag = 0;
                                zstart = r;
                                ystart = t;
                                xstart = s+1;
                        }
                        else {
                                xend = s+1;
                                flag = 1;
                        }
                }
        }
}
glColor3f(0.0, 0.0, 1.0);
glBegin(GL_LINES);
   glVertex3f(-15.0, 0.0, 0.0);    glVertex3f(15.0, 0.0, 0.0);
   glVertex3f( 0.0, 15.0, 0.0);    glVertex3f(0.0, -15.0, 0.0);
   glVertex3f( 0.0, 0.0, 15.0);    glVertex3f(0.0, 0.0, -15.0);
glEnd();
glFlush();
}

void motion(int x, int y)
{
if (mouseState == GLUT_DOWN){
```

```
            if (mouseButton == GLUT_LEFT_BUTTON){
                    rot[1] -= (mouseX - x);
                    rot[0] -= (mouseY - y);
            }
    }
        mouseX = x;
        mouseY = y;
        glutPostRedisplay();
    }

void mouse(int btn, int state, int x, int y)
{
        if (state == GLUT_DOWN){
                    mouseState = state;
                    mouseButton = btn;
                    mouseX = x;
                    mouseY = y;
        }else{
    mouseState = 0;
        }
}

void ChangeSize(int w, int h)
{
GLfloat nRange = 25.0f;
        if(h == 0) h = 1;
    glViewport(0, 0, w, h);
        glMatrixMode(GL_PROJECTION);
        glLoadIdentity();
    if (w <= h)
                glOrtho (-nRange, nRange, -nRange*h/w, nRange*h/w,
                -nRange, nRange);
    else
                glOrtho (-nRange*w/h, nRange*w/h, -nRange, nRange,
                -nRange, nRange);
        glMatrixMode(GL_MODELVIEW);
        glLoadIdentity();
}
```

The resulting solid model from this program is shown in Fig. 7.25 with rotation via the mouse interaction. Note that in the second image there *appears* to be a hole through to the black background of the image - why? Perhaps it would be instructive to look at the data file sphere.txt, and modify the program to account for this condition.

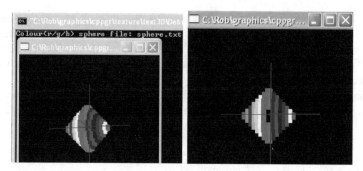

Fig. 7.25 Building a 16 slice model

7.7.2 Building a Solid Model of a Head

We have indicated in the previous section how we can build an object from circular slices made up from small cubes and in Chapter 2 we used the mouse interaction to capture the edge points of a CAT scan of the skull. We now combine these ideas to build a solid model of a shape that is not generated mathematically as was the case for the circles. Each CAT scan image (z) provides the data ($x - y$) to build a slice contribution to the building of a head where the (x, y) coordinates are captured using the mouse as described in Chapter 2. It should be emphasised that this example only works for simple data capture and a more complete and automated edge finder is required for actual systems. The time allowed in a typical 2 semester course is probably insufficient and students will find it beneficial to expand this work in final year projects.

A data file from the mouse input program creates a 24 slice image is provided on the Web site to support this book. In this example we have increase the resolution from 16×16 to 32×32 to improve the visual effect with consequences in terms of processing speed. The image file of RGB values is generated for all $32 \times 32 \times 24$ locations in the volume matrix used to define a head. To generate the matrix we use the file of $x - y$ delimiters to generate RGB values along each y scan line and in this example these are all set to 128 for a grey value. The process is shown below

scan lines	Corresponding RGB values for scan line
	0 0 0 0 0 0 0 0 0 0 0 0 0 0 0 0 0 0 0 0 0 0 0 0 0 0 0 0 0 0 0 0 0 0 0 0 0 0 0 0 0 0 0 0 0 0 0 0
x y	
119 112	0 0 0 0 0 0 0 0 0 128 128 128 128 128 128 128 128 128 128 128 128 128 128 128 0 0 0 0 0
148 112	
110 120	0 0 0 128 128 128 128 128 128 128 128 128 128 128 128 128 128 128 128 128 128 0 0 0
152 120	
0 0 0 0	

where the x-y scan lines values are from the mouse input and the RGB values are generated between these points. Generation of RGB is quite simply achieved by setting all values to zero prior to the first x-value, setting all values to 128 (in groups of 3) between the first and second x-value and finally setting all values to zero after the last x-value (a program to perform this operation is supplied on the Web site accompanying this book). The four zero values for the x-y scan lines indicate the end of data for a given CAT scan slice. The structure 'patches' is used to define the storage of each of the vertices of the cubes used to build the head and variables have been left there for inclusion of the different colours of eyes, lips or other facial features if students so wish. Rotation of the whole object is achieved using the x, y, z keys including upper case as desired with $5°$ intervals.

A function for setting up a lighting environment is also included using ambient and diffuse lighting. Students are encouraged to modify this code by removing comments to include further lighting effects which add realism to the resultant display.

```cpp
#include <stdlib.h>    //Head.cpp
#include <iostream>    //hcubes.txt & cube.dat
using std::cout;
using std::cin;
using std::endl;
using std::ios;

#include <fstream>
using std::ifstream;
using std::ofstream;
#include <math.h>
#include <windows.h>
#include <GL/glut.h>

#define Width 32
#define Height 32
#define Depth 24

static GLubyte image[Depth][Height][Width][3];
static GLuint texName;
float normal[3];
GLfloat rot[]={0.0, 0.0, 0.0};

int r, t, s, rgb, xstart, ystart, zstart, xend, flag;
int mouseX = 0;
int mouseY = 0;
int mouseState = 0;
int mouseButton = 0;
struct patches {
    char type[10];
    char colour;
    float v[4][3];
};
patches cubeface[6];

void makeImage(void)
{
```

```
char filename[25];
int blue, green, red;

cout << "Colour(r/g/b) head file: ";
cin >> filename;
   ifstream inpos(filename, ios ::in);
   if(!inpos) { cout << "File would not open\n";
                                        exit(1);
                            }

for (r = 0; r < Depth; r++) {
        for (t = 0; t < Height; t++) {
                for (s = 0; s < Width; s++) {
                        inpos >> red;
                        image[r][t][s][0] = (GLubyte) red;
                        inpos >> green;
                        image[r][t][s][1] = green;
                        inpos >> blue;
                        image[r][t][s][2] = blue;
                }
        }
}
}

void InputData()
{
int vertex, coord, no_of_faces;
float scale=0.5;
makeImage();
ifstream InPoints("cube.dat", ios::in);
for(no_of_faces=0; no_of_faces<6; no_of_faces++)
{
        //get colour here for cube?
for(vertex = 0; vertex<4; vertex++)
{
        for(coord=0; coord<3; coord++)
        {
                InPoints >> cubeface[no_of_faces].v[vertex][coord];
                cubeface[no_of_faces].v[vertex][coord] =cubeface
                [no_of_faces].v[vertex][coord]*scale;
        }
}
}
}
}
```

```
void Normalise(float vector[3])
{
float length;

    // Calculate the length of the vector
    length = (float)sqrt(((vector[0]*vector[0]) +
                (vector[1]*vector[1]) +
                        (vector[2]*vector[2])));

    if(length == 0.0) length = 1.0;

    // Divide by the length = unit normal vector.
    vector[0] /= length;
    vector[1] /= length;
    vector[2] /= length;
}
// Points p1, p2, & p3 specified in counter clock-wise order
void Normal(float v[3][3], float out[3])
{
    float v1[3],v2[3];
    static const int x = 0, y = 1, z = 2;

    // get two vectors from the three points
    v1[x] = v[0][x] - v[1][x];
    v1[y] = v[0][y] - v[1][y];
    v1[z] = v[0][z] - v[1][z];

    v2[x] = v[1][x] - v[2][x];
    v2[y] = v[1][y] - v[2][y];
    v2[z] = v[1][z] - v[2][z];

    // cross product to get normal vector stored in out
    out[x] = v1[y]*v2[z] - v1[z]*v2[y];
    out[y] = v1[z]*v2[x] - v1[x]*v2[z];
    out[z] = v1[x]*v2[y] - v1[y]*v2[x];

    Normalise(out); // shorten length to one
}

void cube_draw( int x1, int x2, int y, int z) {
int i, no_of_faces, no_of_cubes;
no_of_cubes = x2 - x1;
glColor3ub(128, 128, 128);

for(i = 0; i<no_of_cubes; i++) {
    glPushMatrix();
```

```
    glTranslatef( -Width/2 +(float) x1, -Height/2 + (float) y,
    -Depth/2 + (float) z);
    glBegin(GL_QUADS);
          for(no_of_faces=0; no_of_faces<6; no_of_faces++) {
                  Normal(cubeface[no_of_faces].v,normal);
                  glNormal3fv(normal);
                  glVertex3fv(cubeface[no_of_faces].v[0]);
                  glVertex3fv(cubeface[no_of_faces].v[1]);
                  glVertex3fv(cubeface[no_of_faces].v[2]);
                  glVertex3fv(cubeface[no_of_faces].v[3]);
              }
    glEnd();
    x1++;
    glPopMatrix();
}
}

void display(void)
{
int r, s, t, rgb, flag, xstart, ystart, zstart;
int no_of_faces;

glClear(GL_COLOR_BUFFER_BIT | GL_DEPTH_BUFFER_BIT);
glPushMatrix();
    glRotatef(rot[0], 1.0f, 0.0f, 0.0f);
    glRotatef(rot[1], 0.0f, 1.0f, 0.0f);
    glRotatef(rot[2], 0.0f, 0.0f, 1.0f);

for(r=0; r<Depth; r++) {
    for(t=0; t<Height; t++) {
          flag = 0;
          xstart = 0; xend = 0;
          for(s=0; s<Width; s++) {
              rgb = 0;
              if( (int) image[r][t][s][rgb] ==  0) { //mono only
                  if(flag == 1) cube_draw( xstart, xend, ystart, zstart);
                  flag = 0;
                  zstart = r;
                  ystart = t;
                  xstart = s+1;
          }
          else {
                  xend = s+1;
                  flag = 1;
          }
      }
    }
```

```
    }
}
glPopMatrix();   // Restore matrix state

glColor3f(0.0, 1.0, 0.0);
glBegin(GL_LINES);
    glVertex3f(-25.0, 0.0, 0.0);    glVertex3f(25.0, 0.0, 0.0);
    glVertex3f( 0.0, 25.0, 0.0);    glVertex3f(0.0, -25.0, 0.0);
    glVertex3f( 0.0, 0.0, 25.0);    glVertex3f(0.0, 0.0, -25.0);
glEnd();
glFlush();
}


void keys(unsigned char key, int x, int y)
{
// Use x. X. Y. y. z. and Z keys to rotate
if(key =='x' ) rot[0]-= 5.0;
if(key =='X') rot[0]+= 5.0;
if(key =='y') rot[1]-= 5.0;
if(key =='Y') rot[1]+= 5.0;
if(key =='z') rot[2]-= 5.0;
if(key =='Z') rot[2]+= 5.0;
display();
}


void LightEnvironment()
{
    // Light values and coordinates
GLfloat  ambientLight[] = { 0.0, 0.0, 1.0, 1.0 };
GLfloat  diffuseLight[] = { 0.7, 0.7, 0.7, 1.0 };
float specular[] = {1.0, 0.0, 0.0, 1.0};
GLfloat  lightPos[] = {0.0, 25.0, 0.0, 1.0 };
//float emission[] = {0.0, 1.0, 1.0, 1.0};

float specref[] = {1.0, 1.0, 1.0, 1.0};

    glEnable(GL_DEPTH_TEST);
    glFrontFace(GL_CCW);
    glEnable(GL_CULL_FACE);

    glEnable(GL_LIGHTING);         // Enable lighting

     //glLightfv(GL_LIGHT0,GL_POSITION,lightPos);
    // Setup and enable light 0
    glLightfv(GL_LIGHT0,GL_AMBIENT,ambientLight);
    glLightfv(GL_LIGHT0,GL_DIFFUSE,diffuseLight);
```

```
   //glLightfv(GL_LIGHT0,GL_SPECULAR,specular);
   glEnable(GL_LIGHT0);

   // Enable color tracking
   glEnable(GL_COLOR_MATERIAL);

   // Set Material properties to follow glColor values
   glColorMaterial(GL_FRONT, GL_AMBIENT_AND_DIFFUSE);
   //glMaterialfv(GL_FRONT, GL_SPECULAR, specref);
   //glMateriali(GL_FRONT, GL_SHININESS, 1);
   //glMaterialfv(GL_FRONT, GL_EMISSION, emission);

   glClearColor(0.0, 0.0, 0.0, 1.0 );
}

void ChangeSize(int w, int h)
{
   GLfloat nRange = 25.0f;
   if(h == 0) h = 1;

   glMatrixMode(GL_PROJECTION);
   glLoadIdentity();

 if (w <= h)
   glOrtho (-nRange, nRange, -nRange*h/w, nRange*h/w, -nRange, nRange);
 else
   glOrtho (-nRange*w/h, nRange*w/h, -nRange, nRange, -nRange, nRange);

   glMatrixMode(GL_MODELVIEW);
   glLoadIdentity();
}
```

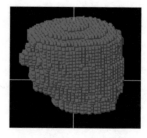

Fig. 7.26 A simple
reconstruction from CAT
scan slices

In Fig. 7.26 the output reconstruction is displayed in blue light after suitable rotations
in the z and x directions.

7.8 Exercises

1. In Section 7.4.8 we mapped the image of a flag onto a sinusoid. Develop this program to increase the frequency of the wave and provide a similar sinusoid in the $x-y$ plane. By adjusting the frequency of each investigate the realism of the ripples in the flag. Students with a sufficiently powerful computer should watch the effects of real time ripple simulation.
2. Use several pictures of an aircraft taken against different backgrounds (runway, sky, etc.) and using the concept of blending (Section 7.6.1), simulate the view through the window of an aircraft taking off or landing.

7.9 Conclusions

In this chapter we have described the process of texturing bit map images on to a number of common geometric surfaces and extended the process to general surfaces. The mapping process is described in terms of a linear transformation between the bit map image and the geometric surface on which it is pasted. We have introduced the idea in order to provide more realistic environments in which the visualisation process may take place. The work forms the basis for developing displays applicable to computer games and in the area of simulation.

In the final section of this chapter we have integrated the work of data capture from images described in Chapter 3.

Chapter 8
Objects to Artefacts

8.1 Introduction

Models are abstractions of real world often described by mathematical equations. In graphics, models are often geometric entities built from lines represented by equations and OpenGL provides primitives from which we can build the user defined objects. Transformations are a hierarchy of relationships, which define objects and how they look and operate.

Object orientated programming has a value in the construction of some types of graphical artefacts – it is what Lego and Meccano are to mechanical toy construction or what mass production is to manufacturing. Where artefacts have forms that are repeated we can reuse the same software again and again as we have already seen with the example of a class used in reading binary image files. As an illustration, a basic object (e.g. rectangle) can be used to construct gear teeth by combining the rectangles with suitable transformations.

8.2 Artefact Hierarchy

Objects are the atomic entities that are used to construct higher-level artefacts by using the objects in suitable combinations. In this section we will use simple objects for illustrative purposes although the reader should not expect OOP to provide an easy solution to the construction of complex geometric shapes – they still have to be modelled!

In constructing an artefact we need to draw basic much used objects, Fig. 8.1 and map out interrelationships to form the total component artefact required. We can imagine an engine made from cylinders, washers, nuts, bolts, pistons etc. Time spent on identifying the repetitively required objects and the data required not only to

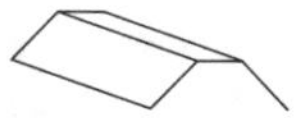

Fig. 8.1 Simple gear tooth made up from three rectangles

specify but also to permit transformations required in building artefacts is a requirement of any graphics system. The complexity of *writing* objects as opposed to *using* objects should not be underestimated.

8.2.1 Construction Double Sided Squares

In this example we create a class, which represents a square that may be coloured on both faces and used to construct walls, make cubes and other solid objects. The square can be considered as the basic building block for geometric entities or artefacts that can be constructed from this shape. Our object class will require the coordinates of the four vertices representing a square plus a parameter to specify the colour (an RGB value or a texture). The squares are located about the origin as shown in Fig. 8.2 with the floor being coloured on both sides (blue and green) for illustrative purposes. Construction of each square requires four calls to glVertex3f() for each vertex and specification of the colour with which to fill the quadrilateral.

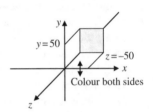

Fig. 8.2 Using a square to build a room object

For the texture facility we have linearly mapped using glTexCoord2f() at the corresponding vertices with rotation of the complete object provided by the keyboard arrow keys.

```
#define Width 256    //oosqu2.cpp
#define Height 256
static GLfloat xRot = 0.0;
static GLfloat yRot = 0.0;

int ww, wh;
static GLubyte Image[Height][Width][4];
static GLuint texName;
#include "cRead_Gen_bmp.cpp"

void LooksLike();
void DrawScene();

class CFace
{
  private:
  unsigned char red, green, blue;
  int colour;
```

```
    float xp0, yp0, zp0, xp1, yp1, zp1, xp2, yp2, zp2, xp3, yp3, zp3;
    public:
CFace(int col, float x0, float y0, float z0, float x1, float y1,
        float z1, float x2, float y2, float z2, float x3,
        float y3, float z3);
          void AreaFill()
          {
  red = 0; green = 0; blue = 0;
  if(colour == 0) red = 255;
  if(colour == 1) green = 255;
          if(colour == 2) blue = 255;
          if(colour == 3) { //Texture one face
                  glEnable(GL_TEXTURE_2D);
                  glTexEnvf(GL_TEXTURE_ENV, GL_TEXTURE_ENV_MODE,
                      GL_REPLACE);
                  glBindTexture(GL_TEXTURE_2D, texName);
glBegin(GL_QUADS);
    glTexCoord2f(0.0, 0.0);  glVertex3f(xp0, yp0, zp0);
    glTexCoord2f(1.0, 0.0);  glVertex3f(xp1, yp1, zp1);
    glTexCoord2f(1.0, 1.0);  glVertex3f(xp2, yp2, zp2);
    glTexCoord2f(0.0, 1.0);  glVertex3f(xp3, yp3, zp3);
glEnd();
          glFlush();
          glDisable(GL_TEXTURE_2D);
          }
  glBegin(GL_QUADS);
  glColor3ub(red, green, blue);
          glVertex3f(xp0, yp0, zp0);
          glVertex3f(xp1, yp1, zp1);
          glVertex3f(xp2, yp2, zp2);
          glVertex3f(xp3, yp3, zp3);
  glEnd();
  }
};
CFace::CFace(int col, float x0, float y0, float z0, float x1,
        float y1, float z1, float x2, float y2, float z2,
        float x3, float y3, float z3) //constructor
        {
        cout << "Initialise points in constructor\n";
        xp0 = x0; yp0 = y0; zp0 = z0;
        xp1 = x1; yp1 = y1; zp1 = z1;
        xp2 = x2; yp2 = y2; zp2 = z2;
        xp3 = x3; yp3 = y3; zp3 = z3;
        colour = col;
        }

void LooksLike()
{
// Light values and coordinates
```

```
GLfloat  ambientLight[] = { 0.9f, 0.9f, 0.9f, 1.0f };
GLfloat  diffuseLight[] = { 0.7f, 0.7f, 0.7f, 1.0f };
float specular[] = {1.0f, 1.0f, 1.0f, 1.0f};
float spec[] = {1.0f, 1.0f, 1.0f, 1.0f};
GLubyte* image_store;
int r, c, i;
ip_bmp_file Read_a_BMP_file;

image_store = Read_a_BMP_file.makeImage();
i = 0;
for (r = 0; r < wh; r++) {
 for (c = 0; c < ww; c++) {
 Image[r][c][2] = image_store[i];
 i++;
 Image[r][c][1] = image_store[i];
 i++;
 Image[r][c][0] = image_store[i];
 i++;
 Image[r][c][3] = (GLubyte) 255;
 }
}
 glClearColor(0.0, 0.0, 0.0, 0.0);
 glShadeModel(GL_FLAT);
 glEnable(GL_DEPTH_TEST);

 glPixelStorei(GL_UNPACK_ALIGNMENT, 1);
 glGenTextures (1, &texName) ;
 glBindTexture(GL_TEXTURE_2D, texName);
 glTexParameteri(GL_TEXTURE_2D, GL_TEXTURE_WRAP_S, GL_REPEAT);
 glTexParameteri(GL_TEXTURE_2D, GL_TEXTURE_WRAP_T, GL_REPEAT);
 glTexParameteri(GL_TEXTURE_2D, GL_TEXTURE_MAG_FILTER, GL_NEAREST);
 glTexParameteri(GL_TEXTURE_2D, GL_TEXTURE_MIN_FILTER, GL_NEAREST);
 glTexEnvf(GL_TEXTURE_ENV, GL_TEXTURE_ENV_MODE, GL_MODULATE);
 glTexImage2D(GL_TEXTURE_2D, 0, GL_RGBA, ww, wh,  0, GL_RGBA,
      GL_UNSIGNED_BYTE, Image);

      glEnable(GL_DEPTH_TEST);
      glFrontFace(GL_CCW);
      glEnable(GL_CULL_FACE);

      glEnable(GL_LIGHTING);       // Enable lighting
      // Setup and enable light 0
      glLightfv(GL_LIGHT0,GL_AMBIENT,ambientLight);
      glLightfv(GL_LIGHT0,GL_DIFFUSE,diffuseLight);
      glLightfv(GL_LIGHT0,GL_SPECULAR,specular);
      glEnable(GL_LIGHT0);

      // Enable color tracking
      glEnable(GL_COLOR_MATERIAL);
```

```
        // Set Material properties to follow glColor values
        glColorMaterial(GL_FRONT, GL_AMBIENT_AND_DIFFUSE);
        glMaterialfv(GL_FRONT, GL_SPECULAR, spec);
        glMateriali(GL_FRONT, GL_SHININESS, 5);

        // Yellow background
        glClearColor(1.0f, 1.0f, 0.0f, 1.0f );
}

void DrawScene(void)
{
// Clear the window with current clearing color
glClear(GL_COLOR_BUFFER_BIT | GL_DEPTH_BUFFER_BIT);

// Save the matrix state and do the rotations
glPushMatrix();
glRotatef(xRot, 1.0f, 0.0f, 0.0f);
glRotatef(yRot, 0.0f, 25.0f, 0.0f);

  CFace sq1(0, 0.0, 0.0, -50.0, 50.0, 0.0, -50.0, 50.0, 50.0, -50.0,
          0.0, 50.0, -50.0);
  sq1.AreaFill();

  CFace sq2(1, 0.0, 0.0, -50.0, 50.0, 0.0, -50.0, 50.0, 0.0, 0.0, 0.0,
          0.0, 0.0);
  sq2.AreaFill();      //Top side of floor

  CFace sq3(2, 0.0, 0.0, 0.0, 50.0, 0.0, 0.0, 50.0, 0.0, -50.0, 0.0,
          0.0, -50.0);
  sq3.AreaFill();      //Underside side of floor

  CFace sq4(3, 0.0, 0.0, 0.0, 0.0, 0.0, -50.0, 0.0, 50.0, -50.0, 0.0,
          50.0, 0.0);
  sq4.AreaFill();
glPopMatrix();
glutSwapBuffers();
glFlush();
}

void ArrowKeys(int key, int x, int y)
{
        if(key == GLUT_KEY_UP)   xRot-= 5.0;
        if(key == GLUT_KEY_DOWN) xRot += 5.0;
        if(key == GLUT_KEY_LEFT) yRot -= 5.0;
        if(key == GLUT_KEY_RIGHT) yRot += 5.0;
        if(xRot > 356.0f) xRot = 0.0;
        if(xRot < -1.0f)   xRot = 355.0;
        if(yRot > 356.0f) yRot = 0.0;
        if(yRot < -1.0f)   yRot = 355.0;
```

```
    // Refresh the Window
        glutPostRedisplay();
}
```

The class in "cRead_Gen_bmp.cpp" provides the texture image (Fig. 8.3).

Fig. 8.3 Construction of the
inside of a room

We will now experiment with some further objects and use them in the creation
of a more complex scene.

8.2.2 A Box as a Basic Building Block

We now define a box data structure together with a facility for texturing and use it to
construct a table. Consider the following box with vertices v_0, v_1, v_2, ...v_7 as shown
in Fig. 8.4.

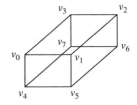

Fig. 8.4 Box data structure

The vertices are stored as a 2D array $v[i][j]$ where i denotes which vertex is being
addressed and j denotes the (x, y, z) co-ordinates at the vertex. Vertices should be
used to texture with the same handedness else you may be texturing the opposite
face to what you intend!
    For instance

$$v_0, v_1, v_2, v_3 \quad \text{Top}$$
$$v_0, v_4, v_5, v_1 \quad \text{Sides}$$
$$v_1, v_5, v_6, v_2$$
$$v_2, v_6, v_7, v_3$$
$$v_3, v_7, v_4, v_0$$
$$v_4, v_7, v_6, v_5 \quad \text{Bottom}$$

will create a box of any dimensions for Fig. 8.4.

The box faces can be coloured or textured in the order defined by the vertex order, Fig. 8.3. Ordering can be expressed in a class both in the ordering of the texturing of individual faces and in the subsequent ordering of the box faces. In following example the box vertices are stored in the array vts[8][3]. OpenGl routines glTexCoord2f() and glVertex3f() are embedded within the class routine FaceTexture to fill in the cube faces.

The data file used in following example to represent the Cartesian coordinates of each vertex looks something like:

x	y	z	
0.0	−40.0	40.0	v_0
40.0	−40.0	40.0	v_1
40.0	−40.0	0.0	
0.0	−40.0	0.0	
0.0	0.0	40.0	
40.0	0.0	40.0	
40.0	0.0	0.0	
0.0	0.0	0.0	v_7

In designing a representation for an object we need also to consider the variability of the object and the uses to which it may be put. Clearly the texture can also indicate the material it is made of while we may use a scale factor to adjust the size. In adition with a number of objects of the same type, position in the scene will also be important. Users will need to make judgements about which factors are held within the class representation and which are more appropriate if held external to the to the class. In the next example we shall for illustrative purposes build a cube (box) class with some facilities included and others not. Readers may wish to vary this organisation in their own applications.

8.2.3 Building a Table

We can now use the box object to build a table with four 'box' legs and a 'box' for the tabletop. Using the common box object for the table construction, the difference between the table legs is a matter of only position since they are all the same, while the tabletop is different in size and position from the legs. Construction can take place from one structure provided we scale it to the desired size and move it to the appropriate location within the total design of the artefact; in this case a table. In this example we could have used glScalef() and glTranslatef(), but for some reason now lost in my memory I provided my own versions – probably because a student asked a question long since forgotten! The change required is of no significance.

The eight vertices are stored in the array vts[8][3] and texturing is applied to each of the six faces of the box using the object class Ccube.

```
float vts[8][3], vts1[8][3];
class CCube
{
    private:
    unsigned char red, green, blue;
    int i, colour;
    float vts[8][3];
    public:
            CCube(int col, float vts[8][3]);    //constructor declaration
                CFace(floats)
            void FaceTexture(float vts[8][3] )
            {
    int i;
 glBegin(GL_QUADS);
   {
     glTexCoord2f(0.0, 0.0); glVertex3f(vts[0][0], vts[0][1], vts[0][2]);
     glTexCoord2f(1.0, 0.0); glVertex3f(vts[1][0], vts[1][1], vts[1][2]);
     glTexCoord2f(1.0, 1.0); glVertex3f(vts[2][0], vts[2][1], vts[2][2]);
     glTexCoord2f(0.0, 1.0); glVertex3f(vts[3][0], vts[3][1], vts[3][2]);

     glTexCoord2f(0.0, 0.0); glVertex3f(vts[4][0], vts[4][1], vts[4][2]);
     glTexCoord2f(1.0, 0.0); glVertex3f(vts[7][0], vts[7][1], vts[7][2]);
     glTexCoord2f(1.0, 1.0); glVertex3f(vts[6][0], vts[6][1], vts[6][2]);
     glTexCoord2f(0.0, 1.0);  glVertex3f(vts[5][0], vts[5][1], vts[5][2]);

   for(i=0; i<3; i++) {
     glTexCoord2f(0.0, 0.0); glVertex3f(vts[i][0], vts[i][1], vts[i][2]);
     glTexCoord2f(1.0, 0.0); glVertex3f(vts[i+4][0], vts[i+4][1], vts[i+4][2]);
     glTexCoord2f(1.0, 1.0); glVertex3f(vts[i+5][0], vts[i+5][1], vts[i+5][2]);
     glTexCoord2f(0.0, 1.0); glVertex3f(vts[i+1][0], vts[i+1][1], vts[i+1][2]);
     }

     glTexCoord2f(0.0, 0.0); glVertex3f(vts[3][0], vts[3][1], vts[3][2]);
     glTexCoord2f(1.0, 0.0); glVertex3f(vts[7][0], vts[7][1], vts[7][2]);
     glTexCoord2f(1.0, 1.0); glVertex3f(vts[4][0], vts[4][1], vts[4][2]);
     glTexCoord2f(0.0, 1.0); glVertex3f(vts[0][0], vts[0][1], vts[0][2]);
  glEnd();
   }
  }
};
CCube::CCube(int col, float vts[8][3])  //constructor
{
            cout << "Initialise points in constructor\n";
    colour = col;
}
```

The scaling and positioning of the table components is hard coded for purposes of demonstration in this example but in practice this would be interactively altered through mouse movements and part of the class.

8.3 Integrating to a System

In the previous example we built what might be three walls of a room and we will now make use of this construction by placing our table in the room, placing the Utah teapot on the table, providing movement of the table around the room and demonstrating lighting effects on *one* of the textured walls. We will revisit a number of topics already covered and show how by integrating each we are developing a simple room layout facility. This program is a partially developed system, which readers can use as a foundation for developing ideas associated with virtual tours and room design. The system allows independent movement of the teapot and table in relation to the room walls, which are also moveable to permit different views. The matrix operations for each of these movements must be separated by means of glPushMatrix () and glPopMatrix () and required texture enabled for each part of the room and contents.

```
glPushMatrix()
//Enable appropriate textures for walls and floor
//Move walls, floor, contents to required view
glPopMatrix()
glPushMatrix()
//Enable appropriate texture for teapot
//Build table from box object
glPushMatrix()
//Enable appropriate texture for table
//Place teapot on table
glPopMatrix()
glPopMatrix()
```

The table and teapot are within a common glPushMatrix(), glPopMatrix() code section since they move together with movement being provided in the x-direction and rotation around the room. If our example the linear movement is via the F9 key while rotation of the table is via F7 & and F8 keys. The arrow keys rotate the whole scene.

Note should also be taken of the effect of lighting on one wall only when the colour parameter is set to 3. For this case we have introduced GL_MODULATE in glTexEnvf(GL_TEXTURE_ENV, GL_TEXTURE_ENV_MODE, GL_ MODU-LATE); in place of GL_REPLACE. The parameter GL_REPLACE replaces the colour of an object by the texture image identified by integer name in texName[0] of glBindTexture(GL_TEXTURE_2D, texName[0]). GL_MODULATE multiplies each texel by the object colour after lighting calculations and thus the textured image appear to be shaded as the walls are rotated. glTexEnvf() has a range of range of parameters and readers are advised to consult the OpenGL reference manual for fuller details.

```cpp
#define Width 256              //ooptstotal.cpp
#define Height 256
static GLfloat xRot = 0.0;
static GLfloat yRot = 0.0;

static GLfloat yFurnitureRot = 0.0;
static GLfloat xFurnitureMv = 0.0;

int ww, wh;
static GLubyte Wall[Height][Width][4];
static GLubyte Table[Height][Width][4], Tpot[Height][Width][4];
static GLuint texName[3];
ifstream cubexyz("c:\\rob\\Graphics\\lectures\\book\\programs
    \\CubeData.txt", ios ::in);

#include "cRead_Gen_bmp.cpp"

void LooksLike();
void DrawScene();

class CFace
{
  private:
  unsigned char red, green, blue;
  int colour;
  float xp0, yp0, zp0, xp1, yp1, zp1, xp2, yp2, zp2, xp3,
        yp3, zp3;
  public:
        CFace(int col, float x0, float y0, float z0, float x1,
        float y1, float z1, float x2, float y2, float z2,
        float x3, float y3, float z3);
void AreaFill()
        {
  red = 0; green = 0; blue = 0;
  if(colour == 0) red = 255;
  if(colour == 1) green = 255;
        if(colour == 2) blue = 255;
        if(colour == 3) { //Texture one wall face
                glEnable(GL_TEXTURE_2D);
                glTexEnvf(GL_TEXTURE_ENV, GL_TEXTURE_ENV_MODE,
                        GL_MODULATE);
                glBindTexture(GL_TEXTURE_2D, texName[0]);
glBegin(GL_QUADS);
```

```
    glTexCoord2f(0.0, 0.0);   glVertex3f(xp0, yp0, zp0);
    glTexCoord2f(1.0, 0.0);   glVertex3f(xp1, yp1, zp1);
    glTexCoord2f(1.0, 1.0);   glVertex3f(xp2, yp2, zp2);
    glTexCoord2f(0.0, 1.0);   glVertex3f(xp3, yp3, zp3);
glEnd();
        glFlush();
        glDisable(GL_TEXTURE_2D);
        }
        glBegin(GL_QUADS);
                glColor3ub(red, green, blue);
                glVertex3f(xp0, yp0, zp0);
                glVertex3f(xp1, yp1, zp1);
                glVertex3f(xp2, yp2, zp2);
                glVertex3f(xp3, yp3, zp3);
            glEnd();
    }
};
CFace::CFace(int col, float x0, float y0, float z0, float x1,
        float y1, float z1, float x2, float y2, float z2,
        float x3, float y3, float z3) //constructor
        {
                cout << "Initialise points in constructor\n";
    xp0 = x0; yp0 = y0; zp0 = z0;
    xp1 = x1; yp1 = y1; zp1 = z1;
    xp2 = x2; yp2 = y2; zp2 = z2;
    xp3 = x3; yp3 = y3; zp3 = z3;
    colour = col;
        }

float vts[8][3], vts1[8][3];
class CCube
{
  private:
  unsigned char red, green, blue;
  int i, colour;
  float vts[8][3];
  public:
        CCube(int col, float vts[8][3]);    //constructor
        declarationCFace(floats)
        void FaceTexture(float vts[8][3] )
            {
    int i;
glBegin(GL_QUADS);
 {
  glTexCoord2f(0.0, 0.0); glVertex3f(vts[0][0], vts[0][1], vts[0][2]);
  glTexCoord2f(1.0, 0.0); glVertex3f(vts[1][0], vts[1][1], vts[1][2]);
  glTexCoord2f(1.0, 1.0); glVertex3f(vts[2][0], vts[2][1], vts[2][2]);
  glTexCoord2f(0.0, 1.0); glVertex3f(vts[3][0], vts[3][1], vts[3][2]);
  glTexCoord2f(0.0, 0.0); glVertex3f(vts[4][0], vts[4][1], vts[4][2]);
```

```
 glTexCoord2f(1.0, 0.0); glVertex3f(vts[7][0], vts[7][1], vts[7][2]);
 glTexCoord2f(1.0, 1.0); glVertex3f(vts[6][0], vts[6][1], vts[6][2]);
 glTexCoord2f(0.0, 1.0);  glVertex3f(vts[5][0], vts[5][1], vts[5][2]);

for(i=0; i<3; i++) {
 glTexCoord2f(0.0, 0.0); glVertex3f(vts[i][0], vts[i][1], vts[i][2]);
 glTexCoord2f(1.0, 0.0); glVertex3f(vts[i+4][0], vts[i+4][1],
   vts[i+4][2]);
 glTexCoord2f(1.0, 1.0); glVertex3f(vts[i+5][0], vts[i+5][1],
   vts[i+5][2]);
 glTexCoord2f(0.0, 1.0); glVertex3f(vts[i+1][0], vts[i+1][1],
   vts[i+1][2]);
 }

 glTexCoord2f(0.0, 0.0); glVertex3f(vts[3][0], vts[3][1], vts[3][2]);
 glTexCoord2f(1.0, 0.0); glVertex3f(vts[7][0], vts[7][1], vts[7][2]);
 glTexCoord2f(1.0, 1.0); glVertex3f(vts[4][0], vts[4][1], vts[4][2]);
 glTexCoord2f(0.0, 1.0); glVertex3f(vts[0][0], vts[0][1], vts[0][2]);
 glEnd();
  }
 }
};
CCube::CCube(int col, float vts[8][3])  //constructor
{
                cout << "Initialise points in constructor\n";
  colour = col;
}
//-----------------------------------------------

void Shiftxyz(float x, float y, float z)
{   // shift vertices to new position
int i;
  for (i = 0; i < 8; i++) {
    vts1[i][0] = vts1[i][0]+ x;
    vts1[i][1] = vts1[i][1]+ y;
    vts1[i][2] = vts1[i][2]+ z;
  }
}

void Scalexyz(float xscl, float yscl, float zscl)
{
int i;
// =diagonal of identity matrix multiplication
for (i = 0; i < 8; i++) {
 vts1[i][0] = vts[i][0] * xscl;
 vts1[i][1] = vts[i][1] * yscl;
 vts1[i][2] = vts[i][2] * zscl;
 }
}
```

```
void LooksLike()
{

// Light values and coordinates
GLfloat  ambientLight[] = { 0.9f, 0.9f, 0.9f, 1.0f };
GLfloat  diffuseLight[] = { 0.7f, 0.7f, 0.7f, 1.0f };
float specular[] = {1.0f, 1.0f, 1.0f, 1.0f};
float spec[] = {1.0f, 1.0f, 1.0f, 1.0f};
GLubyte* image_store;
int r, c, i;
ip_bmp_file Read_a_BMP_file;

image_store = Read_a_BMP_file.makeImage();
i = 0;
for (r = 0; r < wh; r++) {
 for (c = 0; c < ww; c++) {
 Wall[r][c][2] = image_store[i];
 i++;
 Wall[r][c][1] = image_store[i];
 i++;
 Wall[r][c][0] = image_store[i];
 i++;
 Wall[r][c][3] = (GLubyte) 255;
 }
}
 glClearColor(0.0, 0.0, 0.0, 0.0);
 glShadeModel(GL_FLAT);
 glEnable(GL_DEPTH_TEST);

 glPixelStorei(GL_UNPACK_ALIGNMENT, 1);
 glGenTextures (1, &texName[0]) ;
 glBindTexture(GL_TEXTURE_2D, texName[0]);
 glTexParameteri(GL_TEXTURE_2D, GL_TEXTURE_WRAP_S, GL_REPEAT);
 glTexParameteri(GL_TEXTURE_2D, GL_TEXTURE_WRAP_T, GL_REPEAT);
 glTexParameteri(GL_TEXTURE_2D, GL_TEXTURE_MAG_FILTER, GL_NEAREST);
 glTexParameteri(GL_TEXTURE_2D, GL_TEXTURE_MIN_FILTER, GL_NEAREST);
 glTexImage2D(GL_TEXTURE_2D, 0, GL_RGBA, ww, wh,  0, GL_RGBA,
       GL_UNSIGNED_BYTE, Wall);

        glEnable(GL_DEPTH_TEST);
        glFrontFace(GL_CCW);
        glEnable(GL_CULL_FACE);

        glEnable(GL_LIGHTING);       // Enable lighting
        glLightfv(GL_LIGHT0,GL_AMBIENT,ambientLight);
        glLightfv(GL_LIGHT0,GL_DIFFUSE,diffuseLight);
        glLightfv(GL_LIGHT0,GL_SPECULAR,specular);
        glEnable(GL_LIGHT0);
```

```
      // Enable color tracking
      glEnable(GL_COLOR_MATERIAL);
      // Set Material properties to follow glColor values
      glColorMaterial(GL_FRONT, GL_AMBIENT_AND_DIFFUSE);
      glMaterialfv(GL_FRONT, GL_SPECULAR, spec);
      glMateriali(GL_FRONT, GL_SHININESS, 5);

image_store = Read_a_BMP_file.makeImage();
i = 0;
for (r = 0; r < wh; r++) {  //Wood table finish
 for (c = 0; c < ww; c++) {
 Table[r][c][2] = image_store[i];
 i++;
 Table[r][c][1] = image_store[i];
 i++;
 Table[r][c][0] = image_store[i];
 i++;
 Table[r][c][3] = (GLubyte) 255;
 }
}

for (r = 0; r < wh; r++) {  //Red teapot
 for (c = 0; c < ww; c++) {
 Tpot[r][c][0] = (GLubyte) 245;
 Tpot[r][c][1] = (GLubyte) 0;
 Tpot[r][c][2] = (GLubyte) 0;
 Tpot[r][c][3] = (GLubyte) 255;
 }
}

glPixelStorei(GL_UNPACK_ALIGNMENT, 1);
glGenTextures (1, &texName[1]) ;
glBindTexture(GL_TEXTURE_2D, texName[1]);
glTexParameteri(GL_TEXTURE_2D, GL_TEXTURE_WRAP_S, GL_REPEAT);
glTexParameteri(GL_TEXTURE_2D, GL_TEXTURE_WRAP_T, GL_REPEAT);
glTexParameteri(GL_TEXTURE_2D, GL_TEXTURE_MAG_FILTER, GL_NEAREST);
glTexParameteri(GL_TEXTURE_2D, GL_TEXTURE_MIN_FILTER, GL_NEAREST);
glTexImage2D(GL_TEXTURE_2D, 0, GL_RGBA, ww, wh,  0, GL_RGBA,
     GL_UNSIGNED_BYTE, Table);

glPixelStorei(GL_UNPACK_ALIGNMENT, 1);
glGenTextures (1, &texName[2]) ;
glBindTexture(GL_TEXTURE_2D, texName[2]);
glTexParameteri(GL_TEXTURE_2D, GL_TEXTURE_WRAP_S, GL_REPEAT);
glTexParameteri(GL_TEXTURE_2D, GL_TEXTURE_WRAP_T, GL_REPEAT);
glTexParameteri(GL_TEXTURE_2D, GL_TEXTURE_MAG_FILTER, GL_NEAREST);
glTexParameteri(GL_TEXTURE_2D, GL_TEXTURE_MIN_FILTER, GL_NEAREST);
glTexImage2D(GL_TEXTURE_2D, 0, GL_RGBA, ww, wh,  0, GL_RGBA,
     GL_UNSIGNED_BYTE, Tpot);
```

```
        glEnable(GL_DEPTH_TEST);
        glFrontFace(GL_CCW);
        glEnable(GL_CULL_FACE);

        glClearColor(1.0f, 1.0f, 0.0f, 1.0f );
if(!cubexyz) {
        cout << "File cube would not open\n";
        return;
}
for(r=0; r<8; r++) {
 for(c=0; c<3; c++) cubexyz >> vts[r][c];
 }
cubexyz.close();
}

void DrawScene(void)
{
// Clear the window with current clearing color
glClear(GL_COLOR_BUFFER_BIT | GL_DEPTH_BUFFER_BIT);

// Save the matrix state and do the rotations
glPushMatrix();
glRotatef(xRot, 1.0f, 0.0f, 0.0f);
glRotatef(yRot, 0.0f, 25.0f, 0.0f);

  CFace sq1(0, 0.0, 0.0, -50.0, 50.0, 0.0, -50.0, 50.0, 50.0, -50.0,
    0.0, 50.0, -50.0);
  sq1.AreaFill();

  CFace sq2(1, 0.0, 0.0, -50.0, 50.0, 0.0, -50.0, 50.0, 0.0, 0.0, 0.0,
    0.0, 0.0);
  sq2.AreaFill();       //Top side of floor

  CFace sq3(2, 0.0, 0.0, 0.0, 50.0, 0.0, 0.0, 50.0, 0.0, -50.0, 0.0,
    0.0, -50.0);
  sq3.AreaFill();       //Underside side of floor

  CFace sq4(3, 0.0, 0.0, 0.0, 0.0, 0.0, -50.0, 0.0, 50.0, -50.0, 0.0,
    50.0, 0.0);
  sq4.AreaFill();

glPopMatrix();
// Save the matrix state and do the moves/rotations
glPushMatrix();
        glRotatef(xRot , 1.0f, 0.0f, 0.0f);
        glRotatef(yRot , 0.0f, 25.0f, 0.0f);
        glRotatef(yFurnitureRot , 0.0f, 25.0f, 0.0f);
        glTranslatef(xFurnitureMv, 25.0, 0.0);
```

```
glPushMatrix();
 glEnable(GL_TEXTURE_2D);
 glTexEnvf(GL_TEXTURE_ENV, GL_TEXTURE_ENV_MODE, GL_REPLACE);
 glBindTexture(GL_TEXTURE_2D, texName[2]);
 glTranslatef(20.0, -2.0, -20.0);
 glColor3f(1.0, 1.0, 1.0);
 glutSolidTeapot(5.0);
glPopMatrix();

 glEnable(GL_TEXTURE_2D);
 glTexEnvf(GL_TEXTURE_ENV, GL_TEXTURE_ENV_MODE, GL_REPLACE);
 glBindTexture(GL_TEXTURE_2D, texName[1]);

  CCube Cube(0, vts); //Table top
        Scalexyz( 0.5, 0.15, 0.5);
        Shiftxyz(10.0, -5.0, -35.0);
  Cube.FaceTexture(vts1);

        Scalexyz( 0.05, 0.5, 0.05);
        Shiftxyz(30.0, -5.0, -35.0);
  Cube.FaceTexture(vts1);

        Scalexyz( 0.05, 0.5, 0.05);
        Shiftxyz(10.0, -5.0, -35.0);
  Cube.FaceTexture(vts1);

        Scalexyz( 0.05, 0.5, 0.05);
        Shiftxyz(10.0, -5.0, -15.0);
  Cube.FaceTexture(vts1);

        Scalexyz( 0.05, 0.5, 0.05);
        Shiftxyz(30.0, -5.0, -15.0);
  Cube.FaceTexture(vts1);

        glDisable(GL_TEXTURE_2D);
        // Restore the matrix state
glPopMatrix();
        // Display the results
glutSwapBuffers();
glFlush();
}

void ArrowKeys(int key, int x, int y)
{
        if(key == GLUT_KEY_UP)   xRot-= 5.0;
        if(key == GLUT_KEY_DOWN) xRot += 5.0;
        if(key == GLUT_KEY_LEFT) yRot -= 5.0;
        if(key == GLUT_KEY_RIGHT) yRot += 5.0;
        if(key == GLUT_KEY_F8)   yFurnitureRot-= 5.0;
```

```
        if(key == GLUT_KEY_F7)  yFurnitureRot+= 5.0;
if(key == GLUT_KEY_F9)  xFurnitureMv+= 5.0;
        if(xRot > 356.0f) xRot = 0.0;
        if(xRot < -1.0f)  xRot = 355.0;
        if(yRot > 356.0f) yRot = 0.0;
        if(yRot < -1.0f)  yRot = 355.0;
    // Refresh the Window
        glutPostRedisplay();
}
```

Fig. 8.5 Texturing, Shading
and movement within a room

8.4 Changing the Furniture Style

In Chapter 7 we textured a cylinder with a picture of the Mona Lisa and now use
this to demonstrate a circular design for a table. We will develop a class description
of a cylinder filled in at both ends involving a textured cylinder plus two textured
circular end plates. The table design is a circular top with three cylindrical legs. Each
cylinder is formed from a class and the table assembled by use of glTranslatef() for
appropriate positioning of the legs. The cylinder class is defined by data for the
radius, height and Cartesian position (x, y, z) in space. The cylinder is filled in at
either end by a textured circle to give a solid appearance. A function OverTexture
performs the geometric definition and transform of texture to Cartesian space as
part of the class CCylinder. The image (s, t) mapping to Cartesian (x, y, z) space
transform relations are derived in the previous chapter and the following code provides 3 table legs, a table top and teapot. The building of the cylinder is shown in
Fig. 8.6. and readers need to be aware that the size of the patches (resolution) in
relation to the cylinder size is important because of rounding errors. Large patches

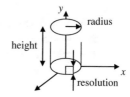

Fig. 8.6 Building a cylinder
class

will cause 'flat' sections on the side of the cylinder and very small patches can lead to patches not quite fitting together. This is because the angle ϕ is a function of $\tan^{-1}$ (radius/height) (see Chapter 7) and if radius/height tends a large number, angle ϕ will be found with some error as the tangent function varies rapidly at $\pm 90°$. The following code implements a textured cylinder object of some radius and height and permits positioning in space.

```
class CCylinder
{
  private:
  float  rad;
  public:
CCylinder(float radius, float height, float xshift, float
          yshift, float zshift);
  int i,j;
  float diameter, tantmp, resolution;
  float x, x1, z, u1, v1, x2, x3, x4;
  float u2, v2, u3, v3, u4, v4, yinc, phi, theta, u, v, y;
  float z1, z2, z3, z4, zinc, xtmp;
void OutsideTexture(float radius, float height, float xshift,
          float yshift, float zshift)
{
float  ustart, uinc, uend, vstart, vinc, vend;
glTranslatef(xshift, yshift, zshift);   //test shift
diameter = 2.0 * radius;
tantmp = atan(radius / height) - 1.5707963;
glEnable(GL_TEXTURE_2D);
  glTexEnvf(GL_TEXTURE_ENV, GL_TEXTURE_ENV_MODE, GL_REPLACE);
  glBindTexture(GL_TEXTURE_2D, texName[0]);
glBegin(GL_QUADS);
 resolution = 0.2;
 vstart = 0.0; vend = resolution;
 vinc = resolution;
 do {                        //cylinder texture
  ustart = 0.0; uend = resolution;
  uinc = resolution;
  do {
   v=vstart;
   for(u=ustart; u<=uend; u=u+uinc) {

    theta = 6.2831853 * u;    //0->2pi
    phi = tantmp * v + 1.5707963;
    x = radius * sin(theta);
    y = radius / tan(phi);
        z = radius * cos(theta);
```

```
            glTexCoord2f(u, v);   glVertex3f(x, y, z);
            }
      v=vend;
      for(u=uend; u>=ustart; u=u-uinc) {

        theta = 6.2831853 * u;      //0->2pi
        phi = tantmp * v + 1.5707963;
        x = radius * sin(theta);
            y = radius / tan(phi);
        z = radius * cos(theta);
                    glTexCoord2f(u, v);   glVertex3f(x, y, z);
            }
        ustart = uend;      //next col
            uend = ustart +uinc;
      } while(uend <=1.0);
      vstart = vend;
      vend = vstart +vinc;
      }while(vend <=1.0);
glEnd();
//circle texturing
glTranslatef(-radius, 0.0, -radius);
x1 = radius * 0.5; x2 = radius * 0.5;
z1 = 0.0; z2 = 0.0;   z3 = 0.0;
zinc = 0.1;
u1 = 0.5; v1 = 0.0;   v3 = 0.0;
u2 = 0.5; v2 = 0.0;
y = 0.0;
glBegin(GL_QUADS);
 do {
  z3 = z3 + zinc;
  z4 = z3;
  xtmp = 2.0 * radius * z3 - z3 * z3;
  if(xtmp < 10E-10) x = 0.0;
    else x = sqrt(2.0 * radius * z3 - z3 * z3);
  x4 = radius - x;
  x3 = radius + x;
  u3 = x3 * 0.5 / radius;
  u4 = x4 * 0.5 / radius;
  v3 = v3 + zinc * 0.5 / radius;
  v4 = v3;
  glTexCoord2f(u1, v1);   glVertex3f(x1, y, z1);
  glTexCoord2f(u2, v2);   glVertex3f(x2, y, z2);
  glTexCoord2f(u3, v3);   glVertex3f(x3, y, z3);
  glTexCoord2f(u4, v4);   glVertex3f(x4, y, z4);
  x1 = x4; x2 = x3;
```

```
  z1 = z4; z2 = z3;
  u1 = u4; u2 = u3;
  v1 = v4; v2 = v3;
  } while(z4 <= diameter);
glEnd();
glTranslatef(0.0, height, 0.0);
x1 = radius * 0.5; x2 = radius * 0.5;
z1 = 0.0; z2 = 0.0;   z3 = 0.0;
zinc = 0.1;
u1 = 0.5; v1 = 0.0;   v3 = 0.0;
u2 = 0.5; v2 = 0.0;
y = 0.0;
glBegin(GL_QUADS);
 do {
  z3 = z3 + zinc;
  z4 = z3;
  xtmp = 2.0 * radius * z3 - z3 * z3;
  if(xtmp < 10E-5) x = 0.0;
    else x = sqrt(xtmp);
  x4 = radius - x;
  x3 = radius + x;
  u3 = x3 * 0.5 / radius;
  u4 = x4 * 0.5 / radius;
  v3 = v3 + zinc * 0.5 / radius;
  v4 = v3;
  glTexCoord2f(u4, v4);  glVertex3f(x4, y, z4);
  glTexCoord2f(u3, v3);  glVertex3f(x3, y, z3);
  glTexCoord2f(u2, v2);  glVertex3f(x2, y, z2);
  glTexCoord2f(u1, v1);  glVertex3f(x1, y, z1);
  x1 = x4; x2 = x3;
  z1 = z4; z2 = z3;
  u1 = u4; u2 = u3;
  v1 = v4; v2 = v3;
  } while(z4 <= diameter);
glEnd();
glTranslatef(radius-xshift, -height-yshift, radius-zshift);
}
};
CCylinder::CCylinder(float radius, float height, float xshift,
                float yshift, float zshift)
{
 rad = radius;
}
```

Fig. 8.7 Circular table
construction

A complete program is provided on the website using a wood grain bit map and a generated black and white squared bit map for the teapot (much more appropriate to flat surfaces!). The output will be as in Fig. 8.7 with the arrow keys being used for rotation.

8.5 Exercises

1. Using the cylinder and box classes discussed in this chapter construct the chassis, axle and wheels of a motor vehicle. Texture the wheels with several colours and animate your car to demonstrate the wheels rotating.
2. Using the box class to represent a building brick, experiment with building a circular chimney and examine the smoothness of the outside in relation to the diameter of the structure. Students may use the angle between successive bricks as a measure of smoothness, which in turn is dependent on brick size.
3. Develop a class to represent a gear wheel with teeth of variable pitch. Using your object class simulate the operation of a gear by having two gear wheels of different radii meshing and rotating. Ensure the rotational speed is correct for the driven gearwheel.

8.6 Conclusion

In this chapter we have begun the process of building reusable objects that can be added together in some form of hierarchy to build more complex artefacts. Facilities for objects must be carefully considered in relation to the application to which the object contributes, in terms of position, size and interaction with other objects or artefacts. Many texts emphasise the value of *using* objects already written elsewhere. This fact should not lull the reader into thinking that general objects are always available. Applications often have very specific requirements and tailoring an object to these requires ingenuity on the part of the programmer.

Chapter 9
Curves, Surfaces and Patterns

9.1 Introduction

The home, office and workplace are full of artefacts that make life pleasing, convenient or are maybe essential to make other tasks possible. The design of objects has to be both aesthetically acceptable and technically possible. Any picture is made up from objects, some of which have a simple geometric representation while others are more complex. Because of the variation and complexity of objects that make up our environment there is no simple way to universally represent them all. The example of representing a football, a flower or a brick wall illustrates both the variation in surface shape, the nature of the material composition and the rigidity of object as challenges when displaying objects graphically. Engineering artefacts can usually be represented on the surface by quadrics, Bezier surfaces and polygons, while naturally occurring objects such as trees, coastlines or surface terrain can be described using fractal methods. Solid objects can also be thought of as composed of a number of small cubes (Chapter 7) and octree structures are a used for storage and display of Tomographic (CT) scans. Readers are referred to the glut library for functions that will draw regular polyhedra.

The representation of surfaces presents a challenge not only in terms of storage and manipulation in a computer but also in terms of machining and manufacture. To model a surface we consider it to be made up from a number of two-dimensional curves, which can be joined by patches to form the surface. For a complex surface the patches may be very small to match rapid changes in shape and in the ultimate, patches would reduce in size to individual pixels. The variation in patch size permits us to construct surfaces with accuracy appropriate to any given application. In this section we will explore the mathematical derivation of curves and surfaces and provide example implementations from which the reader can develop their own applications.

9.2 Fitting a Line or a Curve

Consider a set of data points (x_0, y_0), (x_1, y_1), (x_2, y_2), (x_3, y_3).......... (x_n, y_n) and how we might represent the data in a general form.

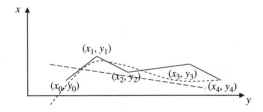

Fig. 9.1 General
representation of data

A number of possible representations of the data are illustrated in Fig. 9.1 from joining every point with straight lines, a single straight line passing as close to all data points as possible, to a smooth curve between the points. All such representations are an approximation as we do not know the context in which the data in Fig. 9.1 was gathered or indeed the purpose of the representation. The physical constraints of say a routing machine are quite different from a mathematical formula where no such restrictions are needed. The choice of what to fit to a set of data points will depend on context and requirements factors such as machining capability, mathematical requirements, marketing and attractiveness of design.

The simplest representation is a straight line where we can construct a flat surface from a number of points. The 'best' line is considered to be one where we try to minimise the distance of the data points from the line and this is referred to as linear regression.

9.2.1 Straight Line Fitting to Data Points

How do we draw the best straight line through a series of points, Fig. 9.2?

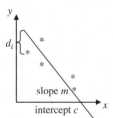

Fig. 9.2 Fitting points to a
line $y = mx + c$

We can imagine finding the best line by placing a ruler on the paper and moving it around until it appears to fit equally between the points and making the sum of the distances between the line and the data points as small as possible, where d_i is the distance between each point (x_i, y_i) and the required line.

The total (distance)^2 of all points from the line is

$$d = \Sigma(y_i - c - mx_i)^2$$

where the summation is over the number of data points. We minimise by partial differentiation with respect to the variables m and c

$$\frac{\partial d}{\partial c} = -2\Sigma(y_i - c - mx_i) = 0$$

$$\frac{\partial d}{\partial m} = -2\Sigma(y_i - c - mx_i)x_i = 0$$

since a function is maxima/minimal when the partial derivatives are zero.

$$\Sigma y_i - nc - m\,\Sigma x_i = 0 \quad \text{and}$$
$$\Sigma x_i y_i - c\Sigma x_i - m\,\Sigma x_i^2 = 0$$
$$\therefore \quad nc = \Sigma y_i - m\,\Sigma x_i$$

Substituting for c in second equation

$$\Sigma x_i y_i - \frac{\Sigma x_i(\Sigma y_i - m\,\Sigma x_i)}{n} - m\,\Sigma x_i^2 = 0$$

$$\therefore \quad m = \frac{n\Sigma x_i y_i - \Sigma x_i \Sigma y_i}{n\Sigma x_i^2 - (\Sigma x_i)^2}$$

The relations for m and c allow one to derive linear relationships for points and construct lines and flat surfaces in space.

9.2.2 Lagrange Polynomials and Curve Fitting

An alternative fit would be to have a smooth curve that passed through every data point. Such a curve is defined by one more point than the n data points and is unique. While this might seem an ideal solution one has to remember that there are usually errors in collecting large numbers of data points and that such a representation is not necessarily any more accurate. Further, the order of the polynomial for n data points is n and this will require terms up to x^n which require $2(n-1)$ multiplications and n additions to represent and evaluate the whole polynomial. This is unattractive both in terms of processing time and rounding errors that may be introduced.

9.2.3 A Practical Approach to Curve Fitting

Some compromise between the linear approximation described and Lagrange polynomials is required for fitting curves to data and this can be achieved by fitting polynomials of a lesser degree to pass through *some* of the data. This is illustrated in Fig. 9.3 where the curve passes through points and is seen to bend between them,

Fig. 9.3 Curves through
some points

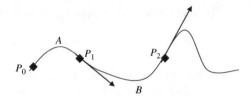

while remaining smooth at each junction. What is required, are different polynomials between each set of points and for the curves to be smooth at the transition
points – called blending. The two curves A and B in Fig. 9.3 join at point P_1 and
for this to be a smooth connection, the gradient dy/dx of both curves at point P_1
must be the same. We can write the values of x and y on the curve in parametric
form as $x(t)$, $y(t)$ where t is a variable parameter. An example of such we have
already met in the use of polar coordinates to transfer to Cartesian coordinates (see
Chapter 7).

9.2.4 Curve Fitting Using Cubic Splines

Spline functions are widely used for curve fitting using a cubic polynomial of the
form

$$x(t) = at^3 + bt^2 + ct + d \quad \text{for } 0 \le t \le 1$$

with similar relations for $y(t)$ and $z(t)$ to specify the curve. The spline must pass
through consecutive points P_i in Fig. 9.3 and satisfy the condition of the same differential at the end point of the previous curve section ensuring that curves both join
and are smooth at the joining point. These conditions are formally written as

1. Two consecutive points x_i and x_{i+1} are equal for $t = 0$ and $t = 1$ between
   sections.
2. The differential dx/dt is known for $t = 0$ and $t = 1$ at section end points.

Differentiating with respect to t, the derivative $x'(t)$ is

$$x'(t) = 3at^2 + 2bt + c$$

We now substitute the values of t into the polynomial and the derivative giving

$$
\begin{aligned}
x(0) &= d \\
x(1) &= a + b + c + d \\
x'(0) &= c \\
x'(1) &= 3a + 2b + c
\end{aligned}
$$

This is a set of four linear equations with four unknowns $(a - d)$. Solving we obtain

$$d = x(0)$$
$$c = x'(0)$$
$$a = 2(x(0) - x(1)) + x'(0) + x'(1)$$
$$b = 3(x(1) - x(0)) - 2x'(0) - x'(1)$$

which can be written in matrix form as

$$\begin{pmatrix} a \\ b \\ c \\ d \end{pmatrix} = \begin{pmatrix} 2 & -2 & 1 & 1 \\ -3 & 3 & -2 & -1 \\ 0 & 0 & 1 & 0 \\ 1 & 0 & 0 & 0 \end{pmatrix} \begin{pmatrix} x(0) \\ x(1) \\ x'(0) \\ x'(1) \end{pmatrix}$$

Similar relations are obtained for $y(t)$ and $z(t)$. The two remaining pieces of data required are the value of the first derivatives $x'(0)$ and $x'(1)$ for the solution of the equations in terms of $a - d$ which then make possible the drawing of the spline curve. The simplest and intuitively most obvious is the Catmull-Rom approach, which derives the gradient (derivative) from the neighbouring data points as shown in Fig. 9.4.

Fig. 9.4 Derivatives for cubic splines

The gradient $\mathbf{P}'_i$ at any point P_i of the curve is given by the average change in x, y or z between the neighbouring points P_{i-1} and P_{i+1} and is a vector where

$$\mathbf{P}'_i = (P_{i+1} - P_{i-1})/2$$

The only two slopes that are missing are those at the first and last points P_0 and P_n. These are often found by introducing a couple of 'dummy' points to initialise the procedure, that are not part of the required curve defined from P_1 to P_{n-1} and use the first and last points to initialise gradient calculations. This approach also permits the construction of closed curves and surfaces by use of P_0 to find the gradient at the end point P_n and P_n prior to P_0 for the first gradient calculation. The author has also found a group of functions known as Tensioned Splines useful in surface drawing (Schweikert, 1966) that permit user control over the curve. The gradient is defined as

$$\mathbf{P}'_i = (1 - \sigma)(P_{i+1} - P_{i-1})/2$$

where σ is the tension factor. The tension factor can be thought of as making the spline behave like an elastic band, where a large σ ($\sim$2) is like a tight band and straight lines are drawn between points while a low σ ($\sim$ $-$1) loosens the elastic and smoother curves are drawn. Care must be exercised with smaller values of tension as extraneous ripples may occur due to the derivatives making the polynomial unstable. There are numerous other methods of adjusting the gradient and readers of referred to other texts on numerical methods for further information (Farin, 1988). In this context the Kochanek-Bartels spline is important where we calculate the gradient differences either side of P_i and weight their effect depending on which is changing most rapidly. This permits the curve to begin before or after P_i depending on the relative gradient magnitudes on either side of P_i.

Functions to perform the spline evaluation follow together with output showing the effect of the tension factor shown in Fig. 9.5. A complete program is supplied on the accompanying web site together with a sample data file for Fig. 9.5.

```
void init(void)
{
char filename[25];
int i;
float x0dx, x1dx, y0dy, y1dy;
glClearColor    ( 1.0, 1.0, 0.0, 0.0 );
cout << "Spline tension (-1->1) = ";
cin >> sigma;
cout << "Name of data points file: ";
cin >> filename;
ifstream inpoints(filename, ios ::in);
if(!inpoints) { cout << "File would not open\n";
                        exit(1);
                        }
inpoints >> no_of_pts;
        for(i=0; i < no_of_pts; i++) {
                inpoints >> xdata[i] >> ydata[i];
            }
step = 0;
for(i=1; i < no_of_pts-2; i++) {     //find gradients with sigma
                                //factor
            x0dx = (1.0 - sigma) * (xdata[i] - xdata[i-1])/2.0;
            x1dx = (1.0 - sigma) * (xdata[i+1] - xdata[i])/2.0;
            y0dy = (1.0 - sigma) * (ydata[i] - ydata[i-1])/2.0;
            y1dy = (1.0 - sigma) * (ydata[i+1] - ydata[i])/2.0;
            step = spline(xdata[i], xdata[i+1], x0dx, x1dx,
                ydata[i], ydata[i+1], y0dy, y1dy);
            }
```

```
}

int spline(float x0, float x1, float x0deriv, float x1deriv,
           float y0, float y1, float y0deriv, float y1deriv)
{
float ax, bx, cx, dx, incr, t;
float ay, by, cy, dy;
// evaluate coefficients a, b, c, d for x & y
ax = 2.0*x0 - 2.0*x1 + x0deriv + x1deriv;
bx = -3.0*x0 + 3.0*x1 - 2.0*x0deriv - x1deriv;
cx = x0deriv;
dx = x0;

ay = 2.0*y0 - 2.0*y1 + y0deriv + y1deriv;
by = -3.0*y0 + 3.0*y1 - 2.0*y0deriv - y1deriv;
cy = y0deriv;
dy = y0;

t = 0.0;
incr = 0.1f;
do {    //evaluate spline values for all t
        x[step] = ax*t*t*t + bx*t*t + cx*t + dx;
        y[step] = ay*t*t*t + by*t*t + cy*t + dy;
        step++;
        t = t +incr;
} while(t <= 1.0);
return (step);
}

void display ()
{         //render spline curve values stored in x [i], y [i]
int i;
glClear ( GL_COLOR_BUFFER_BIT );
glColor3f(0.0, 0.0,1.0);
glPointSize(3.0);
glBegin(GL_POINTS);          //raw data points
        for(i=0; i < no_of_pts; i++)  glVertex3f(xdata[i],
            ydata[i], 0.0);
glEnd();
glColor3f(1.0, 0.0,0.0);
i = 0;
glBegin(GL_LINE_STRIP);
        do {
                glVertex2f(x[i], y[i]);
                i++;
```

```
            } while(i < step);
glEnd();
glFlush();
}
```

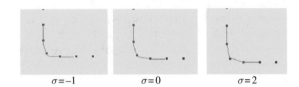

Fig. 9.5 The effect of tension
σ of a cubic spline curve $\sigma=-1$ $\sigma=0$ $\sigma=2$

The polynomial between successive points P_i is different depending on the position and gradient constraints at each junction – called piecewise interpolation. In Fig. 9.5 we see a high tension produces straight lines between the points where with $\sigma = 0$ the curve is smoother. With a low value of σ spurious wobbles begin to appear and this is more apparent if points are widely scattered.

9.2.5 Surface Construction from Contour Maps

The construction of a 3D surface is often governed by the data available and in particular how it is collected. If for example we take a photograph from space of a mountain range, we gain an impression of height from the shadows cast and possibly snow capped mountain peaks or evidence of vegetation. Measurements of height from a 2D photograph can only be made indirectly based on such features or augmented from other sources such as radar reflection times. One method that can enhance understanding is to superimpose a 2D photograph on a contour map of the area concerned. For this exercise we will construct a series of quadrilateral patches to represent terrain and texturing of the surface is previously described in Chapter 7.

Data collection of the contour profile is achieved by laying graph paper over a contour map of a region and reading off positional coordinates (x, z) and the corresponding ground heights (y) using a print of the graph paper on an overhead transparency (see www.mathematicshelpcentral.com). While this is not the most sophisticated or accurate method, it will demonstrate the principles unless more expensive equipment is available! The procedure is illustrated in Fig. 9.6.

The x–z coordinates are read off the graph paper and can be given appropriate distance units depending on the scale of the map. For student exercise purposes the height of mountains can be looked up in a geography textbook and a rough approximation of the elevations used at the x–z points by interpolation from the summit and the ground elevation of the area surrounding a mountain. Thus in each x or z line on the graph paper we are constructing a height contour of the mountain and in the sample data file surf.txt we have five contours each with eight data points.

Fig. 9.6 Mount Fuji from the
space shuttle

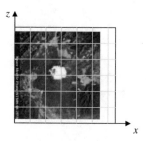

To construct a mesh we now connect the points on a row by row basis as illustrated in Fig. 9.7 where each patch is defined by the locations $x_i \rightarrow x_{i+1} \rightarrow x_{i+n+1} \rightarrow x_{i+n}$.

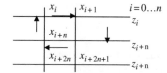

Fig. 9.7 Creating a mesh
from contour measurements

The display function follows together with a sample output in Fig. 9.8.

```
void display ()
{
int i, istart, iend;
glClear ( GL_COLOR_BUFFER_BIT );
glColor3f(0.0, 0.0, 1.0);
glRotatef(rot[0], 1.0, 0.0, 0.0);
glRotatef(rot[1], 0.0, 1.0, 0.0);
glPointSize(3.0);
glBegin(GL_POINTS); //render raw data points in blue
    for(i=0; i < no_of_pts; i++)  glVertex3f(xdata[i],
            ydata[i], zdata[i]);
glEnd();
glColor3f(1.0f, 0.0f,0.0f);
//patching structure access
istart = 0;
iend = 6;
    do {
        glBegin(GL_LINE_STRIP);
            for(i=istart; i <= iend; i=i++) {   //rectangular
                                        //patches
                glVertex3f(xdata[i], ydata[i], zdata[i]);
                glVertex3f(xdata[i+1], ydata[i+1], zdata[i+1]);
                glVertex3f(xdata[i+9], ydata[i+9], zdata[i+9]);
                glVertex3f(xdata[i+8], ydata[i+8], zdata[i+8]);
                glVertex3f(xdata[i], ydata[i], zdata[i]);
```

```
        }
      glEnd();
      istart = istart + 8;              //next row of patches
      iend = istart + 6;
   }  while(iend < no_of_pts-7);
glFlush();
}
```

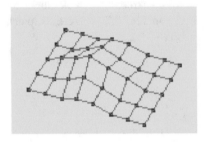

Fig. 9.8 A terrain mesh from
contour measurements

No smoothing has been attempted with this mesh but rather it is presented to
illustrate the generation of a surface from raw data measures. Readers are referred
to Chapter 7 for texture rendering of general meshes.

9.2.6 A Spline Surface Construction

A 3D surface version of the spine function described requires the addition of data
in the z direction and accessing the data in a slightly different order. In the next
example we generate curves spaced in the z-direction to form a hump for perhaps
representation of mountain terrain. Data is input as (x, y, z) coordinates for a fixed
value of z to represent one contour and this repeated with subsequent sets of coordinates with a new value of z for each new contour. There are five contours with
z taking values from 0 to 2 in the sample data file (surf.txt). The first and last data
points on each contour are not drawn in this example since they are dummy points
used to initiate the spline calculation as indicated in the following input code.

```
step = 0;
istart = 1; iend = 6;
do {       //first derivatives including Tension factor
           for(i=istart; i < iend; i++) {
                   x0dx = (1.0 - sigma) * (xdata[i] - xdata[i-1])/2.0;
                   x1dx = (1.0 - sigma) * (xdata[i+1] - xdata[i])/2.0;
                   y0dy = (1.0 - sigma) * (ydata[i] - ydata[i-1])/2.0;
                   y1dy = (1.0 - sigma) * (ydata[i+1] - ydata[i])/2.0;
                   z0dz = (1.0 - sigma) * (zdata[i] - zdata[i-1])/2.0;
```

```
                        z1dz = (1.0 - sigma) * (zdata[i+1] - zdata[i])/2.0;
                        step = spline(xdata[i], xdata[i+1], x0dx, x1dx,
                                          ydata[i], ydata[i+1], y0dy, y1dy,
                                          zdata[i], zdata[i+1], z0dz, z1dz);
            }
            istart = iend + 3;
            iend = istart + 5;
} while( iend < no_of_pts);
```

For display purposes we have also joined the raw data points in the *z*-direction to form quadrilateral patches on the surface. A full program with the data file is supplied on the Web site.

```
void display ()
{
int i, istart, iend;
glClear ( GL_COLOR_BUFFER_BIT );
glColor3f(0.0f, 0.0f,1.0f);
glRotatef(rot[0], 1.0f, 0.0f, 0.0f);
glRotatef(rot[1], 0.0f, 1.0f, 0.0f);
glPointSize(3.0);
        glBegin(GL_POINTS);            //display raw data points
        for(i=0; i < no_of_pts; i++)  glVertex3f(xdata[i],
                ydata[i], zdata[i]);
        glEnd();
glColor3f(1.0f, 0.0f,0.0f);
istart = 1;
iend = 33;
do {                                    //for the patches
        glBegin(GL_LINE_STRIP);
                for(i=istart; i <= iend; i=i+8)  glVertex3f
                        (xdata[i], ydata[i], zdata[i]);
        glEnd();
        istart++;
        iend++;
} while(iend < no_of_pts-1);
i = 0;
do {
        glBegin(GL_LINE_STRIP);
                do {
                        glVertex3f(x[i], y[i], z[i]);
                        i++;
                } while( i%50 != 0);
```

```
        glEnd();
} while(i < step);
glFlush();
}
```

Typical output will look something like Fig. 9.9 after rotation using the mouse.

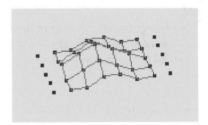

Fig. 9.9 Surface
representation using Splines
in $x-y$ plane only

9.2.7 Bezier Curves

Pierre Bezier invented Bezier curves during early days of CAD system development (1960s) at the Renault car company in France. The Bezier curve is easy to
implement and very widely used in curve and surface generation. The curve is
essentially drawn between two data points (knots) with a number of control points
that can be positioned to alter the shape of the curve in each section. This process is repeated between data point sections to form one continuous curve along
the required surface with blending taking place at the junction between sections.
We now develop a cubic polynomial Bezier curve which is defined by four points.
The first and last points define the section end points and the middle two points
are the control points which govern the shape of the curve in this section. The
Bezier curve only passes through the section endpoints and *not* through the control points. Consider 4 points ($p_0 - p_3$) x_0, x_1, x_2, x_3 and a cubic polynomial $x(t)$
where

$$x(t) = at^3 + bt^2 + ct + d \quad 1 \geq t \geq 0$$

as shown in Fig. 9.1.

For blending constraints the end points are clamped as the curve passes through
these points while the two intermediate points define the curvature at the first and
last points. Thus in the cubic polynomial

$$x(0) = x_0 \quad \text{and} \quad x(1) = x_3$$

Fig. 9.10 Bezier curve
derivation

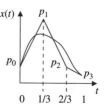

The slope from Fig. 9.10 at the endpoints is given by

$$x'(0) = \frac{x_1 - x_0}{1/3} \quad \text{and} \quad x'(1) = \frac{x_3 - x_2}{1/3}$$

Differentiating the cubic with respect to t gives the slope as

$$\frac{dx}{dt} = 3a\,t^2 + 2b\,t + c$$

When $t = 0$

$$x'(0) = c = 3(x_1 - x_0)$$

and

$$x(0) = d = x_0$$

when $t = 1$

$$x'(1) = 3a + 2b + c = 3(x_3 - x_2)$$

and

$$x(1) = a + b + c + d = x_3$$

Substituting and solving for a, b, c, d we get

$$a = -x_0 + 3x_1 - 3x_2 + x_3$$
$$b = 3x_0 - 6x_1 + 3x_2$$
$$c = -3x_0 + 3x_1$$
$$d = x_0$$

in terms of the four points and we can rewrite this in matrix form as

$$\begin{pmatrix} a \\ b \\ c \\ d \end{pmatrix} = \begin{pmatrix} -1 & 3 & -3 & 1 \\ 3 & -6 & 3 & 0 \\ -3 & 3 & 0 & 0 \\ 1 & 0 & 0 & 0 \end{pmatrix} \begin{pmatrix} x_0 \\ x_1 \\ x_2 \\ x_3 \end{pmatrix}$$

The Bezier curve $x(t)$ can now be written as

$$x(t) = (t^3, t^2, t, 1) \begin{pmatrix} a \\ b \\ c \\ d \end{pmatrix} = (t^3, t^2, t, 1) \begin{pmatrix} -1 & 3 & -3 & 1 \\ 3 & -6 & 3 & 0 \\ -3 & 3 & 0 & 0 \\ 1 & 0 & 0 & 0 \end{pmatrix} \begin{pmatrix} x_0 \\ x_1 \\ x_2 \\ x_3 \end{pmatrix}$$

We can substitute for the coefficients a-d in the equation for $x(t)$ and rearrange in terms of the control point values when

$$\begin{aligned} x(t) &= (x_3 - 3x_2 + 3x_1 - x_0)t^3 + (3x_0 - 6x_1 + 3x_2)t^2 + 3(x_1 - x_0)t + x_0 \\ &= x_0(-t^3 + 3t^2 - 3t + 1) + x_1(3t^3 - 6t^2 + 3t) + x_2(-3t^3 + 3t^2) + t^3 x_3 \\ &= (1-t)^3 x_0 + 3t(1-t)^2 x_1 + 3t^2(1-t)x_2 + t^3 x_3 \end{aligned}$$

Each control point is weighted by a cubic polynomial in t and these terms are referred to as Bernstein polynomials. A listing of a Bezier evaluation follows together with a complete program and sample data for a sine wave on the web site.

```
int bezier(float x0, float x1, float x2, float x3)
{
float a, b, c, d, incr, t;
// determine coefficients for a cubic
a = -x0 + 3.0*x1 - 3.0*x2 + x3;
b = 3.0*x0 - 6.0*x1 + 3.0*x2;
c = -3.0*x0 + 3.0*x1;
d = x0;

t = 0.0;
incr = 0.1f;
do {     //evaluate Bezier curve
         x[step] = a*t*t*t + b*t*t + c*t + d;
         step++;
         t = t +incr;
} while(t $<$= 1.0);
return (step);
}
```

The importance of the control points in curve representation is seen from the data used to represent the sine waves and a half circle very much depends on the curvature of preceding sections of the total curve as shown in Fig. 9.10.

Readers should experiment with the sample control points and see the curvature variations that result.

9.2.8 General Curve Representation

Up to this point we have used a one-dimensional curve $x(t)$, which is very inflexible in general, shape representation where we normally use Cartesian representation in two or three dimensions. Fortunately this is a minor development in that the derivation used for $x(t)$ is similar for $y(t)$ and $z(t)$ but using data in the y–z planes to specify the control points. For the 2D case of a circle the control points will approximately be

0.5 0.0	1.0 0.5	0.5 1.0	0.0 0.5
0.9 0.05	0.95 0.95	0.45 0.9	0.1 0.1
0.95 0.1	0.55 0.9	0.1 0.95	0.2 0.1
1.0 0.5	0.5 1.0	0.0 0.5	0.5 0.0

if we use only four segments to define the circle. Using this data with the following implementation of Bezier curves give the output shown in Fig. 9.11.

```
int step, no_of_pts;
float xdata[50], ydata[50];
float x[5001], y[5001], z[21];

void init(void)
{
char filename[25];
int i, no_of_sections;

glClearColor    ( 1.0, 1.0, 0.0, 0.0 );
cout << "I/P name of data points file: ";
cin >> filename;
ifstream inpoints(filename, ios ::in);
if(!inpoints) { cout << "File would not open\n";
                exit(1);
        }
        inpoints >> no_of_pts;
        cout << no_of_pts <<" raw data (knots)\n";
        for(i=0; i < no_of_pts; i++) {
                inpoints >> xdata[i] >> ydata[i];
                cout << "knot[" << i << "]= " << xdata[i]
                     << "  " <<ydata[i]<< endl;
        }
```

```
no_of_sections = no_of_pts / 4;
step = 0;
for(i=0;  i < no_of_pts;  i= i+4) {
        step = bezier(xdata[i], xdata[i+1], xdata[i+2],
                 xdata[i+3], ydata[i], ydata[i+1], ydata[i+2],
                 ydata[i+3]);
          }
}


int bezier(float x0, float x1, float x2, float x3, float y0,
             float y1, float y2, float y3)
{
float ax, bx, cx, dx, incr, t;
float ay, by, cy, dy;
//cubic coefficients for x & y of Bezier curve
ax = -x0 + 3.0*x1 - 3.0*x2 + x3;
bx = 3.0*x0 - 6.0*x1 + 3.0*x2;
cx = -3.0*x0 + 3.0*x1;
dx = x0;

ay = -y0 + 3.0*y1 - 3.0*y2 + y3;
by = 3.0*y0 - 6.0*y1 + 3.0*y2;
cy = -3.0*y0 + 3.0*y1;
dy = y0;

t = 0.0;
incr = 0.1f;
do {     //evaluate x-y points of  Bezier curve
        x[step] = ax*t*t*t + bx*t*t + cx*t + dx;
        y[step] = ay*t*t*t + by*t*t + cy*t + dy;
        step++;
        t = t +incr;
} while(t <= 1.0);
x[step] = x3;
y[step] = y3;
return (step);
}

void display ()
{
int step, pts_total;
float t, incr,recipincr;
glClear ( GL_COLOR_BUFFER_BIT );
glColor3f(1.0f, 0.0f,0.0f);
glPointSize(5.0);
```

```
glBegin(GL_POINTS);            //draw raw data
        for(step=0; step < no_of_pts; step++)
                glVertex2f(xdata[step], ydata[step]);
glEnd();

glColor3f(0.0f, 0.0f,1.0f);
t = 0.0;
step = 0;
incr = 0.1f;
recipincr = 1.0 / incr;
pts_total =  no_of_pts / 4 * recipincr;
glBegin(GL_LINE_STRIP);
        do {    //draw Bezier representation
                glVertex2f(x[step], y[step]);
                step++;
                t = t + incr;
           } while(step <= pts_total);
glEnd();
glFlush();
}
```

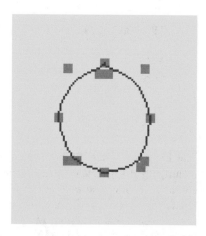

Fig. 9.11 Bezier curves used
to represent a circle

The implementation above can be performed using built in OpenGL functions
glMap1f () and glEvalCoord1f () that perform the same actions as function Bezier ()
in the preceding program. We developed the bezier() function to aid student understanding of how to more effectively use the built in functions. The display function
is given below and a full program is supplied on the web site.

```
void circle(void)
{
int i, j;
 glClear(GL_COLOR_BUFFER_BIT);
 glColor3f(1.0, 1.0, 1.0);

 for(j=0; j<4; j++) {
 glMap1f(GL_MAP1_VERTEX_3, 0.0, 1.0, 3, 4, &cntrlpts[j*4][0]);
 glEnable(GL_MAP1_VERTEX_3);
 glBegin(GL_LINE_STRIP);
     for(i=0; i<= 30; i++) glEvalCoord1f((float) i/30.0 );
 glEnd();
 }
 glPointSize(5.0);
 glColor3f(1.0, 0.0, 0.0);
 glBegin(GL_POINTS);
 for(i=0; i<= 15; i++) {
     switch (i) {
                 case 4: glColor3f(0.0, 1.0, 0.0);
                         break;
                 case 8: glColor3f(0.0, 0.0, 1.0);
                             break;
                     case 12: glColor3f(1.0, 1.0, 0.0);
                                 break;
     }
     glVertex3fv(&cntrlpts[i][0]);
 }
 glEnd();
 glFlush();
}
```

The function glMap1f(GL_MAP1_VERTEX_3, min, max, stride, no_of_points, &cntrlpts[j*4][0]) sets up a one dimensional floating point evaluator for a Bezier-curve where min and max are the range for the linear mapping, stride is number points between successive control points and no_of_points is the number of control points used in each section. In the above example cntrlpts is an array containing the control points and GL_MAP1_VERTEX_3 defines each control point as three floating point (x, y, z) values. The function (glEvalCoord1f) generates the positions along the Bezier curve.

The control points are displayed in different colours to permit readers to experiment and understand the 'pull' of the points in each quadrant section of the circle. It should be noted that quite small changes to the location of the control points can lead to significant distortions. A data file of the well-known cartoon dog 'snoopy.txt'

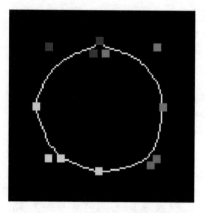

is also provided and if used to replace the control points for the circle gives the result shown in Fig. 9.12.

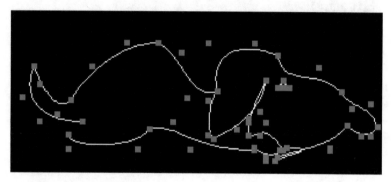

Fig. 9.12 Snoopy using Bezier curves

9.2.9 The Beginning's of a Bezier Surface

A surface may be thought of as made up from different slices in planes separated by some distance. In this example we will develop the skeleton planes, which may be used to subsequently define a surfaces of patches. The 2D curves described previously may easily be extrapolated to 3D surfaces by modifying the function bezier() to include curves for different z values. The equation for $x(t)$ is now repeated in a similar form for both $y(t)$ and $z(t)$ where the coefficients

```
ax = -x0 + 3.0*x1 - 3.0*x2 + x3;
bx = 3.0*x0 - 6.0*x1 + 3.0*x2;
cx = -3.0*x0 + 3.0*x1;
dx = x0;
```

```
ay = -y0 + 3.0*y1 - 3.0*y2 + y3;
by = 3.0*y0 - 6.0*y1 + 3.0*y2;
cy = -3.0*y0 + 3.0*y1;
dy = y0;

az = -z0 + 3.0*z1 - 3.0*z2 + z3;
bz = 3.0*z0 - 6.0*z1 + 3.0*z2;
cz = -3.0*z0 + 3.0*z1;
dz = z0;
```

are the corresponding evaluations for each Cartesian direction. To illustrate the construction of a surface we shall use the circle data file for different z values and use the mouse to rotate the solid cylinder around to provide different views. In this first example the cylinder is built using the program bezierxyz.cpp on the Web site from four identical circles at different z locations (data file circlexyz.txt).

```
void init(void)
{
char filename[25];
int i;

glClearColor ( 1.0, 1.0, 0.0, 0.0 );
cout << "I/P name of data points file: ";
cin >> filename;
ifstream inpoints(filename, ios ::in);
if(!inpoints) { cout << "File would not open\n";
                    exit(1);
        }
inpoints >> no_of_pts;
cout << no_of_pts <<" raw data (knots)\n";
for(i=0; i < no_of_pts; i++) {
        inpoints >> xdata[i] >> ydata[i] >> zdata[i];
        }
step = 0;
for(i=0; i < no_of_pts; i= i+4) {
        step = bezier(xdata[i], xdata[i+1], xdata[i+2],
                        xdata[i+3],
                    ydata[i], ydata[i+1], ydata[i+2], ydata[i+3],
                    zdata[i], zdata[i+1], zdata[i+2], zdata[i+3]);
        }
}

int bezier(float x0, float x1, float x2, float x3,
            float y0, float y1, float y2, float y3,
            float z0, float z1, float z2, float z3)
```

```
{
float ax, bx, cx, dx, incr, t;
float ay, by, cy, dy;
float az, bz, cz, dz;
//evaluate coefficients a-d in x,y,z
ax = -x0 + 3.0*x1 - 3.0*x2 + x3;
bx = 3.0*x0 - 6.0*x1 + 3.0*x2;
cx = -3.0*x0 + 3.0*x1;
dx = x0;

ay = -y0 + 3.0*y1 - 3.0*y2 + y3;
by = 3.0*y0 - 6.0*y1 + 3.0*y2;
cy = -3.0*y0 + 3.0*y1;
dy = y0;

az = -z0 + 3.0*z1 - 3.0*z2 + z3;
bz = 3.0*z0 - 6.0*z1 + 3.0*z2;
cz = -3.0*z0 + 3.0*z1;
dz = z0;

t = 0.0;
incr = 0.1f;
do {    //Bezier surface points in x, y, z arrays
        x[step] = ax*t*t*t + bx*t*t + cx*t + dx;
        y[step] = ay*t*t*t + by*t*t + cy*t + dy;
        z[step] = az*t*t*t + bz*t*t + cz*t + dz;
        step++;
        t = t +incr;
} while(t <= 1.0);
x[step] = x3;
y[step] = y3;
z[step] = z3;
return (step);
}

void display ()
{
int step, pts_total, each_loop, loop_tot;
float t, incr,recipincr;
glClear ( GL_COLOR_BUFFER_BIT );
glColor3f(1.0f, 0.0f,0.0f);

glRotatef(rot[0], 1.0f, 0.0f, 0.0f);
glRotatef(rot[1], 0.0f, 1.0f, 0.0f);
```

```
glPointSize(3.0);
glBegin(GL_POINTS); //display raw data in red
    for(step=0; step < no_of_pts; step++)
            glVertex3f(xdata[step], ydata[step], zdata[step]);
glEnd();

glColor3f(0.0f, 0.0f,1.0f);
t = 0.0;
step = 1;
incr = 0.1f;
recipincr = 1.0 / incr;
pts_total = no_of_pts / 4 * recipincr;
loop_tot = 40;
each_loop = pts_total / 4;
do {    //Bezier curves display
   glBegin(GL_LINE_LOOP);
       do {
             glVertex3f(x[step], y[step], z[step]);
             step++;
             t = t + incr;
         } while(step < loop_tot);
         loop_tot = loop_tot + each_loop;
       glEnd();
} while(step < pts_total);
glFlush();
}
```

The output from this example shows control data points in red that make up the cylinder and rotation allows the viewer to get a clearer grasp of the construction in Fig. 9.13 together with the influence of the control points.

Fig. 9.13 Bezier curves used
to construct a simple surface

9.2.10 Using Rotation to Sweep Out a Ring

In the previous example we built a cylinder in a rather laborious way by repetition of the data defining a circle along the z-axis. Many artefacts such as cups, vases and rings are made from a constant curved cross section which if rotated about an axis forms the object of interest. We can use the data defining a single circle in Cartesian coordinates and rotate these points to various points about an axis to find the new Cartesian values and then recalculate the Bezier values at each of these rotational positions. This is illustrated in Fig. 9.14 where think of rotation about the y-axis coming out of the plane of the paper.

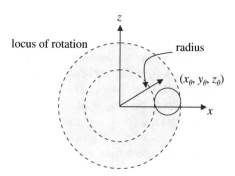

Fig. 9.14 Rotate points of a circle to form a ring

If the coordinates (x, y, z) that are used to define the Bezier curve that make up each quadrant of the circle, then we can find the corresponding values for x and z at each rotational point θ using the relations

$$x_\theta = (x \pm \text{radius}) \cos\theta$$
$$z_\theta = (x \pm \text{radius}) \sin\theta$$

since the circle is perpendicular to the locus of rotation for a constant cross section ring. If we perform this calculation on all the defining data points for the circle on the x axis in Fig. 9.11, we can then generate the defining (16) points at each angle θ and form the skeletal slices at these positions while the y coordinates are the same for each circle in the ring.

We now use the function bezier() to evaluate the points for the four quadrants of the circle and in our example we produced 40 Bezier coordinates per circle at 30° intervals from 0 to 360 degrees. Clearly the number of raw data points used in the initial definition of each circle (16) depends on the quality and accuracy with which curve is required. The resulting output is shown in Fig. 9.15.

9.2.11 Patching a Surface

The final part of object construction is to use the skeletal points defining each circle to form patches, which may be textured as appropriate to the object concerned. In

Fig. 9.15 Circles used to construct a ring – points in red define each circle

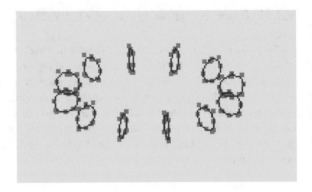

this example we form rectangular patches between adjacent circles by joining corresponding points on the circles and then skipping a number of points and repeating the process. In the example each circle is defined by 16 raw data points and drawn from the 40 Bezier points. The patch formation is illustrated in Fig. 9.16 where the circle defining the ring is rotated at a distance radius, and the coordinates of each patch vertex are (x_i, y_i, z_i) where $i = 0 \ldots 39$. The size of each patch is governed by the number of points (skip) between each side of the rectangle and thus the ring is now constructed from a series of cylinders defined by adjacent circles separated by the angle θ and joined by the patches.

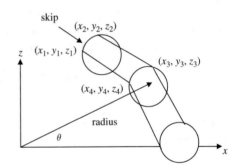

Fig. 9.16 Patch formation

```
void display ()
{
int step, pts_total, each_loop, loop_tot, skip, last_slice;
float incr,recipincr;
glClear ( GL_COLOR_BUFFER_BIT );
glColor3f(1.0f, 0.0f,0.0f);

glRotatef(rot[0], 1.0f, 0.0f, 0.0f);
glRotatef(rot[1], 0.0f, 1.0f, 0.0f);

glPointSize(3.0);
glBegin(GL_POINTS);
```

```
        for(step=0; step < no_of_pts; step++) glVertex3f
                (xdata[step], ydata[step], zdata[step]);
glEnd();

glColor3f(0.0f, 0.0f,1.0f);
step = 0;
incr = 0.1f;
recipincr = 1.0 / incr;
pts_total =  no_of_pts / 4 * recipincr;
loop_tot = 40;
each_loop = pts_total / 4;
        /*      do {    //circles only
                glBegin(GL_LINE_LOOP);
                do {
                        glVertex3f(x[step], y[step], z[step]);
                        step++;
                } while(step < loop_tot);
                step++;
                loop_tot = loop_tot + 40;
                glEnd();
        } while(step < pts_total);  */
skip = 13;
step = 0;
do {
        glBegin(GL_LINE_STRIP);
        do {
            glVertex3f(x[step], y[step], z[step]);
            glVertex3f(x[40+step], y[40+step], z[40+step]);
            glVertex3f(x[40+step+skip], y[40+step+skip],
                    z[40+step+skip]);
            glVertex3f(x[step+skip], y[step+skip],
                    z[step+skip]);
            glVertex3f(x[step], y[step], z[step]);
            step = step + skip;
        } while(step < loop_tot-skip);
        step++;
        loop_tot = loop_tot + 40;
        glEnd();
} while(step < pts_total-40);

//Now back to start
loop_tot = 40;
last_slice = (no_of_slices - 1) * loop_tot;
step = 0;
glBegin(GL_LINE_STRIP);
```

```
    do {
        glVertex3f(x[step], y[step], z[step]);
        glVertex3f(x[last_slice+step], y[last_slice+step],
            z[last_slice+step]);
        glVertex3f(x[last_slice+step+skip], y[last_slice+
            step+skip], z[last_slice+step+skip]);
        glVertex3f(x[step+skip], y[step+skip],
            z[step+skip]);
        glVertex3f(x[step], y[step], z[step]);
        step = step + skip;
    } while(step < loop_tot-skip);
glEnd();
glFlush();
}
```

The function display() given above implements the facilities described with a patching rectangle width of 13 Bezier points. Although this is too wide for an accurate representation of the ring it does permit the user to see the patches and a full program plus data file is provided on the web site with typical output shown in Fig. 9.17. Movement of the ring is provided in the program by using the mouse.

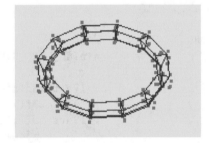

Fig. 9.17 Constructing a ring from circles

Various parts of this function may be commented out to improve the image (e.g. plotting red data points) and rotations are implemented using mouse movement. Students will find it instructive to define the profile of shapes other than a circle in order to build different artefacts.

9.3 Complex Shapes and Fractal Geometry

In the first part of this chapter we dealt with curves and surfaces described by a classical mathematical description that can be used to represent the surface. We shall now enter a world where we can begin to represent more random shapes such as coastlines, clouds and objects in nature such as leaves. Such shapes are not easily represented and the variations in structure require a different approach to graphical display. The relation between such large systems as say a cloud and the attraction between the water molecules that make up the cloud, is not well understood particularly when other forces such as wind, temperature or density come into play. Similarly the shape of leaves and their relation to biological content let alone the evolutionary environment in which they developed can only be described at a macroscopic level at this time. Other shapes such as that of the coastline or snowflakes result from both material composition and the effect of forces over long periods of time, which still remain to be quantified. Fractal geometry is a language used to attempt to describe some of the complex shapes seen in nature and we describe here some of the capabilities that are used to contribute to scenes in computer graphics. For a fuller treatment the reader is referred to Barnsley, 1988, Becker and Dorfler, 1989 and Crownover, 1995.

A fractal is a geometrically complex shape, which arises from repetition of a given form over a range of sizes – a form of symmetry. Examples might be trees or lightning, which are symmetrical, not at the level of microscopic detail but at the macro level. A twig, a branch and a tree trunk are similar each being a repetition or subdivision of each other. Similarly lightning may be thought of as composed of sparks, shorts flashes. These are examples of what we call **dilation symmetry**and are all called fractal. Fractal complexity is the repeat of the same design or pattern over and over for different sizes.

Fractal complexity is hard to characterize because each object is different, as examples such as food stains, coastal erosion, clouds or leaves illustrate. We shall now visit a number of examples where knowledge of fractals enables us to build models of object surfaces not easily described by any other method. The fractal designs permit the introduction of objects into graphical displays that would not otherwise be possible.

9.3.1 Introductory Concepts

We begin by looking at some seemingly simple equations that behave in an unstable fashion for what seem to be very minor changes in the values of parameters.

Example 1
Consider the equation $y = kx(1 - x)$ with $k = 2$ or rewriting as $x_{i+1} = kx_i(1 - x_i)$

If we start with $x_0 = 0.3$ and substitute in the equation we see that $x_1 = 0.42$. Now use x_1 as next x and we find that $x_2 = 0.487$ and repeating process y successively becomes 0.49967232, 0.49999978 (i.e. the equation for $y(x_{i+1})$ tends to a value of 0.5 – try with other values of x between 0 and 1 and see what happens). The value 0.5 is called the **attractor** of sequence, that is, the sequence is attracted to a value of 0.5 and this sequence is said to have **one attractor.**

Example 2
Again we will use the same equation $x_{i+1} = kx_i(1 - x_i)$
but with the constant $k = 3$ and starting with an initial $x_0 = 0.7$

We perform the same iteration and different pattern emerges despite only changing the multiplier constant k of the equation. After about a sequence of 15 terms we
get values of 0.635, 0.695 repeating – **two attractors.**

Example 3

Again we use the equation $x_{i+1} = kx_i(1 - x_i)$ but with $k = 3.5$ and starting with
$x_0 = 0.7$. If we iterate a different pattern emerges and after about 40 terms we get:
0.383, 0.827, 0.5, 0.875 repeating – **four attractors.**

If we increase k by small amounts the number of attractors will keep increasing and the grouping we call scaling or self-similarity. Readers are encouraged to
experiment and find that before $k = 4$ the sequence appears to be random – what
we call **chaos**. The intricate and seemingly unpredictable behaviour exhibited by
this and other apparently simple equations together with computer power becoming
available in 1960s spawned a number of studies in complex systems in Biology,
Meteorology, Economics and Population numbers.

If k were dependent say on temperature and the equation represented weather
conditions, then we might be able to say whether the weather was to be predictable
(1 attractor) or unsettled and chaotic. In this case small changes in k seem to have
very significant effects on the value of our equation. This has led to questions as
to what an equation was assumed to represent and how well did we understand its
behaviour when small parameter changes occurred. Popular examples of the time
asked questions such as: does the flapping of a flies wings in the UK ever cause
Tornadoes in the USA, is there a model for the neuronal branches in our brains, how
do we measure the length of the coastline etc.

Analysis of quadratic systems such as the preceding equation is quite difficult
as stable and unstable behaviour is closely intertwined, and the transition between
the two is hard to predict. This behaviour is the foundation of what is called Chaos
Theory.

9.3.2 Reduction Copying

Consider the rectangles in Fig. 9.18 below where we reduce the size of each rectangle by a half as we move from the left to right hand side of the diagram. This is akin
to photo reduction and the process of generating a copy is termed a *self-similarity*
operation.

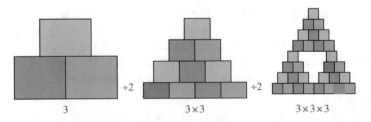

Fig. 9.18 Reduction copying

The process works with any shape not just rectangles, and is independent of first image and always tends to final composite image called a **Sierpinski Gasket** The reduction in size is the same in x and y directions and is called a **linear** or **affine** transformation, which in this example is a scaling factor of 0.5.

The scaling of each point is an affine transformation (see Chapter 4) where the scale factor is the diagonal of the matrix. Consider the triangles in Fig. 9.19 and the affine

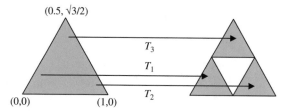

Fig. 9.19 The linear or affine transformation transformation

transformation of each point where the scale factor of $\frac{1}{2}$ is the diagonal of the matrix.

$$T_1 \begin{bmatrix} X_1 \\ Y_1 \end{bmatrix} = \begin{bmatrix} 0.5 & 0 \\ 0 & 0.5 \end{bmatrix} \begin{bmatrix} X_1 \\ Y_1 \end{bmatrix} + \begin{bmatrix} 0 \\ 0 \end{bmatrix}$$ This transformation for the 3 vertices forms vertices for lower LHS triangle

$$T_2 \begin{bmatrix} X_2 \\ Y_2 \end{bmatrix} = \begin{bmatrix} 0.5 & 0 \\ 0 & 0.5 \end{bmatrix} \begin{bmatrix} X_1 \\ Y_1 \end{bmatrix} + \begin{bmatrix} 0.5 \\ 0 \end{bmatrix}$$ This transformation for the 3 vertices forms vertices for lower RHS triangle

$$T_3 \begin{bmatrix} X_3 \\ Y_3 \end{bmatrix} = \begin{bmatrix} 0.5 & 0 \\ 0 & 0.5 \end{bmatrix} \begin{bmatrix} X_1 \\ Y_1 \end{bmatrix} + \begin{bmatrix} 0.25 \\ \sqrt{3}\sqrt{4} \end{bmatrix}$$ This transformation for the 3 vertices forms vertices for top triangle

Scale **Translate**

More generally we can write an iterative set of affine operations to form the reduction triangle copies. If P_0 are the set of 3 original vertices points, then P_1 is the next set of vertices given by

$$E_1 = T_1(P_0) \cup T_2(P_0) \cup T_3(P_0)$$
$$\cdots\cdots\cdots\cdots\cdots$$
$$E_n = T_1(P_{n-1}) \cup T_2(P_{n-1}) \cup T_3(P_{n-1})$$

for each successive smaller set of triangles.

This is called an **Iterated Function System** which under some circumstances can be **Fractal**. The above set of **IFS** mappings have an output that is called the **attractor** (the Sierpinski Gasket in this case), where the mapping is composed of a scaling (contraction) plus a movement of position (translation).

9.3.3 Implementation of a Sierpinski Gasket

Our implementation of the deterministic (IFSD) will use recursively-generated triangles, although any basic shape can be used. This is a general way of fragmenting space and subdividing length of triangle sides by 2.

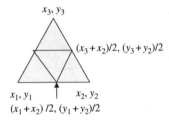

After drawing first triangle we find the mid points of each side (a scaling transform of 0.5 for matrix diagonal) and a translation to move it to required position.

Then we draw the 3 triangles associated with each vertex (1, 2, 3)

This is now repeated for the 3 triangles recursively. At each level of recursion we draw 1, 3, 9, 27, 81 ... triangles, each half the size of previous set as given in the following program fragment.

```
void Sierpinski (void) {
int x, y;
glClear ( GL_COLOR_BUFFER_BIT );
float x1, y1, x2, y2, x3, y3;
int level = 5;
x1 =1.0; y1 =1.0; x2 = 200.0; y2 = 1.0;
x3 = 100.0; y3 = 200.0;
glBegin(GL_LINE_STRIP);
  glVertex2f(x1, y1); glVertex2f(x2, y2);
  glVertex2f(x2, y2); glVertex2f(x3, y3);
  glVertex2f(x3, y3); glVertex2f(x1, y1);
glEnd();
Triangle( x1, y1, x2, y2, x3, y3, level);
}


void Triangle(float x1, float y1, float x2, float y2, float x3,
    float y3, int level)
{
float xm1, ym1, xm2, ym2, xm3, ym3;
if (level $>$ 0) { //mid point subdivision
  xm1 = (x1 + x2) / 2.0; ym1 = (y1 + y2) / 2.0;
  xm2 = (x3 + x2) / 2.0; ym2 = (y3 + y2) / 2.0;
  xm3 = (x1 + x3) / 2.0; ym3 = (y1 + y3) / 2.0;
```

```
   glBegin(GL_LINE_STRIP);
     glVertex2f(xm1, ym1); glVertex2f(xm2, ym2);
     glVertex2f(xm2, ym2); glVertex2f(xm3, ym3);
     glVertex2f(xm3, ym3); glVertex2f(xm1, ym1);
   glEnd();
   glFlush();
   Triangle( x1, y1, xm1, ym1, xm3, ym3, level-1);
   Triangle( x2, y2, xm2, ym2, xm1, ym1, level-1);
   Triangle( x3, y3, xm3, ym3, xm2, ym2, level-1);}
   }
```

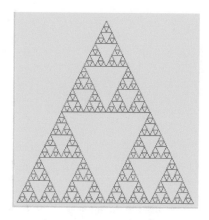

Fig. 9.20 Sierpinski gasket –
recursively

It is instructive in understanding recursion to comment out one of the Triangle
() function calls in the previous program when the output will omit the triangles
initiated by the corresponding vertex [(x_1, y_1) in this case].[1]

---

[1] On a personal note the author has found that teaching recursion in programming courses using
examples from graphics has been an aid to student understanding.

```
void Sierpinski (void) {
int x, y;
glClear ( GL_COLOR_BUFFER_BIT ) ;
glBegin(GL_POINTS);
for(y = 0; y <= 255; y++) {
        for(x = 0; x <= 255; x++) {
        if ((x & y) == 0) glVertex2f(x + 5, y + 5);
    }
}
glEnd();
glFlush();
}
```

9.3.4 Pascal's Triangle

Although probably known in China some centuries previously, Pascal's triangle was used to study gambling odds and forms one of the foundations of Probability theory.

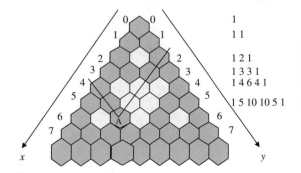

Fig. 9.21 Pascal's triangle

The shape in Fig. 9.20 will remind readers of the Pascal Triangle above! The rows can represent the coefficients of the expansion of $(1 + x)^n$

$$(1 + x)^2 = x^2 + 2x + 1$$
$$(1 + x)^3 = x^3 + 3x^2 + 3x + 1$$

By setting the hexagon position to white when a coefficient is even begins to give us a picture that looks like a Sierpinski gasket.

If we take the point $A(4,2)$ in Fig. 9.21 and consider the binary values $(100,010)$ and set the cell colour to white if two 1's occur else set to black, then we have our Sierpinski gasket produced by the following code fragment.

9.3.5 The Sierpinski Gasket in 3 Dimensions

We now will produce the 3D version (Angel, 2006) of the gasket. Each of the three vertices representing each triangular face combine to define the four vertex Tetrahedron or pyramid, Fig. 9.22. Each face is made up from a combination three of the above vertices and a colour although we omit the colour in this example.

At the base level of recursion we draw each of these triangles and the logic is

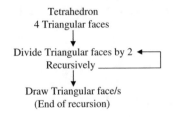

The Tetrahedron function call will initially use input vertices of main Tetra-hedron. If recursion occurs (levels > 0) then we set up a new set of coordinates which are the halfway positions between previous vertices of each triangular face and define our next level (1/2 size) Tetrahedron.

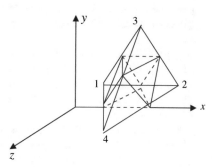

Fig. 9.22 Tetrahedron
subdivision – first level

The recursive process is identical to that for a 2D triangle except we now have four faces to consider. We define the mid points of the three edges of each triangular face by

$$x_i = (x_1 + x_2)/2.0 \qquad y_i = (y_1 + y_2)/2.0 \qquad z_i = (z_1 + z_2)/2.0$$

and similarly for each of the other faces, where the subscripts refer to the corre-sponding vertices of the Tetrahedron. In the following example (serppyr3D.cpp) we have provided a rotation movement, as this seems to give a 'better feel' to the shape and nature of the recursive process not seen in the flat 2D view alone.

```
void Sierpinski (void) {
glClear ( GL_COLOR_BUFFER_BIT );
float x1, y1, z1, x2, y2, z2, x3, y3, z3, x4, y4, z4;
int level = 3;
x1 =1.0; y1 =1.0; z1=1.0;
x2 = 200.0; y2 = 1.0; z2 = 1.0;
x3 = 100.0; y3 = 200.0; z3= 100.0;
x4 = 100.0; y4 = 1.0; z4= 200.0;
glPushMatrix();
glTranslatef(-20.0, -10.0, 1.0);
glRotatef(xRot, 1.0f, 0.0f, 0.0f);
glRotatef(yRot, 0.0f, 1.0f, 0.0f);
//4 faces of pyramid
glBegin(GL_LINE_STRIP); //face 1
  glVertex3f(x1, y1, z1); glVertex3f(x2, y2, z2);
```

```
  glVertex3f(x2, y2, z2); glVertex3f(x3, y3, z3);
  glVertex3f(x3, y3, z3); glVertex3f(x1, y1, z1);
glEnd();
glBegin(GL_LINE_STRIP); //face 2
  glVertex3f(x1, y1, z1); glVertex3f(x4, y4, z4);
  glVertex3f(x4, y4, z4); glVertex3f(x3, y3, z3);
  glVertex3f(x3, y3, z3); glVertex3f(x1, y1, z1);
glEnd();
glBegin(GL_LINE_STRIP); //face 3
  glVertex3f(x1, y1, z1); glVertex3f(x4, y4, z4);
  glVertex3f(x4, y4, z4); glVertex3f(x2, y2, z2);
  glVertex3f(x2, y2, z2); glVertex3f(x1, y1, z1);
glEnd();
  glBegin(GL_LINE_STRIP); //face 4
  glVertex3f(x2, y2, z2); glVertex3f(x3, y3, z3);
  glVertex3f(x3, y3, z3); glVertex3f(x4, y4, z4);
  glVertex3f(x4, y4, z4); glVertex3f(x2, y2, z2);
glEnd();
// Display the results
Pyramid_Face( x1, y1, z1, x2, y2, z2, x3, y3, z3, x4, y4, z4, level);
glPopMatrix();
glutSwapBuffers();
}


void Pyramid_Face(float x1, float y1, float z1, float x2, float y2,
    float z2, float x3, float y3, float z3, float x4, float y4,
    float z4, int level)
{
float xm1, ym1, zm1, xm2, ym2, zm2, xm3, ym3, zm3, xm4, ym4, zm4;
float xm5, ym5, zm5, xm6, ym6, zm6;
if (level > 0) { //mid points of edges
  xm1 = (x1 + x2) / 2.0; ym1 = (y1 + y2) / 2.0; zm1 = (z1 + z2) / 2.0;
  xm2 = (x3 + x2) / 2.0; ym2 = (y3 + y2) / 2.0; zm2 = (z3 + z2) / 2.0;
  xm3 = (x1 + x3) / 2.0; ym3 = (y1 + y3) / 2.0; zm3 = (z1 + z3) / 2.0;
  xm4 = (x1 + x4) / 2.0; ym4 = (y1 + y4) / 2.0; zm4 = (z1 + z4) / 2.0;
  xm5 = (x4 + x3) / 2.0; ym5 = (y4 + y3) / 2.0; zm5 = (z4 + z3) / 2.0;
  xm6 = (x2 + x4) / 2.0; ym6 = (y2 + y4) / 2.0; zm6 = (z2 + z4) / 2.0;
  glBegin(GL_LINE_STRIP);
   glVertex3f(xm1, ym1, zm1); glVertex3f(xm2, ym2, zm2);
   glVertex3f(xm2, ym2, zm2); glVertex3f(xm3, ym3, zm3); //face 321
   glVertex3f(xm3, ym3, zm3); glVertex3f(xm1, ym1, zm1); // for pyramid
  glEnd();
  glBegin(GL_LINE_STRIP);
   glVertex3f(xm3, ym3, zm3); glVertex3f(xm4, ym4, zm4); //face 134
   glVertex3f(xm4, ym4, zm4); glVertex3f(xm5, ym5, zm5);
   glVertex3f(xm5, ym5, zm5); glVertex3f(xm3, ym3, zm3); // for pyramid
```

```
glEnd();
glBegin(GL_LINE_STRIP);
  glVertex3f(xm1, ym1, zm1); glVertex3f(xm6, ym6, zm6);
  glVertex3f(xm6, ym6, zm6); glVertex3f(xm4, ym4, zm4); //face 142
  glVertex3f(xm4, ym4, zm4); glVertex3f(xm1, ym1, zm1); // for pyramid
glEnd();
glBegin(GL_LINE_STRIP);
  glVertex3f(xm2, ym2, zm2); glVertex3f(xm5, ym5, zm5);
  glVertex3f(xm5, ym5, zm5); glVertex3f(xm6, ym6, zm6); // for pyramid
  glVertex3f(xm6, ym6, zm6); glVertex3f(xm2, ym2, zm2); //234 face
glEnd();
glFlush();
//*4 for each face
  Pyramid_Face( x1, y1, z1, xm1, ym1, zm1, xm3, ym3, zm3, xm4, ym4,
  zm4, level-1);
  Pyramid_Face( x2, y2, z2, xm2, ym2, zm2, xm1, ym1, zm1, xm6, ym6,
  zm6, level-1);
  Pyramid_Face( x3, y3, z3, xm3, ym3, zm3, xm2, ym2, zm2, xm5, ym5,
  zm5, level-1);
  Pyramid_Face( x4, y4, z4, xm4, ym4, zm4, xm6, ym6, zm6, xm5, ym5,
  zm5, level-1);
  }
}
```

Output is displayed in Fig. 9.23.

In the Pyramid_Face function readers might like to try replacing the glBegin (GL_LINE_STRIP) with glBegin(GL_POLYGON) and introduce some colour to the different levels of pyramids to understand the construction process in more detail.

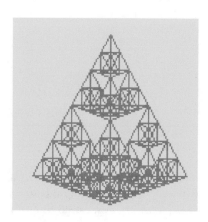

Fig. 9.23 A fractal pyramid

9.3.6 Order Out of Chaos – A Non-deterministic Gasket?

A further method of drawing the Sierpinski gasket comes from what one might see as an unlikely source. Consider a dice with six faces with the values 1, 2, 3 replicated on each face, that correspond to the sides of a triangle shown in Fig. 9.24.

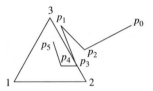

Fig. 9.24 A fractal pyramid

From some starting location p_0 we throw the dice and move from the start point to the halfway point to either vertex 1, 2 or 3 point, depending on the throw. We repeat at each point this process as shown in Fig. 9.24.

9.3.6.1 Moving Towards a Vertex

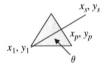

Distance between two points

$$= \sqrt{(x_s - x_1)^2 + (y_s - y_1)2}$$

Divide by 2 for halfway

$$\frac{x_p - x_1}{0.5^* \text{ distance}} = \cos(\theta)$$

and

$$\frac{y_p - y_1}{0.5^* \text{ distance}} = \sin(\theta)$$

The calculation is needed for other vertices x_2, y_2 and x_3, y_3 depending on which vertex we are moving towards as a result of each throw of the dice. We can use a random number generator to simulate a dice, with 1–3 representing each vertex duplicated on faces using modulo 3 arithmetic. The above calculation was in the first quadrant and we need to take account of the sign of the sin (θ) or cos (θ) if start point is in a different quadrant in relation to each vertex. The following code fragment from SerpRand.cpp implements these relations.

```cpp
void Serp (void) {                    //SerpRand.cpp
int xstart, ystart, xpos, ypos, i, rn;
float dist, xs, ys;
float xp1=100.0, yp1= 100.0, xp2=200.0, yp2=100.0, xp3=150.0,
      yp3=187.0;
points values;
glClear ( GL_COLOR_BUFFER_BIT );
glBegin(GL_POINTS);
glPointSize(4.0);
glColor3f(0.0, 0.0, 1.0);
glVertex2f(xp1, yp1);
glVertex2f(xp2, yp2);
glVertex2f(xp3, yp3);

glPointSize(1.0);
glColor3f(1.0, 0.0, 0.0);
xstart = 200.0; xs = xstart;
ystart = 200.0; ys = ystart;
for(i = 1; i< 1200; i++) {
rn =  1 +(int) ( rand() % 3);
switch (rn)
 {
 case 1:
        dist = sqrt((xs - xp1) * (xs - xp1)
                    + (ys - yp1) * (ys - yp1));
        values = Quadrant(xs, ys, xp1, yp1, dist);
 //new xs & ys
        xpos = (int) values.xrands;
        ypos = (int) values.yrands;
        glVertex2i(xpos, ypos);
        xs = xpos;  xstart = xs;
        ys = ypos;  ystart = ys;
        break;
 case 2:
        dist = sqrt((xs - xp2) * (xs - xp2)
                    + (ys - yp2) * (ys - yp2));
        values = Quadrant(xs, ys, xp2, yp2, dist);
 //new xs & ys
        xpos =  (int) values.xrands;
        ypos =  (int) values.yrands;
        glVertex2i(xpos, ypos);
        xs = xpos;  xstart = values.xrands;
```

```
        ys = ypos;   ystart = values.yrands;
        break;
 case 3:
        dist = sqrt((xs - xp3) * (xs - xp3)
                    + (ys - yp3) * (ys - yp3));
        values = Quadrant(xs, ys, xp3, yp3, dist);
 //new xs & ys
        xpos = (int) values.xrands;
        ypos = (int) values.yrands;
        glVertex2i(xpos, ypos);
        xs = xpos;   xstart = xs;
        ys = ypos;   ystart = ys;
        break;
   }
}
glEnd();
glFlush();
}


points Quadrant(float xst, float yst, float xp, float yp,
                float dist)
{
points valueof;
float sinth, costh, distby2, xs, ys;

distby2 = dist * 0.5;
if(dist < 0.00001) dist =0.01;
if(xst >= xp && yst >= yp) {  // Quad 1
        sinth = (yst - yp) / dist;
        costh = (xst - xp) / dist;
  //new xs & ys
        xs = distby2 * costh;
        ys = distby2 * sinth;
        xst = xst - xs;
        yst = yst - ys;
  }
if(xst < xp && yst > yp) {  // Quad 2
        sinth = (yst - yp) / dist;
        costh = -(xst - xp) / dist;
  //new xs & ys
        xs = distby2 * costh;
        ys = distby2 * sinth;
        xst = xst + xs;
        yst = yst - ys;
  }
```

```
if(xst < xp && yst < yp) {  // Quad 3
        sinth = -(yst - yp) / dist;
        costh = -(xst - xp) / dist;
  //new xs & ys
        xs = distby2 * costh;
        ys = distby2 * sinth;
        xst = xst + xs;
        yst = yst + ys;
  }
if(xst > xp && yst < yp) {  // Quad 4
        sinth = -(yst - yp) / dist;
        costh = (xst - xp) / dist;
  //new xs & ys
        xs = distby2 * costh;
        ys = distby2 * sinth;
        xst = xst - xs;
        yst = yst + ys;
  }
valueof.xrands = xst;
valueof.yrands = yst;
return(valueof);
}
```

Our chaotic to ordered pattern of Fig. 9.25 may seem no more than an interesting curiosity! In the reduction copy we assumed our duplicated dice randomly produced numbers for each move towards a vertex with equal probability. We then plotted this new position (divided by 2) and then used it to find the next position (*Function Serp in the program*). At present in each triangle roughly the same number of points are plotted due roughly an equal probability of moving towards each of the three vertices.

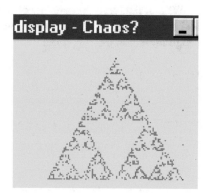

Fig. 9.25 That gasket again

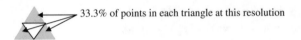

33.3% of points in each triangle at this resolution

whereas at this resolution ~11.1% of points are in each triangle

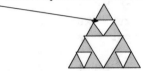

since the probabilities p_1, p_2, p_3 for the dice rolling a 1, 2 or 3 are the same and $p_1 + p_2 + p_3 = 1$. The question may occur to readers as to what happens if we weight the random moves in some other way?

We have just generated the Sierpinski Gasket via random movements towards each vertex that produce a nice pattern, but can we do anything else? We now go back to the shrinking and translation of our multiple reduction-copying machine, which we remember as a scaling, plus a translation for each triangle vertex. In Fig. 9.19 we determined the values in the 3 matrices as

```
0.5 0.0 0.0 0.5 0.0 0.0          First matrices
0.5 0.0 0.0 0.5 0.5 0.0          Second matrices
0.5 0.0 0.0 0.5 0.25 0.433       Third matrices
```

Examples up to this point shown in Fig. 9.25 have all been hard coded but we can also introduce these matrix coefficients from a file (data file serpinnsk.txt) and achieve the same result.

$$T_3 \begin{pmatrix} x_1 \\ y_1 \end{pmatrix} = \begin{pmatrix} 0.5 & 0 \\ 0 & 0.5 \end{pmatrix} \begin{pmatrix} x_1 \\ y_1 \end{pmatrix} + \begin{pmatrix} 0.25 \\ 0.433 \end{pmatrix}$$

was the transformation using the third matrix

We can randomly initiate any of the three matrix operations by using rand() %3 and generate the corresponding point in the gasket as illustrated in the following program.

```
void Data_In()
{               //get transformation matrix coefficients
int r, c;
ifstream indata("c:\\serpinsk.txt", ios ::in);
if(!indata) { cout << "File would not open\n";
        return;
        }
for (r=0; r < ntransforms; r++) {
```

```
                  for (c=0; c < 6; c++) {
                  indata >> Coeff[r][c];
                  }
}
}

void DrawTriangle()
{
int j, r;
float x, x0=10.0, y, y0=10.0;
glClear ( GL_COLOR_BUFFER_BIT ) ;
for(j=1; j< npts; j++) {
   r= (int)rand()%ntransforms;
   x = Coeff[r][0]*x0 + Coeff[r][1]*y0 + Coeff[r][4];
   y = Coeff[r][2]*x0 + Coeff[r][3]*y0 + Coeff[r][5];
   glBegin(GL_POINTS);
           glVertex2i(x*100, y*100);
   glEnd();
   x0 = x;
   y0 = y;
   }
glFlush();
}
```

What are important are the coefficients in the transformation T_n in the stored matrix Coeff[][]. If we know the right values for these and the number of transformations (3 for triangles) then we can draw a remarkable number of fractal patterns in this apparently random manner. We generalise the affine transformation matrix

$$C = \begin{pmatrix} a_1 & b_1 & c_1 & d_1 & e_1 & f_1 \\ a_2 & b_2 & c_2 & d_2 & e_2 & f_2 \\ & \cdot & & & & \\ & \cdot & & & & \\ a_n & b_n & c_n & d_n & e_n & f_n \end{pmatrix}$$

and use this matrix of coefficients for some of the following fractal patterns. The following are but three sets of coefficients for the transformation, with the variable ntransforms in the above program set to the value given.

Crystal.txt

0.255 0.0 0.0 0.255 0.3726 0.6714   ntransforms = 4

0.255 0.0 0.0 0.255 0.1146 0.2232

0.255 0.0 0.0 0.255 0.6306 0.2232

0.37 -0.642 0.642 0.37 0.6356 -0.0061

Tree.txt

0.195 -0.488 0.344 0.443 0.4431 0.2452   ntransforms = 5

0.462 0.414 -0.252 0.361 0.2511 0.5692

-0.058 -0.07 0.453 -0.111 0.5976 0.0969

-0.035 0.07 -0.469 0.022 0.4884 0.5069

-0.637 0.0 0.0 0.501 0.8562 0.2513

Twig.txt

-0.467 0.02 -0.113 0.015 0.4 0.4   ntransforms = 3

0.387 0.43 0.43 -0.387 0.256 0.522

0.441 -0.091 -0.009 -0.322 0.421 0.505

Another way to think of the coefficients is that they define the storage data required for the twig image with 18 floating point numbers, each occupying 4 bytes. This particular image has a size of $94 \times 80 \times 3 = 22560$ bytes, giving a compression of $22560/72 = 313:1$. Fractal compression is a growth research area.

9.3.7 An Alternative Idea for a Tree or Plant

We will now use our ideas of fractals and recursive similarity to explore and generate approximations to other *natural* shapes. The letter Y is a simple twig like shape, so lets draw it recursively and see what happens. The twig is defined by coordinates on the left xl, yl, on the right by xr, yr, the middle xm, ym and the starting point xstart, ystart as shown in Fig. 9.26.

Fig. 9.26 Simple twig
definition

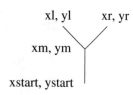

- We set suitable values for coordinates
- Function YBranch draws the letter Y
- We then scale the length of each branch by 0.5 and perform a recursive call

Depending on the depth of the recursion we get a more complex tree and we need to build our tree on both left and right branches of the twig, in the same way as we built our triangles. The code for this process follows with output shown in Fig. 9.27.

```
void YTree(void) {
glClear ( GL_COLOR_BUFFER_BIT );
float xstart, ystart, ys, xs;
int rdepth = 5;
xstart = ww / 2.0;  ystart = wh / 2.0;
xs = ystart /2.0; ys = ystart;
YBranch( xstart, ystart-ys, xs, ys,rdepth);   //RHS
YBranch( xstart, ystart-ys, -xs, ys,rdepth);  //LHS
}

void YBranch(float xY, float yY, float bx, float ay,  int level)
{
float xm, ym, xl, yl, xr, yr, scly, sclx;
if (level > 0) {    //define coordinates of next Y twig
          xm = xY; ym = yY + ay*0.5;
          xl = xm - bx; yl = ym + ay*0.5;
          xr = xm + bx; yr = ym + ay*0.5;
          scly = ay / 2;
          sclx = bx / 2.0;
          glBegin(GL_LINES);
           glVertex2f(xY, yY); glVertex2f(xm, ym);
           glVertex2f(xm, ym); glVertex2f(xl, yl);
           glVertex2f(xm, ym); glVertex2f(xr, yr);
           YBranch( xr, yr, sclx ,scly, level-1);
           YBranch( xr, yr, -sclx, scly,level-1);
          glEnd();
   }
glFlush();
}
```

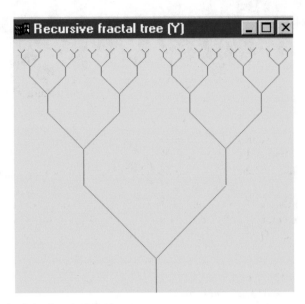

Fig. 9.27 Result of simple twig definition

Experimenting with a 'narrower' shaped Y produces different natural approximations to a plant.

9.4 Koch Curves

Up to this point we have discovered that affine transformations can lead to some extraordinary shapes that mimic what we see in nature. We will now turn to a different set of self-similar operations that will permit representations of naturally occurring shapes. The Swedish mathematician H. Koch in 1904 discovered a shape made by drawing four line segments to make up a side of a triangle with each side constructed as in Fig. 9.28.

The side of a triangle is replaced by four line segments, each 1/3 of the length of the original side. This process can be defined recursively, the base level being the largest line we decide to draw, we then divide the side by three, and drawing

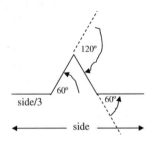

Fig. 9.28 The Koch curve

the four lines above, superimposed on the side concerned. The graphical repetition of recursion is called **self-similarity** where each curve is the same shape but on a different size scale. In the 1970s Benoit Mandelbrot used the term *fractal* for this self-similarity. The process is

> Draw line (turn left 60°) – Draw line (turn right 120°) – Draw line
> (turn left 60°) – Draw line
> line size = line size/3
> ⌞——— repeat

The movement of **forwards – back – left – right** is also called **turtle geometry** after Seymour Papert. We can redraw upon the new lines with a further subdivision to whatever level we choose. The process forms a series of rules called a **tree grammar** (or an L-system) denoted by symbols or **productions**

$$F \rightarrow FLFRRFLF$$

where L and R stand for ±60° movements.

```
void startat()      //KockSnow.cpp
{ //specify an origin at which to start
tangle = 0;
xstart = 50; ystart = 50;
turtx = 50; turty = 50;
}

void DrawKock()
{       //define starting triangle
int level = 3;
glClear(GL_COLOR_BUFFER_BIT | GL_DEPTH_BUFFER_BIT);
 startat();
 turn(0);
 Drawit(step, level);
 turn(120);
 Drawit(step, level);
 turn(120);
 Drawit(step, level);
}
void Drawit(int step, int level)
{
if(level == 0) {
        forward( step, tangle);
}
```

```
else {
glBegin(GL_LINES);
        Drawit( step /3, level-1);
        turn (-60);
        Drawit( step /3, level-1);
        turn (120);
        Drawit( step /3, level-1);
        turn (-60);
        Drawit( step /3, level-1);
glEnd();
}
glFlush();
}


void turn(int angle)
{       //angle turned through
 tangle = (tangle+ angle) % 360;
}
void forward( int step, int tangle)
{       //movement
float xstep, ystep, pi = 3.14159265;
xstep = step * cos(( tangle * pi) /180) ;
ystep = step * sin(( tangle * pi) /180) ;
turtx = turtx + floor(xstep+0.5);
turty = turty + floor(ystep+0.5);
glBegin(GL_LINES);
        glVertex2f(xstart, ystart);
        glVertex2f(turtx, turty);
        xstart=turtx; ystart = turty;
glEnd();
glFlush();
}
```

The basic shape or axiom, the triangle, is specified in function DrawKoch. In function forward() we draw a line between two points at an angle specified by the grammar: in this case multiples of ±60° in function turn().

Level = 0   1   2   3

If the level of subdivision is to large, the vectors become too small to draw. The rules that describe the drawing movements required at each level are

```
The first rule is    FLLFLLF                          at level 0
Now we can replace F with FLFRRFLF on any side of triangle
Thus    (FLFRRFLF) LL (FLFRRFLF) LL (FLFRRFLF)        at level 1
And [(FLFRRFLF) L (FLFRRFLF) RR (FLFRRFLF) L (FLFRRFLF)]
LL [(FLFRRFLF) L (FLFRRFLF) RRĚĚĚĚ..                  at level 2
```

9.4.1 Further Thoughts on the Koch Snowflake

Consider the area of each triangle of side length a

then $h = a\sqrt{3}/2$ and Area $= a^2\sqrt{3}/4$
Now let side length of curve be $a/3$

that is new "a" $= a/3$ and Area $= a^2\sqrt{3}/36$
Now let side length be $a/9$

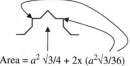

that is new "a" $= a/9$ and Area $= a^2\sqrt{3}/324$
And similarly with side of length $a/27$ the Area $= a^2\sqrt{3}/(4 \times 27^2)$

Area $= a^2\sqrt{3}/4 + 2x\ (a^2\sqrt{3}/36)$

and similarly for smaller triangles.

Area

$$\begin{array}{cccc} 1 & 3 & 12 & 48 \end{array}$$
$$a^2\sqrt{3}/4 + a^2\sqrt{3}/36 + a^2\sqrt{3}/324 + a^2\sqrt{3}/(4 \times 27^2)$$
$$= a^2\sqrt{3}/4\left\{1 + \tfrac{3}{9} + \tfrac{12}{9^2} + \tfrac{48}{9^3} \cdots \cdots \cdots \right\}$$
$$= a^2\sqrt{3}/4 + a^2\sqrt{3}/12\left\{1 + \tfrac{4}{9} + \tfrac{4^2}{9^2} + \cdots \cdots \cdots \cdots \tfrac{4^{n-1}}{9^{n-1}}\right\}$$

The sum of the geometric series is $S_n = \frac{1-(4/9)^n}{1-4/9}$
and when $n \to \infty$, $S = 9/5$.

Thus the total area $A = a^2\sqrt{3}/4 + a^2\sqrt{3}/12 \times 9/5 = 2\sqrt{3}/5a^2$ where the area of the Koch snowflake is a visual geometric representation of a geometric series. The representation of a geometric shape from an infinite series is called Point set topology.

9.4.2 Self-similarity

We noted previously that the Kock curve is a representation of an infinite geometric series

$$\sum_{n=0}^{\infty} r^n = 1 + r + r^2 + r^3 + r^4 \ldots$$
$$\therefore \quad r\sum_{n=0}^{\infty} r^n = r + r^2 + r^3 + r^4 \ldots$$
$$\sum_{n=0}^{\infty} r^n = 1 + r\sum_{n=0}^{\infty} r^n$$

the self similarity of a geometric series demonstrated in recursion.

The Koch snowflake has a finite area but an infinite length through subdivision of the sides and it was this idea, noted by Mandelbrot, of how fractals might allow us to represent the coastline of a country or indeed any irregular shape and measure the length.

So how long is the coastline of United Kingdom? Well it depends on how you measure it and with what resolution, although there are estimates of 4500–5000 miles. When you realise the parts of the coast are made up of bits that are parts of the units we use (miles, feet, inches, metres...) we can never get small enough, even with grains of sand as the outline! Take as an example the simple outline in

Fig. 9.29 Measuring the perimeter of an irregular shape

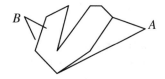

Figure 9.29 with two compasses of different spans S_A and S_B. The steps of compass A with the largest span S_A around the shape will be fewer but will omit the finer detail. The shorter span S_B of compass B will require more steps and permit measurements of indentations not resolved by A and is likely to measure a longer perimeter. The relationship of length measurement of outline perimeter L to compass setting S would provide a means of measurement based on the span resolution. What is required is a set of measurements of length for different compass spans and a graphical plot with a test perimeter of known length, in this case a circle.

It must be remembered that because of the relative sizes involved, where a coastline may be thousands of miles and a compass on a map is only inches, errors will occur. We start the problem with a log – log plot (beware as such plots straighten out most things with variable errors!) of perimeter L against compass span S.

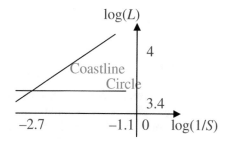

The term $1/S$ is called the precision and we can use this graph to forecast coastal perimeter for different compass precision spans. The circle perimeter L is given by a horizontal line and for any fixed precision at the intercept with $\log(L)$ axis. The coastline is represented by the sloping line, where as S gets smaller and log $1/S$ gets larger, the value of $\log(L)$ increases $(= L)$.

From our graph we have a simple power law relation

$$\log(L) = m \ \log(1/S) + c$$

9.4.2.1 Power Law Digression

If $y = ax^p$ then taking logs of both sides

$$\log(y) = p \ \log(x) + \log(a)$$

which is of same form as

$$L = a(1/S)^m$$

where a is some constant (intercept on graph) and m is the gradient. From our graph for coastline of Britain $m \sim 0.36$ or

$$\text{Length } L \propto 1/S^{0.36}$$

Thus as $S \to 0$ the coastline has a length, which is measured at the size of grains of sand or atoms as you walk round them! The power will be different for different countries depending on general shape and irregularity of the coastline.

The length of Kock snowflake or island increments by a factor of 4/3 for each level of recursion.

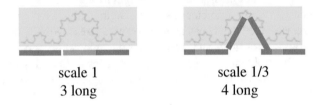

scale 1   scale 1/3
3 long   4 long

9.4.3 Random Koch Fractals

So far our Koch curve has been deterministic and we now introduce a degree of 'randomness' that allows us to generate the first simple 'natural' shapes. A simple change is to permit two different orientations for each step of the drawing

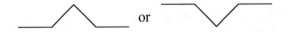

or

and using the change in the sign of the angular turn we choose which way to draw randomly. A modified version of Drawit function follows to permit this operation with typical output.

```
void Drawit(int step, int level)
{
int sign;
sign = rand() % 2;
if(sign == 1) sign = 1;
   else sign = -1;
if(level == 0) {
          forward( step, tangle);
  }
else {
```

```
glBegin(GL_LINES);
        Drawit( step /3, level-1);
        turn (60 * sign);
        Drawit( step /3, level-1);
        turn (-120 * sign);
        Drawit( step /3, level-1);
        turn (60 * sign);
        Drawit( step /3, level-1);
glEnd();
glFlush();
}
```

level = 2

level = 4

We can build a Kock island by using a basic shape such as a triangle or square and use the random orientation drawing function for shaping the edges of the island. Care is needed in relation to rounding errors as the step size gets smaller and a typical result is shown in Fig. 9.30.

Readers may find it interesting to experiment with specifying the basic shape of a country and drawing an outline based on this process. With a very small number of points specifying the outline of a country, remarkable likenesses of form can be achieved.

level = 4

Fig. 9.30 A sample Koch Island

9.4.4 Back to Trees and Bushes

In Fig. 9.27 we recursively drew a simple tree, but it was rather inflexible and we now return to the grammar we used to develop the Koch snowflake and specify the angle between the branches in this example. The building of a tree follows the following stages (levels)

Level = 0   1   2   3   4...

With equal length branches (step) our tree might look like this in terms of a grammar

```
    F                                        Level = 0
F(LFBRRF)                                            1
(LFBRRF)L  (LFBRRF)BRR  (LFBRRF)                     2
        .                                    .
        .                                    .
        .                                    .
```

by recursively drawing 'Y' through replacement at the end of each forward move-ment by (LFBRRF). In the following example we have limited the branching to left and right (LR) to ±10°, Fig. 9.31.

```
void startat()
{ //specify an origin
  tangle = 90; //upright
  xstart = 50; ystart = 50;
  turtx = 50; turty = 50;
}

void turn(int angle)
{
  tangle = (tangle + angle) % 360;
}

void DrawTree()
{
int level =2;    //try 0 1 2 3 ..5 to see recursion
glClear(GL_COLOR_BUFFER_BIT | GL_DEPTH_BUFFER_BIT);
  startat();
  Movefb(step); //trunk
  Drawit(step, level);
}
void Drawit(int step, int level)
```

```
{
if(level > 0) { //grammar describing moves
          turn (-10);
          Movefb(step);
          Drawit( step, level-1);
          Movefb(-step);
          turn (20);
          Movefb(step);
          Drawit( step, level-1);
          Movefb(-step);
          turn (-10);
   }
}

void Movefb( int step)
{        //+ forward - backward
float pi = 3.14159265, d2r= 0.0174532925;
float xstep, ystep;
xstep = step * cos( tangle * d2r) ;
ystep = step * sin( tangle * d2r) ;
turtx = turtx + floor(xstep+0.5);
turty = turty + floor(ystep+0.5);
glBegin(GL_LINES);
        glVertex2f(xstart, ystart);
        glVertex2f(turtx, turty);
        xstart=turtx; ystart = turty;
glEnd();
glFlush();
}
```

Fig. 9.31 Recursive tree building

It should be noted that rounding errors could occur with deep levels of recursion and distort the tree. An interesting modification is to shorten the step length on one side of the tree, which gives an appearance of a tree blowing in the wind, Fig. 9.32.

```
void Drawit(int step, int level)
{
if(level > 0) {
            turn (-10);
            Movefb(step);
            Drawit( step, level-1);
            Movefb(-step);
            turn (20);
            Movefb(step);
            Drawit( step/2, level-1);
            Movefb(-step);
            turn (-10);
    }
}
```

Fig. 9.32 Blowing in the wind effect

Some readers may be now raising the question as to the three dimensional nature of plants. The same principles also hold with the addition of the z-coordinate values in generating a 3D bush. We do this by using spherical polar coordinates and the following simple example acts as an introduction.

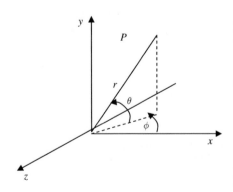

Fig. 9.33 Spherical polar coordinates

From Fig. 9.33 we see that Cartesian point $P(x, y, z)$ may be represented in polar coordinates as

$$x = r \, \cos\theta \, \cos\phi, \qquad y = r \, \sin\theta, \qquad z = r \, \cos\theta \, \sin\phi$$

where P is a point at one end of a line, which we use as the end of a branch. Our grammar can be similar to that for a 2D tree, except we introduce a third branch at every fork in the tree and maintain self-similarity. The function Drawit used in the preceding example now has to be modified to include the angle ϕ in defining the branch end points and a third recursive call of Drawit is included at each tree fork.

```
void DrawTree()
{
int level =5;      //0 1 2 3  to see recursion
glClear(GL_COLOR_BUFFER_BIT | GL_DEPTH_BUFFER_BIT);
 startat();
 glRotatef(xRot, 1.0, 0.0, 0.0);
 glRotatef(yRot, 0.0, 1.0, 0.0);
 Drawit(step, level);
}
void Drawit(float step, int level)
{
levtemp = level;
if(level > 0) { //grammar specifying moves
          turn (-10, -60);
          Movefb(step);
          Drawit( step, level-1);
          Movefb(-step);
          turn (20, 0);
          Movefb(step);
          Drawit( step, level-1);
          Movefb(-step);
          turn (-10, 60);
          Movefb(step);
          Drawit( step, level-1);
          Movefb(-step);
 }
}
void Movefb( float step)
{         //+ forward - backward
float d2r= 0.0174532925;
float xstep, ystep, zstep;
        //spherical polars -> cartesian
xstep = step * cos( tangle * d2r) * cos( tphi * d2r);
```

```
ystep = step * sin( tangle * d2r);
zstep = step * cos( tangle * d2r) * sin( tphi * d2r);
turtx = turtx + floor(xstep+0.5);
turty = turty + floor(ystep+0.5);
turtz = turtz + floor(zstep+0.5);

glBegin(GL_LINES);
        glVertex3f(xstart, ystart, zstart);
        glVertex3f(turtx, turty, turtz);
        xstart=turtx; ystart = turty; zstart = turtz;
glEnd();
glutSwapBuffers();
}


void turn(float angle, float phiangle)
{
 tangle = (int) (tangle + angle);
 tphi = (int) (tphi + phiangle);
}
```

By rotating the 'bush' we can now observe more of a 3D object, Fig. 9.34 and readers might wish to replace the 'line' branches with textured cylinders as objects of varying radii (see Fig. 7.9) to simulate more realistic branches.

Fig. 9.34 Plan and side view of a recursive bush construction

9.5 Brownian Motion

In 1828 Robert Brown noticed that particles of pollen floating on water made small erratic movements when viewed through a microscope. The movement was later discovered to be due to the thermal agitation by collisions from water molecules and it was also noted that the larger the pollen particles the less random and more uniform was the movement. The total movement of each particle of pollen is related to the number of collisions by water molecules. We can simulate this in software by using the rand() function to generate values about a mean and progressively sum the movements to give the overall movement at any given time. Time in this case is represented by the x-axis.

```
void DrawIt()
{
int i, npoints = 100, x;
float y;
float scalefactor = 5.0, frand;
glClear(GL_COLOR_BUFFER_BIT | GL_DEPTH_BUFFER_BIT);
glTranslatef(30.0, 0.0, 0.0);
y = 0.0;
glBegin(GL_LINE_STRIP);
for( i = 0; i<= npoints; i++) {
            x = (-1 + (float) i / (npoints / 2)) * npoints;
            frand = rand() / 32768.0;
            y =  y + scalefactor * (frand - 0.5);
            glVertex2i(x, y);
}
glEnd();
glFlush();
}
```

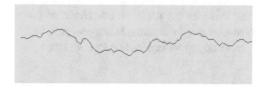

Provided the particle is small compared with the perturbation object (water molecules) the function above will illustrate the progressive movement of the pollen with time.

9.5.1 Fractalised Lines

The construction of the Koch curve permitted us to outline objects and even produce outlines of what might represent an island. In this section we are going to extend these ideas to form contours and surfaces that might represent a simple landscape. The Brownian curve can be thought of as a representation of a coastline or a contour line of height if it were a cut through a landscape surface. We will use the random number function rand() to generate a series of random numbers r_i at point's x_i along a line. Since a landscape can rise and fall we generate r_i such that $0.5 \geq r_i \geq -0.5$ and scale this to that required by the units of height used in an application. Previously we thought of Brownian movement as the impact between two particles and we are now going to modify this idea to represent it as a small perturbation from a

Fig. 9.35 Line fractalisation
process

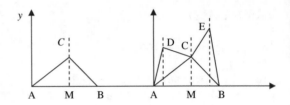

line. We can represent a height profile as the sum of the contribution of the heights r_i
up to any point along the line of the profile. Consider a line AB between two points
A and B and we wish to divide the line in half and add a perturbation at the centre
point as shown in Fig. 9.35.

The point C is the result of a random displacement generated by a random number generator function rand() and this process is repeated recursively for points D
and E to any depth of recursion. We make the displacement of C from the original
line is proportion to the length of the line $|B–A|$. Since C lies on a line vector per-
pendicular to AB, the displacement from the mid point M of AB is $|t||$ B–A| (Hill,
2001), where t is a random Gaussian number. We generate values of t over the
number of points we wish to fractalise the original line by summation and subtract
half this number of points from t to shift the Gaussian variable t to lie between ± 1.
We recursively repeat this process for all subdivisions of the line to generate the
corresponding perturbation displacements. If the points A, B, C, M are represented
by locations (x, y) with corresponding letter subscripts then

$$t(y_b + y_a) \approx x_c - x_m$$

and

$$t(x_b + x_a) \approx y_c - y_m$$

where the length of the line AB effectively weights the offset perturbations. The
value of t is generated as in the previous example when we considered particles
rather than line sections. Hill, 2000, provides a function based on Brownian displacements given below.

```
void lineto( GLPoint A, GLPoint B ) {
glBegin(GL_LINES);
  glVertex2i(A.x, A.y);
  glVertex2i(B.x, B.y);
glEnd();
glFlush();
}
```

```
void fract(GLPoint A, GLPoint B, double stdDev) {
// generate a fractal curve from A to B.
int i;
double xDiff, yDiff, t;
xDiff = A.x - B.x, yDiff = A.y - B.y;

if(xDiff * xDiff + yDiff * yDiff < minLenSq) lineto(A, B);
else {
        stdDev *= factor; // scale stdDev by factor
        t = 0;
        for( i = 0; i < 12; i++) t += rand()/32768.0;
        t = (t - 6) * stdDev; // shift the mean to 0
        C.x = 0.5 * (A.x + B.x) + t * (B.y - A.y);
        C.y = 0.5 * (A.y + B.y) + t * (B.x - A.x);
        fract(A, C, stdDev);
        fract(C, B, stdDev);
        }
}

void DrawFractal() {
        lineto(A, B);
        fract(A, B, 0.1);
}
```

Fig. 9.36 Fractalisation of a
line segment

The above code will produce such a profile as shown in Fig. 9.36 and a complete listing is provided on the website. The profile can be used with straight-line sections of coastline that correspond to the macro features of a country to give remarkably similar outlines to that seen on actual maps.

9.5.2 Fractal Surfaces

We will now develop these ideas to represent a fractal landscape where we calculate the elevation based upon randomly generated values based upon an average of two calculated at locations equidistant from the location concerned as illustrated in Fig. 9.37. The method is based on that presented by Becker and Dorfler, 1989.

At points a and b in Fig. 9.37 we generate two random numbers and the elevation is the average at these locations and dependent on the distance apart of a and b. Points a and b are chosen to be equidistant in x and y from the point where we

Fig. 9.37 Generation of a
fractal surface elevation

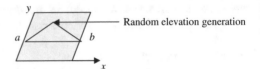

generate the elevation and so we specify a 2D array whose dimensions are a power
of 2 in x and y to store the elevation values. We can then fill an array that is the
size of the surface with these values that represent elevation in a similar fashion to
those for the fractalised line Fig. 9.36. If we consider the following three points at
locations (0,0), (32,0) and (32,32) then we will require a 64 × 64 mesh array for our
surface, where we calculate the random elevation as shown in Fig. 9.38.

Each of the points is recursively defined in terms of two other points situated
equidistant from it with recursion ceasing when we have filled our array with elevation values. The second level of recursion is when we scale by 2 and calculate points
at ±16 either side of the first triangle filling elevations at (16,0), (16,32), (16,48),
(48,0), (48,16) and (16,16). We can formalise this procedure to fill an array with
elevations to represent terrain using the following relations based on the triangle
description in Fig. 9.38.

specify array size
startat = array size / 2
    x = startat

       $elevation_{x,y} = choosefrom(elevation_{x-startat, y}, elevation_{x+startat, y})$
       $elevation_{y,y} = choosefrom(elevation_{x-startat, y}, elevation_{x+startat, y})$
       $elevation_{x, \text{array size}-y-x} = choosefrom(elevation_{x-startat, \text{array size}-y-x+startat},$
                                    $elevation_{x+startat, \text{array size}-y-x-startat})$
    array size = array size / 2
    startat = array size / 2
    until startat = array size

The function choosefrom() returns a random value elevation based on the average
of the elevation of the points from which it is to be calculated and area of the sub
array (32, 16, 8, 4, 2 ,1) in which we are working.

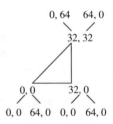

Fig. 9.38 Random elevation
from two points

```cpp
int RandomChoice (int a, int b)        //mountain2.cpp
{
int height;
height = (a + b) / 2 + rand() % Picsize - Initial;
return(height);
}

void fill()
{
int x, y;
y = 0;
do {
        x = Initial;
        do {
                    heights [x][y] = RandomChoice (heights[x -
                            Initial][y], heights[x + Initial][y]);
                    heights [y][y] = RandomChoice (heights[y][x -
                            Initial], heights[y][x + Initial]);
                    heights [x][Parts - x - y] = RandomChoice (
                            heights[x-Initial][Parts-x-y+Initial],
                            heights[x+Initial][Parts-x-y-Initial]);
                    x = x + Picsize;
                    } while( x <= (Parts - y));
            y = y + Picsize;
} while( y < Parts);
}

void Elevations()
{
int i, j;
for( i=0; i<= Parts; i++) {
        for( j= 0; j<= Parts; j++)
                    heights [i][j] = 0;
}
        Picsize = Parts;
        Initial = Picsize / 2;
        do {
                    fill();
                    Picsize = Initial;
                    Initial = Initial / 2;
        } while( Initial != Picsize);
}

void Draw()
{
```

```
int x, y, skip;
glClear(GL_COLOR_BUFFER_BIT | GL_DEPTH_BUFFER_BIT);
glTranslatef(-70.0, -50.0, 0.0);
glBegin(GL_LINE_STRIP);
skip = 8;
y = 0;
for( y = 0; y<=Parts ; y=y+skip) {
    glBegin(GL_LINE_STRIP);
    for( x = 0; x<= Parts ; x=x+skip) {
                    glVertex2i(x+y, y + heights[x][y]*Factor);
                    glVertex2i(x+skip+y, y + heights[x+skip]
                            [y]*Factor);
                    glVertex2i(x+y+skip+skip, y+skip + heights
                            [x+skip][y+skip]*Factor);
                    glVertex2i(x+y+skip, y+skip + heights[x]
                            [y+skip]*Factor);
                    glVertex2i(x+y, y + heights[x][y]*Factor);
            }
    glEnd();
    }
glFlush();
}
```

In this program we have drawn the terrain skipping every eight points to show
more clearly the fractal patches with a scale factor of 0.5 used in Fig. 9.39

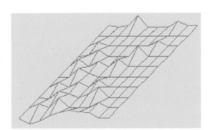

Fig. 9.39 A fractal landscape

9.6 Exercises

1. Use an appropriate bit map image to texture the fractal surface described in
   Section 9.5.2. Readers might consider using the elevation to introduce a second
   texture to mimic lakes in the lower areas of the terrain.
2. In Section 9.2.9 we have provide data for a single plane of snoopy dog. Using
   this basic shape as a template, expand the data file to include further planes and

so construct a 3D solid of snoopy. Hint: Linear scaling of the data will reduce the work required!
3. In Section 9.4 we described the construction of the Koch curve between points. taking a suitable map

9.7 Conclusion

In this chapter we have investigated some of the methods of representing objects though surface representation. The nature of the surface together with the accuracy of required reproduction will govern the storage, rendering speed and realism requirements. The section describing fractal methods is but a small part of a very large subject and we have tried to focus of those parts that have applicability to general graphical rendering. The Web site provides complete working programs in all cases but readers will benefit from using these as a starting point for their own applications.

Appendix A

Getting started with any new systems can be a frustrating process business and it is usually best to find someone whose 'done it before'. In this section we shall attempt some practical help with systems and the installation of OpenGL. Of necessity this will vary across systems and further references, locations and useful libraries are provided on the accompanying website with this book. The Mesa libraries, which I compiled using MS C++ v6 are supplied on the accompanying website and named as:

GLU32.DLL
GLUT32.DLL
OPENGL32.DLL
OMESA32.DLL

Copy these libraries into C:\WINDOWS\system32 and C:\WINDOWS\system for Windows 98, 2000, XP and into C:\WINDOWS for Vista systems. Although this should not be needed, I have found such variation in student machine set-up, that this has ironed out most problems and given me a quieter life over the years!

Look into c:\ Program Files \ Microsft Visual Studio \ VC98 \ Include to ensure all the references to the GLUT are available. A sample GL directory is provided on the Web site and may be copied to this directory if required.

A. 1 Starting up VC++ 6.0

After installing the MS C++ compiler that comes with Dietels' book we click on the start button at the bottom left hand corner of the screen that will look something like the following:

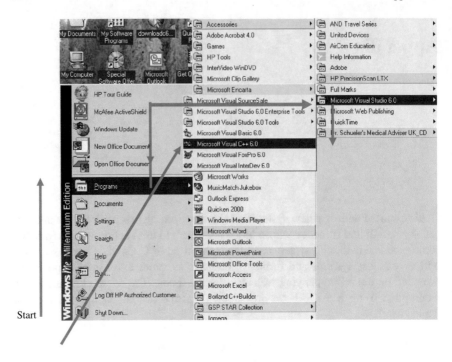

and click here to start up your compiler
which starts up VC++ with a window like

close the pop up

Now click on **File** & **New / Open** and either type in your program or open one that you are using from the web site. After typing in the program below

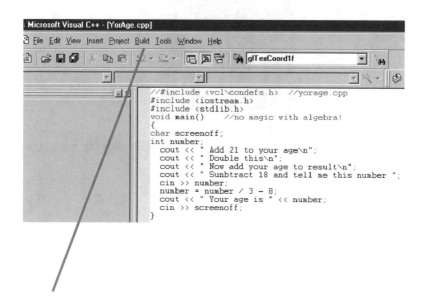

```
//#include <vcl\condefs.h>   //yorage.cpp
#include <iostream.h>
#include <stdlib.h>
void main()    //no magic with algebra!
{
char screenoff;
int number;
   cout << " Add 21 to your age\n";
   cout << " Double this\n";
   cout << " Now add your age to result\n";
   cout << " Sunbtract 18 and tell me this number ";
   cin >> number;
   number = number / 3 - 8;
   cout << " Your age is " << number;
   cin >> screenoff;
}
```

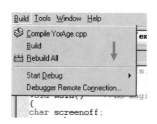

Click on **Build** tab and click on **Build / Rebuild All** after correcting any errors.

You will find a directory called 'Debug' in the area where your source code resides after the first build and you must now copy the four. DLL files above into the Debug directory.

Now your program has compiled click on the **Build** tab again a then click on **Execute**

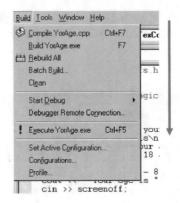

The program will now execute giving a console (DOS) and graphics window.

Appendix B

B. 1 Bresenham's Line Algorithm – General Conditions

If a line has a slope m then the change in pixel representation depends on whether m is greater or less than 1 (45°) in the first quadrant.

> If $m < 1$ then pixels are turned on for increasing x for each y increment (octant 1).
>
> If $m > 1$ then pixels are turned on for increasing y for each x increment (octant 2).

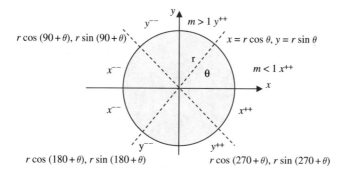

By symmetry the reverse is true in the third quadrant.

For the second quadrant if the slope of the line lies in the third octant, then we decrement y a number of times dependent on gradient, for each x decrement, while in the fourth octant decrement x for a number of times for each y decrement.

By symmetry the reverse is true for lines with a gradient in quadrant four.

Appendix C

C. 1 Matrix and Vector Algebra

In this section we shall briefly describe operations used in this text.

C. 2 Matrix Addition or Subtraction

$$
\overset{\mathbf{A}}{\begin{pmatrix} a_{11} & a_{12} & a_{13} \\ a_{21} & a_{22} & a_{23} \\ a_{31} & a_{32} & a_{33} \end{pmatrix}} + \overset{\mathbf{B}}{\begin{pmatrix} b_{11} & b_{12} & b_{13} \\ b_{21} & b_{22} & b_{23} \\ b_{21} & b_{22} & b_{23} \end{pmatrix}} = \overset{\mathbf{C}}{\begin{pmatrix} c_{11} & c_{12} & c_{13} \\ c_{21} & c_{22} & c_{23} \\ c_{31} & c_{32} & c_{33} \end{pmatrix}}
$$

where matices are normally represented by letters in bold and the subscripts denote the row and column location of each matrix element a_{rc}. The elements of matrix $\mathbf{C}$ are $c_{rc} = a_{rc} + b_{rc}$

$$
\mathbf{A} + \mathbf{B} = \mathbf{C}
$$

C. 3 Matrix Multiplication

$$
\begin{pmatrix} a_{11} & a_{12} & a_{13} \\ a_{21} & a_{22} & a_{23} \\ a_{31} & a_{32} & a_{33} \end{pmatrix} \times \begin{pmatrix} b_{11} & b_{12} & b_{13} \\ b_{21} & b_{22} & b_{23} \\ b_{21} & b_{22} & b_{23} \end{pmatrix} = \begin{pmatrix} c_{11} & c_{12} & c_{13} \\ c_{21} & c_{22} & c_{23} \\ c_{31} & c_{32} & c_{33} \end{pmatrix}
$$

$$
\mathbf{A} \times \mathbf{B} = \mathbf{C}
$$

and the corresponding elements c_{rc} are

$$\begin{pmatrix} a_{11} \times b_{11} + a_{12} \times b_{21} + a_{13} \times b_{31} & a_{11} \times b_{12} + a_{12} \times b_{22} + a_{13} \times b_{32} & a_{11} \times b_{13} + a_{12} \times b_{23} + a_{13} \times b_{33} \\ a_{21} \times b_{11} + a_{22} \times b_{21} + a_{23} \times b_{31} & a_{21} \times b_{12} + a_{22} \times b_{22} + a_{23} \times b_{32} & a_{21} \times b_{13} + a_{22} \times b_{23} + a_{23} \times b_{33} \\ a_{31} \times b_{11} + a_{32} \times b_{21} + a_{33} \times b_{31} & a_{31} \times b_{12} + a_{32} \times b_{22} + a_{33} \times b_{32} & a_{31} \times b_{13} + a_{32} \times b_{23} + a_{33} \times b_{33} \end{pmatrix}$$

Matrix multiplication is non commutative, $\mathbf{AB} \neq \mathbf{BA}$

C. 4 Matrix Vector Multiplication

$$\begin{pmatrix} a_{11} & a_{12} & a_{13} \\ a_{21} & a_{22} & a_{23} \\ a_{31} & a_{32} & a_{33} \end{pmatrix} \times \begin{pmatrix} b_{11} \\ b_{21} \\ b_{31} \end{pmatrix} = \begin{pmatrix} c_{11} \\ c_{21} \\ c_{31} \end{pmatrix}$$

where c_{rc} is the same as the first column in the previous example.

A vector is a set of quantities that describe an object:

Cartesian 3D space is describes in terms of three dimensions (x, y, z).
A motor car may be described in terms of five quantities: weight, colour, year of manufacture, horse power, and fuel consumption.
The universe is said by some to consist of eleven dimensions

$$\text{Thus we write a vector as } \mathbf{v} = \begin{pmatrix} v_1 \\ v_2 \\ v_3 \\ \cdot \\ \cdot \\ v_n \end{pmatrix}$$

where the quantities in the brackets v_i, are the components that describe the object. The vector $\mathbf{v}$ is sometimes referred to as an n-tuple. Vectors can be written either in columns or in rows.

A matrix is written as a rectangular array of rows and columns – for example:

$$\mathbf{a} = \begin{pmatrix} 2 & 3 & 4 & 5 \\ 7 & 8 & 9 & 6 \\ 6 & 1 & 7 & 2 \end{pmatrix}$$

is a 4×3 matrix. In computer graphics we shall make much use of 4×4 square matrices. The identity matrix

$$\begin{pmatrix} 1\ 0\ 0\ 0 \\ 0\ 1\ 0\ 0 \\ 0\ 0\ 1\ 0 \\ 0\ 0\ 0\ 1 \end{pmatrix}$$

is provided by OpenGL with glLoadIdentity ( ); where the diagonal is set to one.

To multiply matrices they must be conformable; that is the number of elements in a row of the multiplying matrix must be the same as the number of column elements in the matrix to be multiplied.

C. 5 Example of Matrix Multiplication

$$\overset{\mathbf{A}}{\begin{pmatrix} 2\ 3\ 5 \\ 4\ 1\ 9 \\ 7\ 6\ 8 \end{pmatrix}} \overset{\mathbf{B}}{\begin{pmatrix} 2\ 4 \\ 1\ 9 \\ 5\ 6 \end{pmatrix}} = \overset{\mathbf{C}}{\begin{pmatrix} 32\ 65 \\ 54\ 79 \\ 60\ 130 \end{pmatrix}}$$

The result is from row and column multiplication of elements in matrices. Thus

$$4 \times 4 + 1 \times 9 + 9 \times 6 = 79$$

and in general

$$c_{rc} = \sum_k a_{rk}\, b_{kc}$$

where $_{rc}$ indicates the element of the rth row and c^{th} column of the matrices summing the products over the number of columns in $\mathbf{A}$ and rows in $\mathbf{B}$ ($k = 1, 3$ in this case).

Except in special cases matrix multiplication is non commutative.

If we were to imagine three multiplications, say

$$\mathbf{ABC} \neq \mathbf{BAC}$$

we can see that the order of the operations becomes important. If $\mathbf{A}$ were a rotation and $\mathbf{B}$ a translation, then quite different results would occur depending on the order of operations.

C. 6 Shearing Matrices

Shearing is a process where a shape that can be considered to be made up in layers, is distorted by what appears as layers sliding to oneside relative to each other.

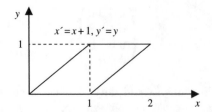

The linear shift in x between the two layers illustrated is one unit. In matrix notation this can be written as

$$\begin{pmatrix} x' \\ y' \\ 1 \end{pmatrix} = \begin{pmatrix} 1 & s_x & 0 \\ 0 & 1 & 0 \\ 0 & 0 & 1 \end{pmatrix} \begin{pmatrix} x \\ y \\ 1 \end{pmatrix}$$

where $s_x = 1$.

Appendix D

D. 1 Equation of a Plane

The general equation of any plane is given by the relation

$$Ax + By + Cz + D = 0$$

where A–D are constants. To find the equation we need the plane to pass through three points and solve for the "4" unknowns (A–D). Although there are only three eqations and four unknowns we can cancel out the constant D to get a result as shown in the following example.

Find the equation of the plane which passes through the points $(3, 4, 1)$, $(1, 1, -7)$ and $(2, 2, -4)$.

Sunstituting into the general equation we have

$$3A + 4B + C + D = 0$$
$$A + B - 7C + D = 0$$
$$2A + 2B - 4C + D = 0$$

which solving gives

$$C = D/10$$
$$A = -D/10$$
$$B = -2D/10$$

Substituting back into the general equation gives

$$-D/10x - 2D/10y + D/10z + D = 0$$
$$x + 2y - z - 10 = 0$$

The coefficients A, B, C are called the direction ratios of the normal to the plane and the plane can be wriiten in perpendicular for by dividing it by $\pm\sqrt{A^2 + B^2 + C^2}$ to give

$$\frac{A\,x}{\pm\sqrt{A^2+B^2+C^2}} + \frac{B\,y}{\pm\sqrt{A^2+B^2+C^2}} + \frac{C\,z}{\pm\sqrt{A^2+B^2+C^2}} = \frac{-D}{\pm\sqrt{A^2+B^2+C^2}}$$

The coefficients on the left hand side of this equation are the direction cosines of the normal drawn through the origin to the plane. The length of the normal between a point (x_1, y_1, z_1) and the plane is given by

$$\frac{A\,x_1 + B\,y_1 + C\,z_1 + D}{\pm\sqrt{A^2+B^2+C^2}}$$

If the positive sign is chosen when D is positive and the negative sign when D is negative, this relationship give a positive result when (x_1, y_1, z_1) and the origin are on the same side of the plane, and a negative result indicates they are on oppposite sides of the plane.

References

Angel, E., Interactive Computer Graphics, Addison Wesley, 2006.

Barnsley, M., Fractals Everywhere, Academic Press, 1988.

Becker K. H., and Dorfler, M., Dynamical Systems and Fractals, CUP, 1989.

Crownover, R., Introduction to Fractals & Chaos, Jones & Bartlett, 1995.

Deitel, H., and Deitel, P., C++ How To Program, Prentice Hall, 4th Ed, 2003.

Farin, G., Curves and Surfaces for Computer Aided Geometric Design: A Practical Guide, Academic Press, 1988.

Hill, F. S., Computer Graphics Using Open GL, Prentice Hall, 2001.

Kilgard, M., OpenGL Programming for the X Window System, Addison Wesley, 1996.

Leuven, Eyetronics scanning systems nv, kapeldreef 60, 3001 Belgium, 2007.

Mandelbrot, B., Fractal Geometry of Nature, Freeman, 1983.

Miano, J., Compressed Image File Formats, Addison Wesley, 1999.

Rogers, D., Procedural Elements for Computer Graphics, McGraw Hill, 1998.

Schweikert, D. G., An Interpolation Curve Using a Spline in Tension, Journal of Mathematics and Physics, 45, 312–313, 1966.

Shreiner D., OpenGL Reference Manual, Version 1.4, Addison Wesley, 2004.

Shreiner, D., Woo, M., Neider, J., Davis, T., Open GL Programming Guide, Addison Wesley, 2006.

Wright R., OpenGL Superbible, 3rd Edition, Sams, 2005.

Index of Functions

The following index indicates where functions are first used or discussed in more detail. Together with the *OpenGL Reference Manual* and *OpenGL Programming for the X Window System* readers will be able to find complete explanations of these and other OpenGL facilities.

Graphical Functions

glBegin, 5, 6, 7, 9, 11, 12, 14, 18, 19, 20, 24, 26, 29, 33, 44, 47, 66, 79, 81, 84, 93, 99, 100, 102, 109, 111, 127, 129, 135, 137, 150, 155, 160, 163, 166, 167, 168, 175, 180, 183, 188, 190, 192, 194, 198, 205, 209, 211, 213, 216, 217, 223, 224, 229, 234, 236, 237, 244, 245, 246, 255, 257, 259, 266, 270, 273, 278, 279, 281, 283, 285, 289, 291, 294, 299, 301, 304, 305, 310

glBindTexture, 173, 174, 175, 180, 183, 187, 190, 192, 194, 197, 198, 204, 205, 208, 209, 229, 230, 236, 239, 240, 242, 244

glBitmap, 15, 16

glBlendFunc, 194, 197, 203, 204, 208

glClear, 5, 9, 10, 14, 16, 24, 25, 44, 65, 78, 79, 80, 83, 92, 99, 100, 106, 110, 118, 128, 135, 144, 150, 154, 160, 163, 175, 180, 187, 191, 194, 205, 209, 212, 223, 231, 241, 255, 259, 264, 272, 278, 281, 285, 289, 291, 293, 300, 303, 305, 310

glClearColor, 5, 6, 9, 16, 112, 118, 130, 135, 138, 145, 156, 161, 167, 174, 180, 194, 197, 200, 204, 208, 225, 230, 231, 239, 241, 254, 263, 268

glColor, 34

glColorMaterial, 156, 161, 225, 231, 240

glDisable, 13, 172, 175, 181, 184, 188, 190, 193, 195, 199, 210, 229, 237, 242

glDrawPixels, 207, 211

glEnable, 12, 13, 14, 130, 156, 160, 161, 167, 172, 174, 175, 180, 183, 187, 190, 192, 194, 197, 198, 200, 203, 204, 205, 208, 209, 224, 225, 229, 230, 236, 239, 240, 241, 242, 244, 266

glEnd, 5, 6, 7, 9, 11, 14, 18, 20, 22, 25, 26, 30, 33, 45, 46, 47, 66, 79, 81, 84, 93, 99, 101, 102, 109, 111, 127, 129, 135, 138, 150, 155, 160, 164, 167, 168, 175, 181, 184, 188, 190, 192, 195, 198, 205, 209, 210, 211, 213, 216, 217, 223, 224, 229, 234, 237, 238, 245, 246, 255, 256, 257, 259, 260, 265, 266, 270, 273, 274, 278, 279, 282, 283, 286, 289, 291, 294, 299, 301, 304, 305, 310

glEvalCoord1f, 265, 266

glFlush, 5, 6, 9, 11, 14, 18, 19, 20, 25, 26, 30, 45, 66, 79, 81, 84, 93, 99, 101, 102, 109, 127, 135, 138, 168, 175, 181, 184, 188, 190, 193, 195, 198, 205, 209, 210, 211, 213, 217, 224, 229, 231, 237, 242, 256, 260, 265, 266, 270, 274, 279, 283, 286, 289, 291, 294, 299, 301, 305, 306, 310

glFrontFace, 156, 157, 160, 167, 205, 224, 230, 239, 241

glFrustum, 139, 143, 144, 145

glGenTextures, 173, 174, 180, 194, 197, 204, 208, 230, 239, 240

glGetFloatv, 122, 135, 136

glGetString, 5, 6

glLightfv, 154, 156, 160, 163, 224, 230, 239

327

glLineStipple, 12
glLineWidth, 9, 112, 137
glLoadIdentity, 5, 6, 9, 17, 79, 99, 103, 106, 112, 118, 130, 135, 136, 138, 145, 167, 175, 181, 195, 198, 199, 206, 210, 217, 218, 225, 321
glMap1f, 265, 266
glMaterialfv, 161, 225, 231, 240
glMateriali, 161, 225, 231, 240
glMatrixMode, 5, 6, 9, 17, 79, 99, 103, 106, 112, 118, 125, 130, 135, 136, 138, 145, 167, 175, 181, 195, 198, 199, 206, 210, 217, 218, 225
glOrtho, 17, 34, 112, 130, 134, 136, 137, 138, 139, 143, 144, 145, 167, 218, 225
glPixelStorei, 173, 174, 180, 194, 197, 204, 208, 230, 239, 240
glPixelZoom, 206, 211
glPointSize, 5, 6, 24, 25, 29, 44, 110, 167, 192, 255, 257, 259, 264, 266, 270, 272, 285
glPolygonStipple, 13, 14
glPopMatrix, 103–104, 105, 106, 110, 111, 114, 119, 120, 129, 144, 155, 160, 164, 168, 195, 205, 210, 213, 216, 223, 224, 231, 235, 242, 282
glPushMatrix, 103–104, 105, 106, 110, 111, 118, 119, 129, 144, 154, 160, 163, 167, 194, 205, 209, 212, 216, 222, 223, 231, 235, 241, 281
glRasterPos3f, 110
glRasterPos3i, 206, 211
glReadPixels, 206, 211
glRectf, 111
glRotatef, 18, 20, 99, 100, 102, 105, 110, 111, 119, 129, 135, 154, 160, 191, 194, 198, 217, 223, 231, 241, 257, 259, 269, 272, 281, 303
glScale, 11, 14, 24, 25, 96, 111, 113, 119, 233
glShadeModel, 112, 118, 150, 174, 180, 204, 230, 239
glTexCoord2f, 172, 174, 175, 180, 181, 183, 188, 190, 192, 195, 198, 205, 210, 228, 229, 233, 234, 238, 245, 246
glTexCoord3f, 213
glTexEnvf, 175, 180, 183, 187, 192, 194, 198, 204, 209, 229, 230, 235, 236, 242, 244
glTexImage2D, 174, 175, 180, 194, 197, 204, 208, 230, 239, 240
glTexParameteri, 173, 174, 180, 194, 197, 204, 208, 230, 239, 240
glTranslatef, 93, 100, 102, 105, 106, 111, 118, 119, 175, 181, 195, 198, 209, 210, 216, 223, 233, 241, 243, 244, 245, 246, 281, 305, 310

gluCylinder, 111, 143, 144
gluDeleteQuadric, 177
gluLookAt, 143, 144, 163, 164, 167, 205, 206
gluNewQuadric, 111, 144, 177
gluOrtho2D, 5, 6, 9, 11, 44, 45, 134
gluPerspective, 34, 118, 139, 143, 146, 175, 181, 195, 199, 206, 210
gluQuadricDrawStyle, 111, 144, 177
gluQuadricNormals, 111, 144, 177, 178
gluQuadricTexture, 177, 178
gluSphere, 177, 178
glVertex, 5, 6, 7, 9, 11, 14, 18, 19, 20, 22, 24, 25, 26, 30, 33, 34, 45, 46, 47, 57, 58, 66, 79, 81, 84, 93, 99, 100, 102, 109, 111, 127, 129, 135, 137, 138, 150, 153, 155, 158, 160, 164, 167, 168, 172, 174, 175, 176, 180, 181, 183, 188, 190, 192, 195, 198, 205, 209, 210, 211, 213, 216, 217, 223, 224, 228, 229, 233, 234, 237, 238, 245, 246, 255, 257, 259, 265, 266, 270, 273, 274, 278, 279, 281, 282, 283, 285, 286, 289, 291, 294, 301, 304, 305, 306, 310
glViewport, 17, 79, 112, 118, 127, 128, 129, 131, 175, 181, 195, 218

GLUT library functions

glutBitmapCharacter, 110
glutCreateWindow, 4, 5, 9, 45, 120, 130, 138, 200
glutDisplayFunc, 4, 5, 6, 9, 45, 120, 130, 138, 200, 203
glutInit, 3, 4, 5, 9, 45, 120, 130, 138, 200
glutInitDisplayMode, 3, 4, 5, 9, 45, 120, 130, 138, 200
glutInitWindowPosition, 3, 4, 5, 9, 120, 138
glutInitWindowSize, 3, 4, 5, 9, 45, 120, 138, 200
glutKeyboardFunc, 4, 37, 193
glutMainLoop, 4, 5, 9, 45, 120, 130, 138, 200
glutMotionFunc, 35, 36, 78, 196, 200
glutMouseFunc, 4, 35, 36, 78, 196, 200
glutPostRedisplay, 4, 36, 37, 79, 107, 112, 114, 115, 117, 118, 130, 145, 156, 161, 168, 196, 199, 213, 218, 232, 243
glutSolidCube, 111
glutSpecialFunc, 34, 36, 130, 144
glutSwapBuffers, 106, 111, 120, 129, 144, 150, 155, 160, 164, 168, 193, 199, 205, 210, 231, 242, 282, 304
glutTimerFunc, 105, 107
glutWireCube, 113, 119

Index

Affine transformation, 96, 277, 289
Ambient light, 152
API, 1, 34–37
Archimedean spiral, 21
Arms, robots, actuators, 113–114
Artefact hierarchy, 227–235
Attractor, 275, 277
Audio video, 39
AVI file format, 51–59

Bernstein polynomials, 262
Bezier curves, 260–263
Bitmap File, 39–50
Blending, 202–206
Bresenham's Algorithm, 25–27
Brownian motion, 304–310
Buffon's needle problem, 31

C++, 1
Callback functions, 1, 4, 34, 78
Cartesian space, 3, 80, 88, 171, 172, 179, 191, 214, 243
Catmull-Rom, 253
CAT scan, 82, 85, 219, 225
Collision detection, 120–124
Colour, 148–149
Component (object) labelling, 73–77
Computer tomography, 212
Convex polygons, 13
Convolution, 64–66
Cylindrical coordinates, 185

Data Types, 2–3
Diffuse light, 152
Digital Difference Analyser, 23–25
Dilation symmetry, 275

Edge detection, 62
Electromagnetic Spectrum, 147–151

Embossing, 49–50
Engineering drawings, 128–132

Foreshortening, 139
Fractal, 19, 249, 274, 275, 277, 283, 284, 305, 307, 310, 311
Fractal geometry, 274–292
Fractal surfaces, 307–310
Frame buffer, 3, 34, 202, 211

Gouraud shading, 94, 150, 151

Histogram equalisation, 71–73
Homogenous representation, 95

Impulse response, 64
Internal combustion engine, 107–113
Iterated Function System, 277

Keyboard interaction, 36–37
Koch curve, 292–304, 305

Lagrange polynomials, 251
Laplacian of Gaussian, 69
Laplacian operator, 66–70
Lighting and illumination, 151–161
Limb movement, 114–116
Linear mapping, 172, 178, 183, 186, 266
Linear transformations, 95
Logarithmic spiral, 19–21

Magnetic resonance imaging, 212
Mandelbrot, 293
Mercator lines, 176–177
Mesa libraries, 2
Mexican Hat operator, 70
Mixing colours, 149–150
Model, 3, 103, 134, 136
Modelview, 125

Modulo 2 arithmetic, 47
Monte Carlo, 31–33
Mouse interaction, 35–36
Movement of composite objects, 104

Normalising, 91

Orrery, 104–107
Orthographic projection, 131, 134

Papert, 293
Parametric definition, 21
Pascal's Triangle, 280
Perspective projection, 139–143
Point, 87–94
Polar angles, 178
Polygon, 6, 10, 11, 150, 164, 166
Polylines, 7
Projection, 125–146
Projection matrix, 131, 136, 146
Projection view, 17, 125, 136

Quadric Surfaces, 177–178

Recursion, 278–279, 291
Rendering, 3, 4, 6, 151, 214

Resource Interchange File Format, 51
Rotation, 35, 96–98, 99–102, 121, 196
Run-length encoding, 58

Scalar, 87
Self similarity, 19, 276, 293, 296–298
Shadows, 164–168
Sierpinski Gasket, 278–279, 280–283
Sobel operator, 63, 64, 66
Specular light, 157–161
Spherical triangle, 177
Spline functions, 252
Straight line fitting, 250–251

Tensioned Splines, 253
Texture mapping, 171–226
Tree grammar, 293
Turtle geometry, 293

Vector, 87–94
Vector cross product, 89–91
Vector Dot Products, 89
Vertex coordinates, 162–163
Vertex pipeline, 125–126

Walking robot, 116–120

Printed in the United States
By Bookmasters